DOWN AMONG THE DEAD MEN

DOWN AMONG THE DEAD MEN

AND OTHER ESSAYS

BY

BERNARD VAN DIEREN

NOVERRE PRESS

First published in 1933

This facsimile reprint published in 2013 by
The Noverre Press
Southwold House
Isington Road
Binsted
Hampshire
GU34 4PH

© 2013 The Noverre Press

ISBN 978-1-906830-62-5

To
GERALD COOPER

PREFACE

Conforming to a respectable tradition, I insincerely crave indulgence for these aesthetico-philosophical rambles. The reader may often wonder where he will be dragged next. One moment he will feel that he is being held up intolerably long in obscure corners, the next that he is being rushed past an imposing edifice which he would wish to explore. He may feel disappointed if eventually we come back to the spot from which we started. Still, if that signifies a safe return, it is worth a fatted calf, and that is more than many wanderers get in the end.

I hope no more than that on the circuit I may be able to show some unfamiliar mews, alleys, and subways; short-cuts here and detours there. I do not pretend to take the reader straight from the station to the hotel; I have tried to be a companion, not a guide. I believe I have shown him some queer customers in the bus and the Underground, and loafing at odd corners. Principal buildings and monuments are always in the same places and may be inspected any time.

Music, Philip Heseltine observes in his Delius monograph, is a rum go. For a mathematically planned stroll one must choose places like Chicago, where one can find the way by counting as one does on a chessboard.

If the going seems now and then too rummy altogether, the fault is partly the peculiar character of all writing concerned with music. Musical forms are so elusive that studied reiteration is called for to hold them together. And every reference to them needs recurrent emphasis to impart a semblance of coherence. Why then write about music? Why does one lover after another risk his head for the hand—as the saying is—of the cruel princess? The crew of musical authors are all in one small boat with short rations, and as the chanson might have said,

> *On tire la plume...*
> *Pour voir qui d'eux va, va être mangé.*

CONTENTS

PREFACE
page vii

I. DOWN AMONG THE DEAD MEN
page 1

II. BUSONI
page 20

III. MUSIC AND WIT
page 102

IV. MEYERBEER
page 142

V. SINE NOMINE
page 175

One

DOWN AMONG THE DEAD MEN

WHEN WE ARE OLD ENOUGH TO BE ASKED FOR INFORMAtion by arguing juniors, we learn to dread the strain of ordeal-by-questioning. Hopeful young enthusiasts live in expectation of meeting a man who knows.

Must one confess that the old problems remain lifelong companions? That as time has gone on they have only increased one's uncertainties? The questions rarely permit concise answers. Every one leads a ghostly army of secondary puzzles to which one hardly dares draw attention. Definite replies would require more knowledge of facts than any man could possess, be he ever so persistent in his studies.

What must one say when asked: 'Do you like Bach for his form or for the emotional content?'

'Is Mozart the last of a line or the first of the moderns?'

'Is Handel a greater composer than Gluck?' (Incidentally: 'Was Handel's cook a cook of counterpoint or a contrapuntist amongst cooks?')

When we hear the name of Gluck, the far-off din of old battles rumbles in our ears; yet for most of us the issues have become so blurred that we seldom reflect on the merits involved in that historic clash.

Then there are direct challenges to partisanship:

'Is Weber a great composer?' And the ensnaring ones: 'Do you believe that Wagner wrote spontaneously?' or 'Is it possible to listen to Tchaikovsky without prejudice?'

Even more embarrassing are the obtrusive ones like, 'Do you prefer modern to classic?' and 'Do you like the *very* modern?'

Or, if one shows affection for both old and new: 'How do you reconcile that?' This ticklish problem is expected to trip up every eclectic. A musician in search of a suitable subject once said to me: 'Wasn't it a dreadful thing about Scriabin dying?' He was shocked to find that so far from responding in the right funereal key, I seemed to be irreverent to the memory. So he put it squarely: 'What music *do* you like?' I diffidently mumbled something about Palestrina, and his clamorous appeal to the company—'Did you hear that one?' was rewarded with a ripple of laughter.

Still, this form of examination deals with material to which we all have given some thought. We may not, at the right moment, be able to satisfy every impatient inquisitor, but we ought to welcome the test.

Every one has tortured his elders with importunate and inopportune requests for aesthetic information, in artist rooms, in hotel lifts, and theatre boxes.

The worst forms of intellectual jockeying, hectoring, and dragooning are disguised as conversational argument by the more sophisticated questioners, who pillage libraries for recondite material. They ask those anguishing questions which one asks of oneself. One knows the pitfalls only too well, but that refines the torment. 'Is Dalayrac a better melodist than Philidor?' or 'Could "Tom Jones" ever get into the repertoire again?' And, 'What do you think of Marschner's orchestration: of the shape of Hummel's slow movements? Do you relish Zingarelli's florid graces?' and 'Aren't you irritated by Jomelli's mannerisms?' or 'Is not Hasse to be preferred to the leaden-footed Keiser?'

Who is ready for such posers as, 'Was Graun more gifted than Buononcini? And is Buononcini a worthy rival of Handel? How does either compare with Lully and Rameau?' 'Can Bieber's solo sonatas stand comparison with Bach's?' and, 'What of Stamitz and the Mannheim school?' 'Do you see anything in Rubinstein's "Ocean" Symphony, or is it no more than Mendelssohnian classicism?' And 'How far had Russian music a distinct claim before the Army and Civil Service took it in hand, and brought us over the steppe to the mythology of the Orthodox Church?' 'Does the Muscovite love of fairy tales provide a useful counterweight to Wagnerism?'

Then, how does one deal with questions about Zarlini, Tartini, and Martini? About Fux and Marpurg? The older theories of chord-structure? The alleged existence of undertones and combination-tones. Speaking of undertones, 'Is Bernhard Ziehn's suggestion of the reflection of chord-formation acceptable?'

Most professional critics know the standard replies to the standard questions and can mechanically reel them off. A few can do even more. Those who are fortunately reclining in University Chairs; those who can afford what really would be 'une occupation toujours inutile'. The others have to do too much uncongenial work. If ever they possessed all the information, the pressure of new facts heaped on their harassed memories blots it out. 'The cold steel pen', whose might seduces so many ambitious young musicians, must constantly be reground on the stone Tables of the Law. And in this process the inscriptions become more and more illegible. They are endlessly scrutinized by the optimistic new-comer and by the disillusioned old hand. The one hopes to read the message one day, the other pretends that he might still do so if he were given an honest chance.

They all see the tantalizing light at the far limits of the dark wilderness through which they are hacking their way, very much like Stanley and his company seeking the disappearing missionary. The music critic in search of a mighty, half-forgotten figure repeats Stanley's grim tracking through the jungle, so that in the end he may come face to face with a somewhat disturbed old master and say, 'Mr. Sebastian Bach, I presume.' The account of his search often makes sensational reading, without adding to our knowledge or understanding.

If Livingstone had been a completely obscure figure no Stanley would have been engaged to hunt him. For the same reason it is seldom worth a writer's while to occupy himself with composers whose names are only vaguely familiar.

New publications about the proverbial figures are mostly built on conjecture. The authors rarely have time for voyages of discovery or for tournaments. And, usually, when the years of leisure arrive the old interest has died. Few preserve enough affectionate enthusiasm to refurbish their armour until it shines with something of its early glitter.

The ignorance of relatively well-informed people on matters regarded as common property was amusingly illustrated once by Heseltine when he signed a circular to the musical profession with the name of one of the most renowned writers on counterpoint, Prosdocimus de Beldamandis. Mr. Ernest Newman, apparently the only one who knew the famous *Tractatus de Contrapunctu*, pointed the moral in an entertaining article. But numerous letters were addressed to 'P. de Beldamandis Esq., Anhalt Studios, Chelsea, S.W.'. None of them, with their 'Dear Sir' and 'Dear Mr. Beldamandis', were conceived in a bantering spirit. They were simply businesslike communications sent by one London gentleman to another. A famous British composer, who, moreover, had a reputation as a wit, said to me: 'Interesting fellow this Beldamandis must be—he writes well. Most useful propagandist. Greek young man, I presume?'

'One of my pupils, in fact,' I could not help saying.

'I am glad to hear it,' said the famous composer.

The root of the trouble lies in a soil we all know to our cost. When we have to go to the dictionary, we are, in our chase through *Ef, Eff, Eg, Ega, Ego, Egu*, constantly held up by unforeseen references to strange subjects and names that seem to have been maliciously put there to lead us astray. Very few of us overcome the temptation to interrupt the hunt and read a column or so about some one of whom we had never heard, and who, we find, is not only a 'famous composer', who 'created an immense stir', but whose this-or-that-in-D-minor 'brought tears to the eyes of innumerable audiences'. One man whose very existence we ignored was 'considered by the best judges the unsurpassed master of the period', another had 'a technique without equal'. Opera composers there are by the dozen whose twenty, or thirty, or forty 'best works' kept 'Europe in a state of continual rapture'.

An appalling swarm of nonentitous celebrities reminds us of fleeting time and of our own ignorance. Yet one finds no real solace in the thought that it is all a matter of perspective, that, as the atmosphere pleasantly blurs the outline of distant objects, so the mist of time lends undeserved charm to historical figures. This emergency exit appears too often locked. Many forgotten composers who lead an alphabetical existence in faded catalogues prove to be absorbingly interesting when we look at their works, and very much alive when we perform them.

There is, however, a new danger when we attempt revivals. A friend once asked me whether any of Meyerbeer's music was suitable for concert performance. I suggested the 'Fackeltänze' and the overture to 'Struensee'. The advice was passed on to a conductor, who performed the overture.

'Did he thank you for your suggestion?' I asked later. 'He cuts me dead now,' was the answer; 'he suspects that I am a practical joker, that I hoped he would make himself ridiculous.' This was literally true; the conductor, having only read the score, was shocked when he heard the music. And after a somewhat lukewarm reception he could not believe in the honesty of a different opinion. He presented Meyerbeer as early-Wagner-and-water; if perhaps born before 1820, by no means going strong. He could not forgive the false friend who had seduced him to the revival of a family-album piece.

The connexion of names with periods is dangerous. As we believe in classical and romantic periods, rococo, baroque, and modern, instead of reflecting that there are all sorts of artists in every age, so we think of a composer who lived in the baroque period as a baroque composer as well as a composer of baroque. We make these mistakes automatically as, grown up, we feel most things connected with our childhood must have been childish things—that life has grown serious with our advancing years. The music of which we heard our aunts and uncles speak must have been auntunclish music. It is not easy to recognize the living soul of music which we first see in some mouldy old tome. Our recollection most likely will suggest that it is mouldy old music.

Possibly a man who has never heard of Bach could listen to his music without preconceived ideas. One who knows that Bach is the all-in-all of many lovers of classical music may, according to his predilections, like or dislike him more for that, but the musician who reads in a yellowed copy of Marpurg's treatise on counterpoint about the praiseworthy efforts 'des seligen Herrn Capellmeister Johann S. Bach' feels that this exemplary contrapuntist must have been finally fossilized fifty years before the old teacher who instructs us how to repair our debilities by the contemplation of this good-old-time manliness.

Affectionate application wipes out much of such prejudice. But that is difficult with lesser figures forced on our minds in our school years. Or those to which, during the impressionable years of approaching maturity, we were introduced by respected elders.

If pianists look upon Czerny as exclusively a pedagogue, and violinists upon Casorti as a man with a right hand only, there is also the danger that one knows a considerable composer only as a purveyor of material for teachers to pester their pupils with. Has not almost every modern fiddler learned to hate Rode or Kreutzer with a deep and enduring hatred? Later, when one knows better, does not there remain the suspicion that Viotti's concertos were expressly planned to heap more undeserved misery on the young musician?

It is a cruel fact that pianists consider Muzio Clementi, in spite of his lovely name, unsuitable for performance. In their youth they saw too much and understood too little of him. How comically dangerous the crossing of names and reputations can be, I once saw demonstrated when a not-too-cultured musician burst out laughing at a tarantella by Sydney Smith. Inquiry for the cause of his mirth elicited the explanation that Sydney Smith was a great wit, 'and can't you hear it?' He mixed up the composer of drawing-room music and the celebrated divine. Most musicians will say that no such thing could ever happen to them. I advise them to try and think not of what they themselves would do or say, but of what they have heard *other* musicians say, when no doubt every one will be able to find in his repertoire of reminiscences a chastening number of exemplary ineptitudes. The remedy is strenuous occupation with the works, unhampered by irrelevant impressions. Still, personal experience cannot everywhere dispense with the specialist's records. Everybody must remain ignorant of part of the literature, but no one can disregard the danger of the fixed notions which drag their existence from one book of reference to another like an undermining contagious disease. They bind names to images gratuitously, and with the perverse incongruity that all through our lives marks the association of unconnected ideas.

Hear a melody when a name is mentally registered, and the two remain as indissolubly wedded as a colour and a perfume perceived at the same time. I knew a man who mixed up Bach and Schubert. Schubert's songs are so full of a 'Bach' here and a 'Bach' there, that he thought all Bachs derived from Schubert. He was as much justified as non-musicians who confuse Schubert and Schumann because they both start with shoes.

My earliest idea about Verdi was that his music came from over the water. I had heard a band play a selection from 'Aida' at the other side of a lake by which I was seated.

It took me years to separate the idea of Boieldieu and a bridge, because I had heard a quasi-lugubrious chorus in a pantomime singing something about 'the bloody night at the fiery bridge' to the famous melody of 'La Dame Blanche'. As a boy I believed that Rossini's music was composed for piano-organ, having first heard Rosina's air from the 'Barbiere' on that instrument (incidentally, on a late summer evening, so that for many years this melody conveyed strongly an atmosphere of slanting shadows and the far-off, fever-haunted rumours of a tired city turning to repose).

I mention these personal experiences only to soften what might seem censure of a common weakness. They have shown me how pervading and how tenacious are these dovetailed images.

Readers of dictionaries are unavoidably tyrannized in their ideas about composers, known or unknown, whom they met accidentally in hastily scanned articles.

Berlioz had arrived at middle age when one of his champions complained that in Germany he was still confused with de Bériot. The modest von Bülow did much more harm than he meant with his pleasantry about the three B's. Too many people took this seriously, forgetting that despite his own B-ness he concluded, 'les autres sont crétins'. There was literally room for the improving spirit of Moskowski, who mimicked Bülow's album entry (for that is all it was) with a contribution about the 'only three M's', Meyerbeer, Mendelssohn, and himself—'les autres sont chrétiens!' Revue-makers, with their alliterative titles, know what powers are hidden in apt approximation of capitals, in BingBoys, Gay-Girls, and Roystering Raggers. It is saddening to think that serious criticism should adopt a device which legitimately belongs to the lowest regions of the artistic business.

We ought to be grateful for a new ray of light on less-known composers. The big searchlights are concentrated on those of whom we know far too much as it is.

Our participation has been devitalized by the trouble that is taken for us. Personal zest disappears when we become too well informed.

To-day the villain is quite safe when he leaves the stage

door, however much he may regret it. A great actor told me wistfully of bygone times: 'Sir, when I played in the *Nun of Cracow* people came to the stalls with revolvers in their pockets!' Superficially it seems as if *this* were a confusion of life and art; in reality we ourselves, for all our pride in our enlightened century, are mixing up life and art. A search for firearms occurs now, not in the theatre but in the U.S. law-courts when there is a sensational trial. Fights in and about the theatre have become exceedingly rare, and they happen only in outlandish places where fantastic foreigners lead their strange existence.

Musicians appear on the whole humiliatingly ready to accept the settlements historians have made for them. 'Passed into history,' they say. The German with pedantic conclusiveness dismisses such matters as 'überwundener Standpunkt'. It is noteworthy, however, that usually the author who assures us that there is nothing more to be said, appropriately proceeds to do so in several pages.

In recent years a more interesting variant of this fundamental pessimism has become known as the process of 'debunking'. Lytton Strachey indicated how settled questions may be unsettled. Musical authors might profitably interrupt their protracted ruminations for occasional browsing in these anti-Plutarch fields. There is material enough, and to spare.

At the tribunal of history an appeal is possible. The victim of error should obtain more than a 'free pardon', even if a spectacular rehabilitation is likely to be contested again.

There need be no inexorable tradition about dictionary verdicts. Dictionary composers deserve generous interest for the wrongs and injustices under which they suffer.

'Monsieur, êtes-vous Gluckiste?' was the question heard in Paris salons at a time when the first growling of the coming Revolution announced itself in aesthetic wrangles of tradition versus innovation. As one could expect from the ironical revenges of history, Gluck has become one of the eminent classics. Piccinni somehow has not completed the cycle by returning to popular favour. The cause is probably not so much that he had been forgotten as that for many years he was regarded as an ignominiously defeated composer who deserved no charitable succour. Yet Berlioz still conducted extracts from a Piccinni opera, although he was one of Gluck's most uncritical admirers. Since performances, however, are dependent on supposed popular interest, we have for many years had no chance of renewing acquaintance with Piccinni. He has been hounded to the dictionary. At the peak of his career he was singled out for hero-worship by the fervent supporters of the great traditions. And this in a country where tradition attracted the finest of trained intellects. His adherents were critically discerning scholars, not drunk admirers of celebrity.

Our natural impatience with the cultured standard-bearers of estimable convention does not alone account for the persistent neglect of Piccinni so long after the passions involved in the old contest have lost all direct meaning for us. There has grown up another barrier in the intervening years and a very formidable one. If we tried to revive a work of Piccinni we should undoubtedly find that generous intentions by no means suffice; the special technique demanded by his vocal parts is completely outside the competence of our singers. They would have to be coached from the very first step for this single purpose. With what we know of singers and opera impresarios we can understand why such difficulties are practically insurmountable. It is not easy to fill the cast for a Gluck opera, although the style he initiated is one that, by Wagner's work and the propaganda of Bayreuth, has become the basis for all dramatic singing which does not dispense, but dispenses with, 'bel canto' prescriptions. The Wagner cult bears the responsibility for this. Not Wagner himself. Wagner invited Spontini to conduct the 'Vestale' in Dresden. The tone of his 'Erinnerungen' suggests that he had a genuine regard for him. To musicians in general Spontini's style may seem shaped very much like that of Gluck, but the student of the period

WHO WAS PICCINNI?

detects far more intimate connexions between the stylistic features of Spontini and Piccinni.

Piccinni was much more than the prolific writer of agreeable melodies he is assumed to be by the few musicians who know anything of him. He was a strong personality and a considerable intellect, and technically well equipped. His music has an elegant stateliness, an easy flexibility, and a balanced clarity such as are rarely found combined with so much strength and purpose. He has dramatic muscle together with exquisite nervous sensibility. His melody emotionally pulsates with a subtlety that has been rarely equalled before the advent of Verdi.

Piccinni's name was a clarion call whose sound can still be faintly discerned in the modern historian's dissertations. But almost invariably when one mentions him now, musicians say, 'I never knew he had written a work called "Dido", but I know "Manon Lescaut".' And the explanation that he is not a mispronounced *Puccini* seldom fetches a smile of recognition.

Singers, who might have some slight interest in the classics of their art, know next to nothing of the very composers who evolved the art of singing, as distinguished from folk-noises.

Of the great exponents they know from hearsay some of the few that are universally familiar. Even a Lablache, whom most bookworms know, were it only from early *Punch* volumes, lives for singers in his *Méthode de Chant*[1] alone. Patti, perhaps, and a few of the early Wagner heroes, they know by name. We have to go to the students of eighteenth-century histoire-de-coulisses and Court-gossip before we meet Farinelli or Faustina Hasse. Besides, they drew attention by other than vocal prowess, the one negative, the other positive.

When this is the fate of singers, who are so much depen-

---

[1] This work is called poor by the inexorable singing-masters who notoriously cultivate a wiseacreage which would appal any surveyor, but it contains a few melodies that many a modern composer might sell his soul to be able to write.

dent on personality and its publicity value, how feeble must be the chances of survival of other virtuosi.

Who was this 'greatest of guitarrists' who created 'universal excitement'? Or the horn-player of the eighteen-somethings who 'enraptured audiences with his three-part-playing', a feat which to-day is generally regarded as an innovation? What mean their proud names to us? Who are those 'unique talents' and 'immortals' who kept the world enthralled?

As we turn the pages the situation turns from left to right and back, great names and forgotten works, great works and forgotten names; can our judgement find the balance? Glowing accounts of phenomenal successes, incomparable positions, unparalleled achievements. They come fast and thick, and we feel with shame that with unforgivable heedlessness we have talked music in a thick cloud of ignorance.

What knowledge we have, we mostly have come to by mere accident. The average English musician needs French relations to hear of Alkan. The case of Alkan is indeed instructive. In the estimation of the ablest contemporary judges, as well as of those who still study his works, he was equally fascinating as a pianist and as a composer.

None the less, he has now long remained in semi-obscurity. Outside France he has been forgotten, or deliberately ignored.

This throws a peculiar light on the systematized unfriendliness that awaits the man whose name has not established itself in the popular memory. To be long neglected is as bad as a fault. 'Qui quitte perd sa place', the French, with their undeserved renown for thoughtful manners, say; and 'les absents ont toujours tort'. It is sad, but 'only too palpably true'.

One would imagine that the qualities which make Alkan repellent to one musician must at least recommend him to another. But this did not happen. Once Alkan's name had become an empty sound, there seemed to form an occult conspiracy to keep his music away also from ears that could have no reason to object to it.

CHARLES ALKAN

When Busoni, in his early Berlin years, presented a compendium of piano-literature, Alkan was violently abused by all critics. Liszt had been the bugbear of the Berlin fraternity. It vetoed French music, French piano music especially, on principle. So Alkan was decried for his supposed exhibition of the features that sempiternally served as the Aunt Sally of musical patriots. Even then the hostility shown was remarkable. It amounted to a personal proscription whose common denominator may be roughly summed up as follows: 'Busoni insists on dishonouring his talents by the playing of virtuoso's music which serious musicians indignantly reject. Still, he might retain the sympathies of old-timers enamoured of romantic sentimentality and of keyboard fireworks. There is no music so bad that a good word could not be coined to defend the taste of such fervent amateurs. But when it comes to such preposterous rubbish as Busoni tries to ram down our throats with his Alkan, it is time to voice a vigorous protest, to tell him that it simply won't do, and shall not be tolerated.'

Whether the rabid prejudice that rears its ugly head here had echoed as far as London I have no means of telling, but it is a fact that on the few occasions when Busoni or Egon Petri included any Alkan in their programmes there, critics almost unanimously, and with similar vehemence, denounced the composer and his interpreters.

E. D., in the Grove article on Charles Henri Valentin Morhange *dit* Alkan, writes of his 'astounding' opus 35, and while ranking his music below that of Chopin and Liszt 'in point of beauty and absolute musical value', is kind enough to compare him to Rubinstein, and to say that his 'Études' have 'a valid claim to be studied' for 'technical specialities' nowhere else to be found 'in the music of their date'. This is about as far as critics without deliberate enmity will go. And that probably because the 'omni opera' of Alkan are incorporated in the 'matériel d'étude' of the Paris Conservatoire.

Yet, any musician who will trouble to go through some of

DOWN AMONG THE DEAD MEN

Alkan's work is sure to experience one of those rare thrills that come with the discovery of new, strange, and unexpected beauty. Is there anything more overwhelming than the sudden sight of a perfect landscape as seen in some small towns at the turn of an unpromising street? A player who knows what most piano music is, and what may be expected of the average French composer, could seldom meet greater revelations than are to be found on every page of Alkan. When he finds a piano piece called 'The Fire in the Village', previous experience suggests several horrors that must be in store for him. Instead he hears an exquisite tone-painting like one of the movements of 'Harold en Italie.' As an introduction, one might study a short, perfectly shaped, impressionistic picture for piano, with the title 'Le Tambour bat aux Champs'. I seriously doubt whether there is another short composition which in an equally simple form conveys so overwhelming a mood of concentrated tragedy. As a 'piece for piano', it has alone, quite apart from its implications, a singular charm. No one, has he the most primitive appreciation of musical beauties, can fail to be touched by it, and yet there lies in these unadorned phrases a depth of imagery, an incandescence of sentiment, and a universality of meaning which remind one of the most intense lines of Poe or Blake. More astonishing still, this scorching Salvator Rosa-cum-Delacroix piece is executed with a Mozartian precision and grace that few composers attain.

How is it that a man of this imaginative power and this striking technical perfection was unknown outside a limited circle of personal friends, and of archaizing specialists? The total absence of picturesque biographical information is presumably to some extent responsible. If one could tell something about his life beyond the bare facts of birth, appointments, and death, there might be some romantic lure to draw musicians to the works. Unfortunately, there is no material. The best one could do in an attempt to 'make something of' his life would be to suggest that it was wrapped in mystery. Certainly, as far as one can detect, most of it must have been spent in the same fabulous prison where Paganini learnt to perform on a single string. Unless on a larger scale something happened to him of the kind that Borrow relates of his own strange youth. Borrovians will remember that a whole day of his life had been mislaid—in spite of most careful research it could never be traced.

Alkan's admirers are naturally anxious to discover the slightest additional facts that could arouse interest, or even simple curiosity. But persistent probing and snuffling and ferreting has failed to bring to light anything beyond the commonplaces, such as that the most considerable musicians of his day—Liszt to begin with—missed no oportunity of visiting him when they came to Paris. Pianists and composers with intuition for spots where inspiration is likely to be found, never let a chance pass of calling on Alkan, of listening to his conversation, his latest ideas, compositions, and whatever technical suggestions he might make.

He is one of those lonely figures, and one of those peculiarly individual artists that cannot be actually compared to any one, but about whom one must speak in terms of constant reference to familiar names, simply because there is no other means of suggesting anything of character and achievement. If one speaks of his qualities while recalling aspects of the works of other artists, it is not because he 'is rather like that'. One cannot profitably quote whole pages of the music. There is no more dishearteningly ineffectual method anyhow. Therefore one is inevitably reduced to the pathetic procedure of citing other names. As long as it is understood that this is not intended as a bolstering up of a shaky case, there is no great harm done. In spite of this I feel unhappy about the necessity, and therefore tiresomely emphasize the point, in the hope that I may only hurt myself.

The names of which one thinks in connexion with Alkan are indicative of his significance. Some of his detractors have called him a Berlioz of the piano; if it was not intended as a compliment, it was an unconsciously felicitous suggestion. Alkan has much in common with Berlioz, but he also has much in common with Haydn; his music has a lovable ruggedness which recalls some moods of Cervantes or Defoe; but it possesses the distant tenderness of Verlaine or Chopin (the Chopin of the Preludes and the Ballades), and a variety of colour and rhythm, a vivacity of profile combined with wealth of detail such as is perhaps only found in Berlioz himself.

He is markedly methodical in the lay-out of the separate sections and in the deliberate intricacy of instrumental design. In this we find a substratum of pedagogic *arrière-pensée*. But few composers retain his liberty of movement where they have so definite and practical an object in view. There is in many places a dark strain from which we might infer that he was a somewhat enigmatic personality, and yet there are not many equally compelling and immediately attractive composers amongst those with so pronounced and unmistakable an individual tone.

Alkan never shies at the boldest tone-painting; he knows no half-heartedness. But however unreserved a colourist he dares be, he retains a structural purity which should satisfy the most exacting stylists. His technical procedure displays the deliberate precision of an engraver; his lines are chiselled with reasoned and cool accuracy. Yet this never tones down the fascinating glow of his coloration; in the most fantastic pictures the utter truthfulness of his musical temperament convincingly knits together the diverse qualities.

As a teacher he possessed qualities of imagination combined with methodical insight and enthusiastic convictions that made the most gifted eager to learn from him. Any one who has ever given or received instruction will know that this is neither the truism nor the contradiction which the bald statement at first sight appears. The crystalline clarity of his structures, and their rhythmical incisiveness, reveal sufficiently the supple power of thought which must have inspired the select few who could value this exceptional combination and for whom it was a constant spur to higher ambition and elegant discipline. If a teacher with so regulated a mind can show his disciples his own convincing works, he gives them something that cannot be found elsewhere. His personality, we gather, was like his music, strangely varied and consistent; the 'texture' of the gnarled oak-bark next to the silkiness of a lily-petal. He has the acerbity and the strident accents of a Hogarth or Rowlandson, and withal he is a dreamer whose enchanting vignettes have the melancholy sweetness of Watteau.

No composer was less impeded by keyboard limitations than Alkan, who draws from the unpromising 'daily-bread' medium an undreamt variety of colour and a width of expression which, like Berlioz's orchestra, presents tender figures against proud, jagged mountain and rock backgrounds, amidst the clamour of fiery combat. With equal felicity he knows how to improvise on a fugitive, whispering, little piping melody that sounds like the ghost of a devout old supplicant reciting his lyrical canon of simple faith in a silent, sun-warmed village church.

While this poet lived his retired life in some dark corner of Paris, the limelight was for the Steibelts, the Pixises, and the Kalkbrenners. He was the unsurpassable virtuoso, but the others had the public. The sentimental Scheffel, who slobbered together the complete apotheosis of tears-moonlight-violets-and-ichweissnichtwas sadness, has laid it down that 'Es ist im Leben hässlich eingerichtet, Dass bei den Rosen gleich die Dornen stehn'. (Significantly enough, an important role in his tearful 'Trompeter' is filled by 'The Tomcat Hidigeigei', whose dismal melodies follow on the go-a-rovings of the Knight Before. Only, he meant it all very seriously.) I should say that the trouble is not so much the thorns being so near the roses as that some people get all the roses, while others have not enough skin for the thorns, thistles, cactus leaves, and stinging-nettles that are thrust on them in abundance. Here was Alkan with his brilliant light hidden under a bushel, and there was the appropriately named Kalkbrenner—Limeburner!—with rings on his fingers and bells on his toes, like the ladies scorned by the Hebrew minor prophet, having, and bringing, music wherever he went.

This egregious Kalkbrenner—speaking as a composer—once summed up the merits and infantile ambitions of his successful fellows and himself in a memorable description of some 'Grande Fantaisie pour Piano sur Thèmes Caractéristiques' of his own: 'Sehn Se, det Janze ist ein Draum, eine Dreimerei; es beginnt mit Lieuwe, Passion; Disperation, Verzweiflung; und et endigt mit einem Militärmarsch'! One despairs of ever improving on such a confession; if composers would all be so honest we should perhaps discover how many of their works have grown from similar mental images.

Piano music with the spiritual and structural qualities we connect with the symphonies and string quartets of the classical masters is rare enough, but there is none of it with which Alkan need fear comparison, however different his idiom may be. Yet oblivion has overtaken him and his name, partly for lack of biographical glamour, and one shivers to think of the other great works there may be which suffer under the same crippling disability. There must have been composers who did not have, as one mild consolation, the admiring friendship of confrères to draw a little posthumous attention to them.

Another danger, by no means negligible, is that the sympathetic praises of a few insistent lovers of so recondite a figure may be themselves dangerous. They seldom serve any good purpose, however worthy the intentions; and they raise the suspicion of unfriendly critics who happen to be ignorant of the music. The case for the prosecution always seems the more convincing. When one reads law-court reports one hopes that the culprit may get off, but, while one admires the generous ingenuity of his counsel, a conviction seems the only possible conclusion. That, no doubt, is why the defence is allowed the final word.

Alkan and Piccinni illustrate in contrasted ways the hideously doubling effects of ignorance and neglect. Two such remarkable figures are to-day practically unknown, although the one earned fame rarely surpassed—'undying fame' it was called—and the other possessed a most striking and distinguished personality. This should considerably modify our tempers when we set out to pronounce judgement on the composers of our own time, or on the surviving representatives of authentic, if antiquated, ideals.

'Dictionaries are like watches,' wrote Dr. Johnson, 'the worst is better than none, and the best cannot be expected to go quite true', but O my soul, what demon-watches they are to remind us of the uncertainty of the moment, and of the futility of the most ardent human striving, if they happen to be slow or fast!

Lasciate ogni speranza would be a fitting remembrance to print at the head of a lexicon. If we praise and condemn let us remember our uneasy blushes when we read of the immortality or of the imperishable glory of men whose names we should never know if their first letters did not set them in columns where the accident of an irrelevant chase has led us.

Let us also measure future chances by the lame, neutral lines the knowing editor allots to a composer we may happen to know and revere, but who has fallen out of public favour. He is admitted only for the completeness demanded of books of reference which, for a scholar's reward, 'deliver the body dead or alive' to whoever is on a missing artist's tracks.

Still, Hamlet could not even have said 'Alas' but for the grave-digger.

·☙ *Two* ☙·

BUSONI

WHEN PHILEAS FOGG TRAVELLED ROUND THE WORLD IN eighty days the achievement was fantastic enough to make his name proverbial. To-day there is a man living who has achieved the traject in something like five days. He has inspired no poet or novelist. We had become prepared for anything. It seemed a prosaic fulfilment of an obvious promise.

Distance has moved with the times. When Verne wrote, a Serbian with relations in America was a celebrity in his village. He was as remarkable as the Roman patrician who kept lions in his garden. But now we take thought in terms of what every lady-journalist calls 'this far-flung empire' so much for granted that it needs male original genius for a modern writer to dare profess himself a Little Englander.

Internationalism in art has developed along the same lines in the course of the same years. As long as only a composer of means, or a painter with a patron, could afford to travel to Italy for the last phase of his artistic education, it was a refined distinction to acquire technical familiarity with ultramontane styles.

As distances decreased with greater speed of travel, there developed the popular pride in an international outlook on art. Its devotees appeared from phase to phase as naïvely hopeful as the contemporaries of Montgolfière, who began discounting their experiences on the moon as soon as they saw the first balloon rise above the chimney-pots.

When it comes to anticipating probable developments, the most ignorant devise the boldest picture. They know neither how often similar hopes have been destroyed in the past, nor how the reading of that lesson has damped the optimism of less ingenuous thinkers. The better man suffers from his intellectual uneasiness, whereas the sanguine fool retains the gratuitous chance of success in his forecasts. When occasionally the facts bear him out, not only does he look a fool no longer, but he is referred to as a prophet who did not even require that exact information which wiser men were awaiting before they dared prognosticate anything at all.

The artist can permit himself a certain latitude in speculation on the probable development of new departures in artistic form, but a similar relationship exists here between the browsing dilettanti who lightly range over whole fields and the diffident scholar who is somewhat hesitantly occupied within an enclosed space.

The position is necessarily different for those who envisage the question in its widest aspect, who remember interstellar space and sidereal time whenever they look at the clock or the compass. They may be lacking in the command of smaller technicalities. A comprehensive view keeps them alive to the danger that while imperceptible gains are made if one impudently grasps time by the forelock, an incalculable loss may be incurred through reckless interpretation of the final issues.

Musicians more than most artists, and composers more than most musicians, believe that a vertiginous speed of progress is being attained when they themselves cannot recognize the ground under their feet.

The emptiest heads are the last to feel giddiness. Where brains are a handicap, the race is to him who can afford to lose his head, for he need not stop to collect it. He runs on like a decapitated chicken.

Many people who call themselves 'enlightened moderns' know nothing of the fear that besets the cautious thinker. The compleat blockhead, who proudly takes everything on trust, is bound to proceed quickest. He does not mourn tradition; he despises it. He is ever ready to discard old possessions because he is sure new ones will somehow fill the void as it is formed.

Any artist who understands that he participates in a

mission which does not begin with his own appearance, and does not finish with his death, instinctively knows that there are no short cuts, and that the loss of command of one language does not produce the slightest knowledge of another.

In a time that has seen the dissolution of national musical traditions, there have appeared numerous composers who assumed that any bold apostasy was bound to find its reward in the automatic formation of an international tradition grown from the new contacts thus provided. Even if something valuable *could* be gained in this way, it could hardly replace the many precious possessions which had been recklessly abandoned.

No man, of however original genius, could wish for a greater gift than the rationally developed traditions of the country in which he is born and the race from which he descends. From his earliest years he becomes familiar with a completely organized idiom whose constituents are sufficiently balanced to make it a readily flexible medium for the practised hand. From the first he enjoys the advantage that he need not waste time in a struggle with first questions. He does not learn to regret the loss of youth; that torture is reserved for artists who later in life curse their early superstition that the first duty to oneself was to hammer out a language of one's own.

If a young man of talent were wise enough to see the importance and the usefulness of the conventions of his craft, he could start in a unique state of settled harmony between himself and his public. If, on the other hand, he demands of his hearers that they shall learn his new idiom with as much sweat and anxiety, and as many sleepless hours, as he has given to its formation, he will have to overcome the almost personal hatred his demands are bound to engender. If from the first he directs his thoughts along the path of tradition, he can straightforwardly say what he thinks and feels, and the terms he chooses will mostly be intelligible to the average of his hearers. The composer who has the misfortune to be born at a time when almost every one is dissatisfied with existing conditions, will feel obliged to display the utmost grade of impatience that he shares with the advanced thinkers among his public. Then tradition, so far from being a constant help, acts as an automatic brake, hampering his movements the more as they become more impetuous.

The usual consequence of this gloomy state of affairs is that he learns for expediency's sake to ape a tradition on which he should really depend with the confidence of a child in a benevolent and capable father. He constantly works in the danger that he may be wasting what should be his most productive years in a futile, half-concealed fight against ways of thought which in the end he will admire—when he has discovered a personal use of them that lends sufficient fresh colour to his vocabulary.

His own brave, consistent spirit may perceive the rational function in this apparent compromise; to the unwavering radicals among his contemporaries (if they do not accuse him of downright duplicity) it must seem the more insidiously despicable for its non-partisan reasonableness. They consider this no better than flabbiness, and that naturally makes his fight harder than it would be if at least he flattered their expectations. He knows they are waiting for a new language and he might cautiously direct evolution, even if in its course he touches only some of the minor elements of his own projected idiom.

There is another way out of this impasse, but it is an uninviting one that leaves cruel marks on every original spirit. It is the path which offers itself to the exceptionally gifted man who, like Busoni, achieves maturity at too early an age. He sees that which few do in youth—the respectability of traditional teaching. It is not difficult to analyse the causes of future suffering which he lays in store for himself. The early years of the artist should be devoted to fruitful rebellion; the youth whose untimely wisdom makes him forgo this devotes his energy to the conquest of conventional technique instead. Consequently he arrives at a critical judgement of the values of convention at a time when they have already determined his immediate outlook. His attitude towards his craft has then for some time been fixed. He has now to overcome not, like others, the detested prejudice of cocksure teachers, but the ingrained habit of his own mind.

Later, when the revolt against himself comes, he realizes that he has missed something of the elation he should have known in his youth. Mozart probably knew this predicament. Too late for enjoyment there comes the conviction that it would have been a delight to reject without reflection all teachings. That would have acted as an inspiration. When the same sacrifice has to be made so much later, it means a bad wrench first. It is true that some controlled originality has probably been acquired, but any artist should have been reckless in his youth; it profits his soul. He will retain a deeper satisfaction in remembering that he dared to rebel when the very people he most respected were opposed to him. He let that chance pass and must face the consequences. Once he is disappointed in art as he has learned to understand it, he becomes dissatisfied with the world and with his own attainments. He can no longer take pride in seeing them recognized: he comes to admit that he owes this recognition—his very rank in the artistic world—to accepted standards in which he himself has no longer any faith. It becomes painful to him to recall how these standards have been a support to him, now that he would be unhappy to see them applied to any work in his new manner. He is faced at every turn by the reflection that the suspected criterion, though he has come to hate it, was once accepted by him and—what is hardest to bear—accepted with a full intellectual appreciation of all it implied. Indeed, as he has ripened he has recognized more and more the weight and helpfulness of tradition. Yet philosophical speculation always leads him to the conviction that to satisfy his own spirit he must blaze a new path. While wisdom perpetually cautions him against the hasty application of any principles lately formulated, he can never silence the prompting of his artist's disposition. His creative urge remains the final arbiter for his instincts in such agonizing doubts. It may lead him to question his sincerity if he holds back too deliberately the possible results of his recent experiments.[1]

If ever a man was brought up in conditions that would eventually bring home to him all these advantages and disabilities with a vengeance it was Busoni. His parents were both capable musicians of some considerable standing. The father was a brilliant virtuoso with a cynical trust in the usefulness of social relationships. The mother had not only an equally great platform experience, but she was a noted teacher as well. She was, moreover, a devoutly religious woman, whose confident orthodoxy extended to respectful acceptance of worldly conditions and settled reputations.

Since Busoni happened to be an exceptionally precocious child, it cannot cause wonder that, instead of smarting under the relentless artistic discipline applied by both parents, he instinctively prized from the first the tuition he received. If not clearly, then at least obscurely, he understood the rare appropriateness of his beloved and respected elders for the heavy task they were undertaking. He appreciated their responsibilities, which grew with his own, as well as the ambitions of which he himself was the object. Although soon he may have dreamt of independence, he was already at that time endowed with a technique which he could assess at its proper value. This extraordinary perception left no room for the presumptuous expectation that he could ever substitute a method of his own. At least, not one which preserved

---

[1] The aesthetic philosopher knows that it is precisely the artist's mission to hunt with the hounds and to run with the hare. (Shakespeare lives in Iago and in Desdemona; the moral smoothing out at the end of a tragedy, when every one gets his deserts, is a concession to stage convention that finds its ultimate asseveration in the harlequinade.) But it is a terrifying discovery for the artist himself, if he does not yet know how far he need reveal this duality, that is, if he should discover it by reasoning before he is aware of its necessity, and before he knows what application it ought to receive in his several works.

equal advantages, and yet allowed for originality. The dangers of originality might prove greater than any gains.

For many years Busoni remained in this position. The Faustian struggle between knowledge and doubt began for him at an age when deliberate thought has not yet become a habit, even for the most gifted children. He always realized his own unique powers. One need only look at the camera portraits made between his first (*sic!*) and fifth year to be convinced of this.[1] This may seem a preposterous assertion —there is surely no equivalent case—but a look at the actual photographs will convince all cynics. That as far as his memory reached he always felt the power and direction of his own desires we must believe on his own word. His early compositions were too much shaped by the commands of the school in which his thought had been formed to supply evidence. But the alacrity with which he produced them gives proof of an ambition that permits no question of his artistic consciousness. On the evidence collected from the most varied sources one comes to the conclusion that he was aware of his personality long before he was in a position to assert his independence against the masters who trained him to his own precocious satisfaction.

He early foresaw the coming fight, for he instinctively apprehended that he would not remain satisfied with the conventional technique which for the moment proved useful. None the less, even in his extreme youth he was spiritually too mature to anticipate the struggle with a crusader's exaltation. He had held formed artistic convictions, although in miniature; the little philosopher in him sadly divined that they were not above doubt and might one day have to be discarded.

The effects were far-reaching and permanent. When he went through his belated period of revolt he had reached a degree of technical perfection and a corresponding state of

[1] Cf. *Busoni* by E. J. Dent (Oxford University Press). A photograph of the child at less than two years old shows, for those who knew him, the whole man with astonishing completeness.

intellectual superiority from which he could spare no more than a pitying glance for the floundering attempts of youngsters in their first phase of rebellious impatience. Yet he knew that what they attempt is an eternal need for them. Few of the cleverest heads can hope to combine such advantages as his education gave, with a disciplined ambition that has acknowledged artistic liabilities from the outset. Busoni the fully formed artist approved in a fatherly way of the disrespectful labours of young rebels. His approval was for many years only theoretical, and, while he may not have admitted it, his sympathy remained somewhat tepid. His personal interests had long suffered from this superior insight. He had become willing enough to extend to others the tolerance that once would have been beneficial to himself. But he knew too well how extensive must be their incompetence in exactly those matters in which he was most prodigious. Throughout his career he insisted on a precise degree of academic competence. He practically demanded of others that they should have his great craftsmanship before they undertook to set aside the accepted tenets. One might say that he rated them too highly by believing it possible. There cannot have been many musicians after Mozart who possessed anything like his immense technical versatility.

Perhaps he remembered with a certain lasting irony how much he had learned at an age when most toddling artists do not know yet what learning means, and how this was made possible by an abnormal respect which later stood in his way. The superhuman virtuosity he had acquired came near to proving pernicious. It facilitated the technical struggle of his early career so much that the harder spiritual fight only shaped at an age when the years of indefatigable energy had gone. To some extent he was proud of it, as well he might be; but certainly not too proud, since he best knew its natural limitations, and his relative modesty was very genuine. Precisely this surpassingly rare disposition made him justly contemptuous of much respectable achievement, although he never failed scrupulously to pay it the public tribute which he considered all distinction to deserve; as a very enlightened monarch might unstintingly distribute crosses and ribbons to the notabilities who care to claim them. Often his more turbulent disciples, who had good cause to know his severity with himself and themselves, were shocked into protest (not free sometimes from resentment) when they heard him speak with almost humble respect of composers or pianists that seemed to them monsters of successful mediocrity. He gave both Caesar and the devil all they could legitimately ask for; indeed, made a point of it when the 'green', the 'fauve', and the 'anti-philistine man-eaters' around him became too vocal in their reviling of the tall hat, the umbrella, and the decorated buttonhole.

His absolute command of traditional technique ensured for him from the first consideration and respect in the academies. This made him all the more suspect in the rebels' circles. His own late rebellion thus put him in a seemingly false position. The searchlight of conventional appraisement discovered no flaw in his achievement, but for just that reason he did not obtain the whole-hearted suffrage of those younger fighters who regarded the academies as the born enemies of all progress and originality. Beyond the two camps reigns the innocent optimism which expects the best of all innovation. Unfortunately this state of mind discerns no merit in the clairvoyant discontent of a Busoni. If he was a hard judge of his own work, they only remembered his seeming submission to the keepers of the official seals, and they insinuated that there was sycophantic vanity at the bottom of his hesitations. But the simple explanation is that he felt it incompatible with his artistic dignity to join them on terms of equality.

As his career proceeded, this painful antithesis became more pronounced. His conservative admirers shook their heads at his calculated futurism. Those of his adherents who were committed to revolution at any cost, and who still

THE LOAD OF TRADITION

hoped to find a leader in him, distrusted him for his connexions in the other camp. They felt disheartened every time they found that, while he approved of their efforts in principle, he did not express much regard for their actual productions. The fact was that if he did not consider the work of immediate practical account as a demonstration, or of genuine artistic value, he consistently refused to give it public praise although he might privately encourage it.

In his racial and national waverings he found himself in the same predicament.

As a youth he was already too developed a cosmopolitan to be satisfied with the prospect of being an Italian composer. For that one needs a naïve genius that unfolds in the course of a lifetime of relatively obedient handling of available forms. If a man is to adhere with satisfaction to the prescribed paths which lead to success through unquestioning acceptance, he must keep away from speculation on the final truth of the aesthetic principles that guide one there. At the time when Busoni had proved his command of the school's technique by obtaining a reward of the Bologna *Liceo Filarmonico* that had only been awarded to Mozart before him, he was too young and had been too hard-worked to think out at all clearly what he wished his own future to be. As far as one can ascertain he did at that time vaguely identify the immediate future of music itself with his own future; only, while his mind was continually occupied with questions relating to the former, he had not yet arrived at sufficiently precise conclusions to direct his aspirations.

The universal tradition whose abstractions he had till then honoured appeared so venerable to his prematurely developed mind, and had such a hold upon it, that the thought of defection must have seemed impermissible. Even the attempt to strike a purely personal note or to evolve a personal system would appear to him the conceit which he dreaded. One might say that he was so precociously mature as to recognize the physiologically inevitable fact of his immaturity.

It must be emphasized, however, that he renounced any birthright from the loftiest motives only, without ever calculating possible profit. He would have feared for instance that if he adopted a different tradition he might become demonstrably *tedesco*. Where his motives might seem open to suspicion, he instinctively shrank from the appearance alone.

He was too ambitious for the role of an Esau. The mess of pottage meant little to him, however hungry he might have been during the worst years of a youth that was ruthlessly exploited by a born prodigal father. This in spite of his Latin lust for 'here-and-now' instead of the 'later, when!' of more reflectively inclined races.

Since we are dealing with primitive human passions, Biblical metaphors are obviously suitable. Busoni was a Cain who could not bring himself to the slaying of Abel. He was a David too appreciative of the merits of Goliath to advertise his own precocity by the spectacular defeat of so great and estimable a figure. He resembles the different but equally authentic O.T.-David in his generous tolerance of prerogative. He would have cut off that piece of Saul's mantle and sent it back improved by stylistically appropriate embroidery, accompanied by a signed copy of his latest Psalms.

The average boy, when told that he need only begin by stealing an egg to come to stealing a horse before he knows it, and that from there to murdering his mother is but a step, giggles, because he knows better, thanks to a kind Providence. Imagine the fearful contingency that he might be, instead of a reckless little boy, a little great artist, sufficiently serious of purpose to believe that there must be something in it. Think of the unspeakable disillusions he must have when life itself instructs him that this is not how things happen: when he finds that his parents were not even deliberate liars who hypocritically frightened him for their own ends, but just insufficiently intelligent 'grown-ups': that they knew no better than to defend the existing order, with all its mechanical dishonesties and pretensions, simply because they feared the consequences of asserted independence.

Busoni tried in his early manhood to convince himself that his parents' dullness was reasoned policy. To save his soul he made himself believe that his father was not simply a time-serving clarinet-player but a Machiavellian diplomatist at the court of Mammon. He would have felt too unhappy if he had so soon understood that in his youth he had been tyrannized for the sake of remote and threadbare appearances. His dramatic interpretation of the world made it easier for him to think reproachfully of his father as a positively diabolical being. It left him with more faith in the end. He once said to me, discussing Strindberg's 'Totentanz', that the dreadful old fiend who tortures his wife and children with the most exquisite malice reminded him of nothing so much as of his own father, who knew no greater pleasure than to make others suffer. This probably was his endeavour to escape from the preoccupation with the domestic relationships of his earlier years. For he was an exceptionally dutiful son, and he had unwaveringly applied an inexhaustible fund of affection to his parents for so long that he could not help feeling doubly confused when later he saw this sentimental attachment revealed to himself and to a cynical world. There is nothing extraordinary in this attitude. If I dwell upon it here beyond what it seems to require for its simple biographical significance it is for the direct effect it had on his development, and consequently on his work. The same fight between obedience and independence through which he had to go as a son he had to experience again as an artist.

He was taught to admire 'the immortals' before all, and next, to respect those new masters whose success seemed a sufficient guarantee of immortality to come. He lived to question the claims and hopes of the most exalted figures among the immortals, and to despise the epigonic determination of those successors who, like Wagner, started discounting their posthumous credit as soon as a sufficiently respectable following of admirers grew powerful enough to assure eventual victory.

He would sometimes speak of the saddening futility of immortality. Without citing Ozymandias he would point to the ghostly reputation of Homer, and the improbability of any one surviving his own immortality, of more than his name outlasting the civilization from which he derived his mythical prestige. He was convinced that Bach would hardly be remembered to-day if it had not been for the propaganda of the few men like himself who, by adaptation and transcription, revived or kept alive interest in his works. Without that, the occupation of musicians with Bach would in his opinion be artificial, while amateurs would let him participate in the general cult of preciosity for its own sake. He looked upon the Beethoven legend as a typical 'period piece' characteristic for the democratic reaction against a settled order; he liked to recall how Beethoven's popularity diminished as, in his intellectual development, he returned to the spiritual disposition of his formalistic predecessors. Individual romantic figures, like Schubert and Chopin, to whom Busoni would feel naturally attracted when he first attempted to escape from the notions instilled by parental instruction, he came to see afterwards as the ineffectual rebels they must appear when viewed alongside the stately hierarchical procession of the classics.

It has been often observed that it is pernicious for a musician to have a surplus of brains. It is supposed to lead him into the dangerous labyrinth of system. Busoni certainly suffered as much from this implication as any one ever did. There again, he was suspect to opposing parties. The orthodox distrusted his intellect for the time-honoured reason that music evidently does not ask for it in any conspicuous quantity. The unorthodox suspected that he ranged himself on their side, not because his innards moved him to it, but because his mind was driven that way by abstract reflection. This makes a man a doubtful, unwelcome convert. For, however radical his principles, he has, like Mirabeau, to carry in his new position the dead weight of his antecedents and earlier milieu. Really useful converts are of the type represented by Saulus-Paulus, whose undiminished significance derives from this authoritative standing in two capacities. Paulus the Christian advocate knew everything concerning the mania for persecution of Saulus the heretic-hunter. No one could better advise the victorious new rulers about the sound methods of the *ancien régime*. That is why the sifters, the Rabbinical organizers, are so particularly acceptable to every new government. That they are spectacular acquisitions becomes incidental to their bureaucratic usefulness. They owe their welcome to the proved, indispensable efficiency of which they bring the secret with them.

The superstition that brains are a handicap in a musical career has existed long enough to have had distressful consequences. It has become a rare occurrence for any one with a noble purpose and high ideals to devote himself to music exclusively if he is intelligent enough to have a choice of occupations. No other form of human ambition has suffered quite so much under similar disabilities. A peculiarly discouraging feature is that the easiest path to the top seems to be preserved for the popular virtuoso, who, by common consent, should possess the minimum of intelligence called for in the hide-bound specialist.

Busoni was a virtuoso born, but all the more did he dread the danger of becoming a 'popular virtuoso'. He determinedly avoided the facile mannerisms that lead to this contingency. His clear-sightedness saved him from the usual provincial preparations. He did not depend on the local patronage from which a performer slowly emerges into wider territories when tautened expectancy has assured general acclamation.

He did not aspire to the carefully planned explosion in Paris after years of preliminary rumbles reported from Trieste. His simple aim had always been to become an educated and versatile artist before he faced the audiences of the great European centres. He wanted to present himself there not as a musical acrobat but as a matured personality.

What then made him, of all people, settle in Berlin, of all places?

Berlin was the newly established centre of Germany, which by common consent was the promised land of musicians. To the travelling virtuoso of every country it is also attractive by its geographic position. And Busoni found there what in his younger years was notoriously absent from Italian cities: new life, new hope, growing organization, and the absence of a weighty tradition that reproachfully pointed to the old track whenever any one would prospect for himself.

He could not have foreseen at the time that Berlin was to become the centre of the musical industry, and develop an atmosphere which he detested more than the deepest pool of stagnant convention.

Between the eighteen-nineties and the present century musical trade-unionism soared to its zenith in Berlin. The local celebrities of the minor German states, the men who participated in the culture spreading from the small courts, fled from what after the establishment of the Empire threatened to become provincialism. They were attracted by the city which Germans fondly imagined would become what Paris had been before. International virtuosi who for practical reasons chose Berlin as their abode were not so much concerned with questions of prestige. Their intentions had nothing in common with the ideals of native musicians who hailed with excitement the chance of reasserting an unassailable national pre-eminence.[1]

Musicians have, at every period, groped about until they

---

[1] Busoni might have seen a warning in an experience of his Leipzig student days, which, however, at the time chiefly struck him as a grotesque joke. Old Jacob 'Consecutive-fifths' Jadassohn, a hook-nosed, high-shouldered, oily-curled Ghetto Jew who then represented the chaste German tradition, used to say to him: 'D'ye know, Mr. Busoni, an artist is a soldier!' (proudly rolling up the greasy lapels of his chamber cloak) 'Look at me! *I'm* a soldier!'

PARVENU PATRIOTISM

found the road laid by political philosophers a century earlier. The German musical centres, it must not be forgotten, still had some of the old glamour of the musical Zion which made Berlioz write of 'la Sainte Allemagne'. It had not become clear yet that it had exchanged its spiritual for a political Empire. As the Empire discarded the old intellectual mask and asserted itself with the mailed fist it became spiritually more provincial. When it began blustering in the name of its new-found Nationalism, it divulged the mean and ostentatious pride of the parvenu. The imperial capital sweated this greasy offensiveness through all its pores. Musically it grew 'up-to-date' so rapidly, and 'efficient' on such a grand scale, that, before any cosmopolitan musician had time to understand the dreadful facts, it had become the noisy, tinpot heart of music-and-no-nonsense. Its rabid professionals developed an exceptionally fine sense for the detection of blacklegs. Their envious sensitivity registered without fail the defection of rivals who, for the love of art, became as guilty as the veriest amateurs. A pig's flair for truffles could not be more infallible. Their mammoth solidarity was securely based on their professional pride. This held a high rank. Hence their deep resentment and unflagging suspicion of colleagues whose professional status might be beyond question but whose attitude towards art was too obviously idealistic for the herd-prescribed susceptibilities.

Now they saw a man like Busoni, with talents that not the severest critic could deny, a man struggling hard for existence, squandering funds on first performances of manuscript works by obscure rivals. It was enough to cause despair to any one who realized that his success might spoil the market for other composers, Busoni himself included. Another lapse from professional etiquette was his habit of inviting pupils from all over the world to take his time and energy without asking anything in return. That meant robbing hard-working teachers who would for a consideration have gladly given such pupils all those hours which they genteelly advertise as 'still free'.[1] He committed the identical sins which made Liszt lastingly unpopular in professional circles that with their calculated perversity would have daunted the campaigning courage of Don Quixote himself. Poor Liszt helped to make his rival Wagner popular. So popular that he would probably be aghast at the present vulgarization of what to him was one of the highest manifestations of aesthetic ideals. Liszt had to pay a heavy penalty; it is not fully paid yet, and possibly cannot be as long as Wagner's fantastic popularity lasts. It is true that after many years the musical world is renewing its acquaintance with Liszt's scores, but it has lost sight of the order of priority and numerous critics still belittle Liszt for being so like Wagner—as one might reproach Homer for being so obviously reminiscent of Pope.

Busoni's position in Berlin remained difficult; he was not forgiven his championing of Liszt in a city that kept the adored Clara's hatred alive under the guidance of Joachim. When he was acclaimed all over Europe and America as a pianist, he still had to endure the very personal—often unashamedly libellous—attacks on him as a composer by the pundits of the Berlin musical press. These perpetually stood in his way whenever he modestly tried to present his compositions.[2] It happened sometimes that, in spite of his willingness to accept what organizers knew to be nominal fees, they would still demur and haggle if he proposed to play one of his own works in addition to the welcome Beethoven or Mozart concerto. It is unpleasant to couple such banalities with his name, but the necessity should not be shirked. He has been too contemptuously neglected, and too viciously

[1] This does not, of course, alter the fact that 'amateurism' was wholeheartedly detested by Busoni. He took care to put his own works out of its reach. Only the thoroughly trained musician can attempt to touch them. 'We must make the texture of our music such that no amateur can lay hands on it', he once said to me in a moment embittered by some dreadful assault and battery on a Mozart sonata to which we had listened.

[2] I wish we had a musical Dante, exploring at the hand of Virgil-Berlioz the abodes of nasty and not-so-nasty musicians. I like to imagine the lines in which he shows us the all-knowing scribes (seated on a locked box containing dictionaries) condemned to copying out each other's complete writings.

THE LEOPARD'S SPOTS

criticized from motives that ought not to be spared the pillory. One cannot speak of his greatness without remembering how grievously he was made to suffer for his devotion to his ideals. To his last day he unflinchingly faced savage antagonisms which did not cease with his untimely death. After what Germans are pleased to call the 'Revolution' of 1918, his chance seemed to have come. One of his disciples received a post at the Arts Ministry as a reward for socialistic activities. This brought Busoni an official appointment which enabled him to do much valuable work. Characteristically he then abandoned plans for an American tour, and sacrificed chances of repairing a financial position that had become acute during the War. He prepared to concentrate on composition and on the teaching of talented young men who flocked to him in even greater numbers now that he combined official with personal prestige.

He profited from a transient period of liberal thought; one shudders to contemplate what would have happened had he lived long enough to see Germany veer to a régime of fanatic reaction surpassing the rigid formalism of the pre-War period.[1]

To-day it would be remembered that he did not at any time in his career identify himself with the artistic tendencies of the country where, by a freak of circumstance, he had become domiciled. Whatever his descent (much was made in Germany of his maternal grandfather being half-Austrian),

---

[1] It is not generally realized here to what extent the monstrosities exhibited by the rulers of the German 'Third Reich' were a familiar feature of pre-War days. In 1913 the first performance of Mahler's posthumous ninth symphony was greeted with a howling chorus of execration by a vast section of the Berlin public. The conductor happening to be himself a Jew, the occasion was described as an impudent piece of Jewish propaganda!

Nor were the really Nordic musicians of Germany ever tired of voicing grave doubts concerning Busoni's ancestors. A man is more than likely to be a Jew if he has a grandfather indiscreet enough to be called Giuseppe Weiss, it was argued! Wilhelm II's erstwhile pet Chancellor, von Bülow, in his Memoirs still revives the old story of the quarrel of Heine and Börne, and speaks of the Jew-stinkpot that was then opened under delicate German nostrils. Most Germans are so afraid of their possible ancestry that they hardly know how rude to be in order to discard suspicion.

in his own consciousness he was a very Italian Italian, as with growing age he increasingly realized. His conceptions and standards were essentially Latin, and temperamentally far removed from everything Teutonic. It must have been an internal struggle, as well as an outward one, for him to spend his life in Germany among Germans while retaining his independence. His hope originally had been to give the most intimate elements of his art as a spiritual contribution to the nation among whom he lived. The Germans preferred to hold on to the precept of Wagner's Hans Sachs about pure, chaste, German Art, that should keep itself undefiled by pernicious mixture with Latin glitter and frivolity.

He merely asked that he might create an influence which would become active among later generations in whose purposes and plans he was more interested than in immediate results. But it was precisely this vaguely suspected desire which was physiologically resented by the German artistic community. He did not aspire to spiritual naturalization, but in spite of the suggestion that emanates from his ideas of service—otherwise so welcome to German sentimentality—he preserved an independence that connotes overmuch pride in the earnest eyes of men who think of their art as their daily bread, eaten for the greatest good of all the people.

Busoni was far too conscious of his precious inheritance of race and culture to overlook the presumptuousness of these militant implications. He felt hurt by the conditional acceptance offered to his work by people whose appreciation was restricted within the limits of national sympathies.

He was given no respite from these petty resentments because his personality was too strong to leave any one indifferent. He inspired ardent affection in his admirers, often more than he could respond to, and of a kind that proved embarrassing. At the same time he was extensively and intensely hated by many people who had no accountable grudge against him. They hated him for just being Busoni. They felt acutely uncomfortable because he existed. They regarded his designs and undertakings as so many attacks on the peace of their souls. Sometimes one has the impression that they took his activities as direct insults, rather as Chopin imagined that Berlioz composed his works to annoy him. His early death itself was by some musicians regarded as a retribution for obscure sins, an insufficient punishment for his vast nastiness. They tried to improve the occasion by sinister hints and whispered lies. Before his emaciated body was cold they spread the foulest insinuations concerning his habits and the probable causes of his death. Since he was one of the few great artists who never suffered from any venereal disease, they tried to make him out at least an abject drunkard.[1] This was done with such disgusting persistence as to have called for contradiction that otherwise would in itself have been a calumny.

Busoni had to live the devastating life of a performer with its constant travelling and consequent irregularity. But he had a horror of dissipation in any form. Every waking hour was devoted to work, with only the most harmless relaxation, beyond which his chief wish was for as much sleep before midnight as any suburban could desire. I once accompanied him on a journey to Manchester after he had gone through a trying rehearsal in the morning following on a concert the night before. The evening recital over, he had to travel back to be in London for another 10 o'clock rehearsal and a concert in the afternoon. Feeling completely exhausted, he asked me to share a bottle of champagne before our train left, but when the bottle was put before us he found it was of the variety described as 'brut, special for Great Britain'. He went without his innocent stimulant because he had been told that to this wine 'brandy, if not . . . *whisky!*' was added. He had this exaggerated horror of spirits. Yet such is the growth of animosity, once it is rooted

[1] Excesses 'in Baccho et Venere' proceed from an abnormal sensitiveness of the imagination. The vivid image of realization of the wish makes every appeal almost irresistible. It is no wonder then if musicians are frequent sufferers.

in the soil of suspicious conjecture, that his devoted biographer, Professor Dent, had to defend him against the crazy aspersion that he died of delirium tremens.[1]

We all know how freely new weapons are offered to any aggressive publicist who reveals the identity of his target. In New York, in 1911, some German musicians bitterly complained of Busoni's heartlessness towards his colleagues. Heaven knows that he made more sacrifices than perhaps any musician. But what tickled the fancy of some gossip writer was that an unemployed bandsman found he could not reach 'Busoni', although he had a letter of introduction. When eventually by sheer persistence he interrupted one of Busoni's meals, and received no engagement, he widely complained of such callousness. The journalist who lapped up his accusations had perhaps not had it explained to him that there happened to be another Busoni, an agent for restaurant orchestras. The poor fiddler may have been sorry afterwards, but one may be pretty sure that he did not take very much trouble to undo whatever harm he caused by his earlier whining, and anyhow he would have found no more than the most lukewarm interest for his belated rectifications. (Mistaken exposures with scare headings seldom receive more than modest contradiction at the bottom of the dullest page. Every sub-editor knows that a denunciation has news-value, but an apology very little or none.)

Possibly the antipathy of some German critics for Busoni was no better founded, yet a few of them when at a loss for a subject used the occasion for a renewed offensive against the man, his works, and his ideals. They allowed him scant credit for such facts as that he lived in their country, wrote most of his dramatic works to German texts, corresponded and conversed in German as much as Italian, that he studied, performed, and edited with affectionate devotion German

---

[1] Any one with the merest smattering of medical knowledge *would* know—any journalist *should*—how foolish is the accusation in the case of a patient who was for months in bed while treated for nephritic heart trouble. This destroys every possible excuse in *forma pauperis* on behalf of the offending newspapers.

music, and had an extensive and profound knowledge of German literature. But of course he felt, dreamed, and reasoned as a true-born Italian. In the country of his choice it was evidently argued that the 'Lieb' Vaterland' could not 'ruhig sein' as long as there was this foreign body in its organism, although by the irritation it set up it might become the nucleus of a new pearl. His antagonists were not physiologically so conscious as to realize these advantages. Presumably they would rather live up to their self-evolved reputation as 'Spree-Athener', and be proud to raise the old cry: 'Here goes a foreigner! Heave half a brick at him!'

Even those who were not deliberately hostile frequently felt somewhat doubtful. Was he paying them compliments, or the reverse, when he discoursed on German classical music, as in his 'Neue Aesthetik'? Speaking of the relative youth of European music he pointed out the pleasing fact that some of the early masters, such as Bach, Beethoven, and Mozart, would probably never be surpassed. It seemed strange to them that, having seen the light so far, he rejected the popular belief that this proved Germany the blessed soil on which great composers grow, and that one can naturally look forward to an endless succession of them. On the contrary, in his speculations on the probable future developments of music he left no doubt that he expected revitalization or rejuvenation only from a bold reaction against the sterile German conventions. The doubters might have taken heart when later he developed his principle of the new 'classicity', which finds room for all, however readily it admits of false interpretations. He had also revealed his very individual conception of the use to be made of methods derived from classical tradition. Few things so embarrassed his convention-suckled colleagues as the freedom he permitted himself on their hallowed ground. The Teuton who likes to quote a Philistine perversion of Schiller's joyful line[1] and maintains that 'Ernst ist die Kunst', felt endlessly annoyed by Busoni's Latin habit of partly veiled

---

[1] 'Ernst ist das Leben—heiter ist die Kunst.'

sarcasm and elegant irony. They found it irritatingly recurrent in his titles and their descriptive allusions, which teasingly pretend to assume coherent erudition in his hearers. His use alone of the term 'classic' implies 'what it appears to me, hardly what it will be to you'. This disposition permeates his choice of titles with a mocking assumption of modesty. But, in spite of the slight touch of preciosity, they announce his feeling for the greatness of his examples and depreciate the mean conceptions ordinarily associated with them in mean minds. He would call an ambitious work of whose value and importance he was well aware, 'Sonatina', inferring with esoteric pride that one day he might compose 'a Sonata', and till then left to others the use of a title which Beethoven's practice links in our minds with the most monumental manifestations of genius, for some trite arrangement of patterns on the overtrodden academic plan.

This again accounts for the diffident appellations of movements in his works, such as 'fughetta', 'arietta', 'duettino'. Only his measured sense of humour prevented him from calling, as he once intended, the 'Brautwahl', with dimensions on the scale of 'Robert le Diable' and 'Götterdämmerung', an operetta.

The effect of this habit was enhanced by the contemptuous honesty which made him hesitate to denounce in practice things he had disowned in theory. He was profoundly convinced that individual talent is always the deciding factor, whatever the chosen label. He courageously advertised sympathy with the Italian futurists although he questioned the validity of their manifestoes. And this in the face of nationalist and academic opposition, when diplomacy would have demanded concealment. Sympathetic interest in futurism was at that time taken to denote approval of internationalism and of anarchism.

However paradoxical it seems now, it was this brave independence that had made him choose Germany for his home. At the time when he came to Germany it was the chosen domain of progress and cosmopolitanism. Young

Busoni, impatient of the stern canons and strict formalism of his own country, where individualism was anything but a saving grace, encountered a more congenial atmosphere as he travelled north. In Berlin he was attracted by what Mme. de Staël calls its 'total lack of historic traditions, spiritual and material'. Here, if anywhere, it seemed that one might live and work unhampered by the fetters of a tyrannical past. One would not find one's way mapped out at every point by what one's fabulous ancestors had planned. Busoni had seen enough of that as a child and during adolescence. He was horrified to find it again in its full mustiness when much later in life he returned to Bologna as Director of the Liceo. Not only was he expected to look with a tearful eye on the wig of Rossini, but after the arrangements of the lavatories,[1] for no better reason than that Padre Martini had not considered this beneath his contrapuntal dignity.

Young Italians of his generation were obsessed with fear of the spectral old man of the sea who threatened to jump on one's neck from behind every broken pillar. The country to which one could flee to see that ghost laid was modernist Germany, where no dilapidated frescoes reminded one at every step of all that others had done, and of the little one could hope to add. The continual growth and change in Berlin was a constant fascination, which for Busoni held a personal message. Eventually, however, these very surroundings taught him—more than at first he could have believed—how much his national heritage meant to him.

If anything were needed to emphasize his potential unpopularity in his adopted country, it was his preoccupation with his racial beliefs and fears. In his earlier years in Germany he found in its literature and customs just that touch of the exotic that made them romantic for him. His choice of subjects for dramatic works proves it abundantly. Direct

[1] 'Als Abortfrau wurde ich benutzt', he told a German friend. In most German cities, lording it over a dozen private chambers is considered incompatible with male prestige, and therefore left to patient old Whistler's-mother ladies who do not mind sitting and waiting.

touch with the sordid reality of professional life inevitably destroyed the illusion. His German antagonists were wiser than they knew when they perpetually objected to his presence. They had not reasoned it out; his extraordinary talents alone provided a sound basis for their objection. They had good reasons to feel jealous.

Yet, despite Busoni's reiterated assertions of solidarity, Italian musicians could not forget what they regarded as his defection. Perhaps this was what made him so markedly sensitive on that point. Nothing infuriated him more than for an Italian to address him in German. Circumstances had made him a musical Ishmael. He enjoyed his years in Moscow and in Helsingfors, but he never identified himself with Russian or Scandinavian habits of thought. On the contrary, he remembered so much of the dilettantism he had seen there that he found it hard to free himself from an ingrained irritation. 'What is one to expect,' he said several years later, 'of all these composing admirals and generals that are supposed to have kept Russian music alive? I understood that national tradition had begun and died with Glinka.' His knowledge of their works was never extensive, and I heard him inquire of a Russian friend, as late as 1913, whether 'Russlan and Ludmilla' was still a work in 'pure' Russian style or not. Of the uttermost north of Europe he remembered resentfully that people had an ineradicable tendency to highfalutin moral preoccupation, and while he deeply admired the originality of Sibelius's application of traditional forms, he detected in his works 'bleak-and-white' perspectives that to his own ardent temperament seemed barren and ill-favoured. The ineffaceable memory of his own country's abundance and generous climate made him increasingly intolerant of the stonily rectitudinous, Ibsenile blond beasts who had never felt the sweet warmth of the Southern sun. This also explains to some extent the feeling of discomfort which life in America gave him. In his last years this grew almost to an obsession. He had tried hard to show interest in the country where he resided for some years, and where his first son was born, but he never got far beyond the composition of a work founded on Red Indian motives. Occasionally he would give a tendentious interview after a tour, but he nursed his resentment until he could speak with voluptuous pleasure of a planned holiday which should be the excuse for a journey to New York, when he would stay on board ship in the harbour for the sole satisfaction of returning to Europe without having set foot on land. This looks like extravagant insult, unless one recalls his provoking experiences in the United States. He could never forget how, in his early years in Boston, his colleagues reproached him for taking too much trouble with his pupils, thereby adversely influencing conditions of employment. Nor could he dismiss from his mind those agonizing tours when talk was about nothing but fees, professional chances, and social duties. The endless receptions by local committees exasperated him to the breaking point. In revenge he once allowed himself the luxury of refusing an official luncheon, to return at the dessert with a parcel of books, bought during a walk through the town. This was to show that he was sound enough in wind and limb, but that he could think of a better use for his few spare hours. The organizing ladies, with a rare interloping male, would have forgiven him much more than this if they had known how he suffered under the consciousness of having to parade an expected repertoire. He considered this a demoralization, and it lacerated his nervous system. He told me that often his first act on entering his hotel bedroom was to turn round the mirrors on the walls, so as to spare himself the sight of his own face, which reminded him too much of his degrading slavery. He was not irascible by temperament and he had few nervous idiosyncrasies. But he had to endure much. There was, for instance, the ridiculous and painful experience he once had in New York. He felt inspired by the opportunity of a conscientiously rehearsed performance of a Beethoven concerto with Mahler and the Philharmonic Orchestra.

Mahler and Busoni worked with enthusiasm and exceptional application to give a rendering that should owe nothing to stale traditions. After arduous preparation, in a state of prolonged tension, these two servants of the loftiest discipline hoped to resuscitate the very spirit of Beethoven.

The introduction was only just over, when an obese lady, with tortoise-shell rimmed glasses on her millionairish pug-nose, stood up in the first row of stalls, bellowed 'This will *never* do', and removed her expensive body with such ostentatious dignity that it was difficult to preserve the mood of tiptoe-reverence. Another disturbing memory was created by the agent who had arranged Busoni's first tour. He withheld half of the money he owed, simply to force him into signing a fresh contract. In view of such facts one cannot exactly wonder at his criticisms. On the contrary, one admires the detachment which made him insist that his elder son should once, at least, accompany him, to see the beauties of the country of his birth[1]—the country where the father had been told by a distracted impresario that he was so difficult to deal with because he rejected suggestions for 'a little' publicity. Busoni had indeed refused to stage even a motor-car accident. Altogether he had proved maddeningly incapable of understanding the publicity agents' predicaments. He regarded such proposals as indecent; he was shocked when asked to believe that other artists wooed fame by more dramatic devices than floral tributes, or the innocent play-acting to which the nervous tension of the platform might lead.

His exploiters felt irritated. Jenny Lind and Barnum—Art and Blather wedded—had achieved sensational successes. It had been proved that even pianists could be sold to the general public. One must not expect Art alone to suffice. Art, with however much behind or before it, is '——' to the thousands who are in search of an hour's entertainment. A

---

[1] His first son was born in Boston, where Busoni had an appointment at the Conservatoire.

pianist and a piano were never quite enough for that in Paris or Vienna, no longer even in Moscow or St. Petersburg. Why could not he show some rational sense?

In his younger years Busoni was not unwilling to recall Liszt, who when he heard his audience shout for the 'Paraphrase' on 'Robert le Diable' only spluttered 'Cela va sans dire, je suis l'esclave du public', and who travelled with a load of laurel-wreaths to be handed up to him on each platform. Once, when an impresario told Busoni that it was his 'duty' to play at a concert arranged for him in an outrageous place and at an outrageous time, he became murderous, and did not trouble to hide it. His artistic duties to himself and his talent made him resent having to play the very programmes he had made up, if perhaps under some slight pressure. The demands of over-spontaneous galleryites painfully reminded him of the routine improvisations he had to give as an infant prodigy. Anything that touched his composer's sensitiveness made him more aware of his genuine calling, and of the tragic waste of time most of his public appearances signified. But whether an artist feels unhappy is neither here nor there; the one solid fact is that composing music seldom provides an existence unless one has the relative good fortune to be tied to a bear-leader like Diaghilev. And probably that is more humiliating in the end. The 'engaged' composer has not even the right to decide what his own style shall be. The successful virtuoso can at least choose between the whole world plus advertisement, and a few capitals plus what may be more intimate appreciation. When, however, the great cosmopolitan centres are infected by the need for extra-musical aids to attention, shall he find consolation in Leipzig, Warsaw, Amsterdam, the reputed music-spots on the face of the earth? There, after all, he must also repeat his old tricks, whether they be Mozart and Beethoven concertos or variations on once-popular opera tunes. For poorer returns he is showing off the same horses in a smaller circus. Whichever way he chooses, he knows that he will find no interest in unknown work, unless it is so sensational that a child cannot only hear it but will listen to it. Busoni was in these things free from the usual weakness. He went to the other extreme far enough to introduce difficulties for his own delight; if he solved new problems satisfactorily he did not mind that his public had never been aware of them. A characteristic example was when, having moved every one at the final rehearsal in the morning with his rendering of a slow movement, he bewildered the audience in the evening, having, as he proudly informed his friends, managed it 'entirely without pedal'. His audience could not have been expected to share his satisfaction even if they could have understood his ambition. But he would have felt ashamed if he had repeated himself to the few who heard him twice.

When Busoni was touring Europe with Ysaye he complained that Ysaye did not feel like practising new works. His partner said: 'What more do they want than to hear Busoni and Ysaye playing the "Kreutzer" Sonata? Do you want to rehearse as well?' Busoni's pride and ambition were outraged.

He cruelly chided another famous virtuoso for playing the same favourite little pieces in every city of the world. The reply was, 'I hate it so much that I do it as often as I can. Then I shall soon be able to retire and devote myself to My Real Art.' Busoni for once retorted with an observation which showed a shrewd judgement of human failings—on the whole he was too generous and trusting for that: 'You never will retire; you will never think you have enough.' And the fact is that this admirable player is still to-day enchanting vast audiences with his 'charming trifles', whatever, with his immense wealth, he may feel about it. 'This man', Busoni said in one of his rare moments of bitterness, 'will play in a sailors' brothel if only they pay his fees, yet it seems this does not affect his artistic standing.'

He would naturally be reminded of his own integrity which had been the cause of much hardship. He justifiably expected his Berlin public, at least, to take him at his own valuation, and to appreciate his intentions. But only in the concluding years of his career did he attain anything approaching this. Until then, he found that he was condemned for things which were gladly tolerated in others, or that they were praised for feats he had equalled or surpassed without notice being taken. 'When I was a young man', he told me, 'I was infuriated to see my finest efforts ignored. I was neglected, and others were acclaimed for what I had actually performed.'

BUSONI. 'You need not smile; it was precisely as in the tale of Hoffmann. His Klein-Zach, curiously enough, was a dwarf too, and he was admired for every one's merits and actions.'

MYSELF. Are you serious, or intentionally extravagant?

B. I mean every word of it. When the Eisenach courtiers heard the Prime Minister speak they would say, 'Klein-Zach is an orator without equal. Oh, he *is* clever!' If they saw a fine-looking woman they said, 'Isn't Klein-Zach lovely to-day?' You may believe me: the Berlin Press was exactly like that about me.

M. I understand you are referring to . . .

B. Of course I am! It was ghastly. If I surpassed myself in a recital they said, 'Have you ever heard D'Albert play better?' I might play the whole of Liszt's works, and they would say with gasps of worship, 'D'Albert's repertoire is simply astonishing.'

It is a fact that D'Albert acquired a reputation as an opera composer of remarkable originality, although anything more lamely trite than his music would be difficult to imagine. And Busoni's strongly individual contributions to opera hardly received notice. One cannot, therefore, dismiss his account as a delusion of overwrought nerves. Busoni saw the situation as an allegory of his critics' doubts about him. Its effects were anything but unreal. While he could not be expected to discover the obscure causes of this antagonism, and the strange substitutions to which it gave rise, he felt appalled at the draining of force brought about by this nightmare. The dwindling effect of his most heroic labours represented the mechanical exaction of tribute by 'the public's' inexorable stupidity. Its unspoken ethics do not tolerate a musician with more brains and vision than appear sufficient for other famous men. The Lilliputians fear Gulliver's bulk, if they do not resent it.

What is the poor man of genius to do? He might know that he will be petted only after he has been tamed. The monstrous legions of men-in-the-street dread forces that are not properly shackled. It is, everywhere and always, dimly remembered that when licence or power was given to men with original ideas, perturbing and harrowing things started to happen. Prudent citizens were relieved if they managed in time to cut their losses. The Gullivers and Columbuses were lucky if they escaped with life in this cutting process. Statesmen, alchemists, astrologers, explorers, and financiers seldom get a fair bargain. Had Law or Necker been given more than a half-chance they might have led nations to triumph and wealth. Half-heartedness sees the risk of failure constantly in the foreground. Men with bold ideas are therefore feared like forces of nature which cannot be satisfactorily contained, and smirking prudence calls a craven halt before the fruit on the tree of achievement has had time to ripen.

In our days we have seen the case of Clemenceau added to the classic examples. People wish to see elemental forces usefully directed in known channels, otherwise they feel that they must destroy in order not to be destroyed. Alas, when common sense applies its restrictions to genius and forces it into the treadmill, it makes it as ineffectual as Samson with his locks shorn. The hideous process is carried out in a mild enough manner now and then, but the results do not vary. The pathetic decline of Mendelssohn showed how sweetly a gifted man can be cured of his talents. The Philistines caught him in the comfortable movement of aesthetic banality which suspects waywardness wherever there is genius. When they had him well in hand they dully wondered how it was that he no longer charmed them with that graceful originality which they had so much admired in his earlier performances.

'AUX CHRÉTIENS LES LIONS!'

Shades of Alcibiades! Many a young conqueror's *élan* has been broken by the weight of distinctions and rewards hung upon him. The ingenuity of the braid-collared white ants and brass-hatted burying-beetles that do the world's levelling is inexhaustible in its Protean applications. Mythology records how Hercules lifted the redoubtable giant off the earth. Swarms of unassuming nitwits surpass his feat by collectively holding down giants that threaten to soar.

Busoni was always philosophical enough to know all this, even if he did not consider the application to himself. But he felt exasperated when serious attention was denied to him while he used up his mind and body without stint.

Dr. Bierbach, who collected pulse-measurements of pianists after their concerts, has published a record of the condition of Busoni's heart at the end of a few hours playing. It graphically demonstrates how the nervous and physical energy expended equals what normally a man might use up in a week. 'Illness denotes lack of talent', I have heard Busoni say. This aristocratic recklessness may in part account for his early decline. The dissipation with which he has been charged existed in the venomous imagination of a few slander-mongers.

If certain forms of criticism roused his anger it was not from vanity. Busoni judged too sanely to tolerate the affectation of the executant who pretends to scorn success. He saw in such a resignation to obscurity an apology for mental feebleness. In his own case he knew that only success as a pianist could secure leisure for composing. Besides, in spite of his hard saying about illness, he had no illusions concerning his powers of resistance. When he was forty-five he spoke without a shade of sentimentalism of 'the fifteen years I may, with luck, last'.

Every succeeding year made him more acutely aware of his precise situation, social and physical. This unavoidably increased his feeling of loneliness, however much he must to the world have seemed surrounded by friends. The point is of a certain importance since he would speak differently about his work to his numerous acquaintances, and to his few genuine intimates. Here lies a distinction which accounts for many misunderstandings. He often complained that as a child he was too precocious to have friends of his own age, that as a youth he saw comrades grow up to ostensible manhood with unpleasant rapidity, and that when his own full maturity had arrived he felt again that he had left his contemporaries behind. All this is unmistakably reflected in his compositions. Their very sequence suggests how he lived in continuous hopeful anticipation, rarely in touch with actualities. His relations with full-fledged musicians always remained somewhat distant, and, while his love and interest were all for youth, he did not find it easy to meet very young people on terms that precluded embarrassment.

In this connexion his estimation of which were his first genuinely individual works is all the more interesting. Officially his second Violin Sonata is named as the work with which he arrived at a ripened personal style. In frank discussion with a few close companions he made no such claim for any work written before 1910. This means that he dated his birth as an independent composer from the appearance of the piano-pieces 'An die Jugend' (later drawn on for the first Sonatina) and the 'Berceuse' in its initial version for piano.[1]

[1] The subsequent orchestral version was named 'Des Mannes Wiegenlied am Sarge seiner Mutter'. He meant nothing more than that a man's understanding of motherly love deepens until in spirit he tenderly bends over his mother's form, returning a little of the affection he has received. Most people, unfortunately, believed that he was aiming at some Christmas-cracker moral about 'from the Cradle to the Grave'. The title admittedly suggested the inference. A similar misapprehension occurred over his 'An die Jugend'. Here again, strong associations beset the mind. Every musician has seen so many pieces 'für die Jugend' that he may be excused for believing that these simply constructed movements were meant for childish brains and fingers. Busoni intended them as visionary sketches of aspects which, in his belief, music was to assume, and dedicated them to Youth which would see the full growth. On Youth all his hopes centred.

Similar explanations were constantly required, and he was always ready to correct and to enlighten. If one could not say that he chose titles deliberately in order to provide the elucidations afterwards, one must admit that he did not resist the temptation to leave possibilities of confusion. It points to a didactic strain in his mind which avoided the danger of pedantry by an impish sense of humour, and by a romantic delight in erudite, poetic complexities. This Hoff-

THE CURSE OF ORIGINALITY

It was his misfortune that his originality of outlook penetrated everything he did, for, since some part of his erudition was necessarily shared with potential critics, antagonisms were continually reborn.

His recondite interests often proved unacceptable. He insisted for instance on playing Saint-Saëns, not because he considered him a great master, but because his works present a phase that, via Hummel and Chopin, reaches to the legitimate origins of modern piano-music. His intrinsically aristocratic predilections made him respect the Pretender to the old ruling dynasty, not the 'free-lance' usurper. Another cause for displeasure was his advocacy of Bizet. When it moved him to the composition of a 'Sonatina super Carmen' he perpetrated three branding sins simultaneously. He had resumed the despised Lisztian tradition of a Piano Fantasia on operatic fragments, he had chosen a composer whose name, in connexion with chamber music, jarred on Teutonically critical ears, and by his reference to sonata form he intensified the general sinfulness of the proceedings.

Again, critics who were prepared to forgive even as much as this would stand aghast at his Bach paraphrases, and in their indignation forget the unique merits of his scholarly editions of Bach.

Thus in many ways his constantly varying activities made new enemies. On the other hand, his restless roaming over the whole field of pedagogic, editorial, and creative interests left many friends who were not exclusively disciples no time for readjustment. Numerous admirers of his violin sonatas, and even of his Concerto for piano, orchestra, and chorus, were bewildered when they first heard the orchestral version of the 'Berceuse'. They were sufficiently familiar with his orchestral style to know that his technical command was beyond question. Yet, when at a rehearsal in London the

mannesque disposition made the recurrent expounding of his intentions to disciples and critics a kindly and graceful pleasure. He was infinitely patient here, as he was infinitely inventive in the provision of opportunities for the indulgence of this playfully solemn custom itself.

53

conductor put a section of his orchestra at Busoni's disposal, there was a noticeable embarrassment on all sides at the strange impressionistic sound with which we are now familiar enough in the compositions of younger men who have profited by his researches. Probably an unknown composer would have caused no surprise; his work would have been considered strange, but accepted as a sample of the style at which he was aiming. People would have postponed judgement while awaiting further developments in the direction indicated. But Busoni's orchestral writing had become relatively familiar as being founded on that of Beethoven with, in addition, the chromatic brass of Liszt, and the flexibility of the body of sound that was Verdi's specific contribution.[1]

The important work of the intervening years, the 'Brautwahl', had never been heard here. This goes far to explain his critics' failure to grasp the meaning of the changes in his style and the inevitable re-orientation of craftsmanship that followed. But those German critics who knew the 'Brautwahl' score, and had attended the Hamburg performances, felt none the less very dubious when they heard the constantly changing timbres of the 'Berceuse'. One of Busoni's most faithful adherents found it necessary, when writing a programme note, to give a disquisition on modes and the relative artificiality of major and minor, instead of frankly admitting that Busoni had at this period broken with the conception of consonance and dissonance, and at the same time discarded the palette of orchestral colours which ranges all luscious sound on one side and harsh sound opposite.

This method left Strauss-nurtured critics bewildered, for Busoni's dissonance was as often presented in tender sounds as gay moods were conveyed in minor keys. Again, his

[1] Verdi was the first to achieve this with the modern opera orchestra. His problems were quite different from those created by the slowly coiling Wagnerian phrase, pierced here and there by prickly barbs of contrasting sound. The tenderly entwining shoots of melody in Verdi's latest manner are not his speciality. They had been anticipated by Gounod, who seldom receives the credit.

orchestral expletives shunned neither the simplest of homely chords nor departments of the band that are usually reserved for melodic titbits. For those reasons, knowledge of his 'Brautwahl' was desirable. It would have supplied clues to the students of Busoni's music who felt baffled by the new departures at this point of his career. An opera is exceptionally useful in this respect, for when situations are dramatically treated the relationship between musical phrases and orchestral colours, and between harmonies and words, most plainly points the way to the composer's thoughts.

Unfortunately his 'Brautwahl' had only a few performances, although there the composer showed his kindest face and his easiest smile. He himself had hoped that there was a chance of international popularity for this work in particular. He forgot that the humorous complexities of E. T. A. Hoffmann in any case appeal to a very limited circle, and that in translation most of the subtle allusions that abound in the score would be irretrievably lost.[1]

Another drawback from a practical point of view is that the very intimacy of detail which imparts the most delightful qualities to the separate scenes becomes in its totality responsible for dimensions that must frighten almost any producer, and test even the patience of a sympathetic audience. With a translated text the work might acquire a further exotic attraction for a public outside Germany. Against this would have to be set off the inevitable loss of most of the musical finesses. It is a score to be savoured almost bar by bar, but it plays something over four hours, and with all its *leggierezza*, it shows enough of the Beethovenian *patte du lion* to become somewhat of a trial to any but the most determined enthusiasts. If the orchestral score could have been published at a low price, or if a readable miniature score had been technically

---

[1] In his 'Arlecchino' he reverted to the ironically allusive manner at its most abstrusely erudite, and to the deliberately Italian and archaic mien of the Commedia dell'Arte. His musical utterance conveys his immediate feeling. It is constantly modified by innumerable considerations which presume on the receptive faculties of most listeners.

practicable in 1911, there might have been a better chance for the subsequent works.

The 'Brautwahl' reveals all Busoni's theories, all his beliefs, his leanings, hopes, and affections, transmuted by the flame of his unquenchable musical ardour. Yet he shows himself here the complete antipode of the unaffected, instinctive artist. He never aimed at the unreasoning notation of impressions. He was incapable of the state of perpetual awe of a naïve spirit amidst a world of astonishing material. His music reveals a soul that has passed through every fire. He intellectually accounts for all his experiences, and presumes hearers who are at ease amongst the complete range of musical literature. Without that, too much would be lost of his involved, far-roaming thought, reflected in a restlessly searching language full of ellipses, poetical allegations, and stylistic point.

The formation of every detail of his intricate musical conceptions rests on definitely reasoned premises. The hearer must call to his aid the shrewdest erudition if he would appreciate the full meaning of each bar.

In melodic construction Busoni reveals a reasoned approval of Bellini's most broadly developed phrases. But he also recalls those of Beethoven which, as in the slow movement of the 'Pathétique', point to the same origin. The simple clarity of his chromaticism derives from Bach, to whose unendingly varied, unforced polyphonic complexities Busoni applied the motivic caesura of Beethoven's dramatic symmetries. In the extension of his periods he applies the essence of the contrasted ensembles of Cimarosa, Donizetti, and Mozart. He has their controlled rise and fall of lyrical emphasis, spread over the amplest dimensions. But he employs it with the increased subtlety of dramatic alternation that was first shaped by Meyerbeer and Verdi. He possesses the ironical *savoir-faire* and the facetious lyricism of Offenbach, and he pleasantly applies the worldly-wise toying with thematicism that was one of the charms of Italian opera up to the time of Rossini. To the latter he is again indebted for a characteristic tempo and fioritura in his slighter arias and concerted sections.

When something perplexing is found in the more portentous of his shorter compositions, it can nearly always be elucidated by reference to the conversational treatment of comparable matter in his 'Brautwahl'.

This applies also to his 'Arlecchino', but only in as far as the references touch the Italian material, for here more than elsewhere he restricted himself to immediate dramatic needs. But it holds good again for most of his 'Faust', which at a later stage and on a higher plane was another summing-up of all his musical experiences and memories.

It is useful to examine what led him to this regularly recurring stock-taking in his life-work, because it shows the consciousness of his methods. We may regard it as the synthesis which is the natural companion of his habit of incessant analysing. When a composer approaches all music in the severely analytical mood which Busoni the performer brought to bear on every work, he acquires an exceptional insight of its inner relationships. For better or worse he will, in his own compositions, use his experience of the possible treatments of various forms of which he has dissected every fibre.

A harmlessly gay piece of dance music will almost unavoidably in his mind demand something Schubertian or Johann Straussian. In his more gravely disposed instrumental combinations he is certain to recall Beethoven. He cannot be expected to write for the piano without reference to Liszt and Bach, or for the violin without reminiscences of Corelli or Paganini, were it only because he has recognized the sense of technical formalities which guided these composers. Busoni's own realization of this is, as we have seen, piquantly revealed in his choice of titles. His profoundly exhaustive study of other composers' great 'Sonatas' accounts for his modestly named 'Sonatinas'. He emphasizes his independent individuality by calling some ambitiously planned piece simply 'March' or 'Waltz'. He is constantly mindful of the abstract meaning that might be imparted to a form; he deals with the 'march-idea', or the 'waltz-idea', showing how it can still be exploited, or how in the employment of such titles the composer should take account of the associated impressions they carry to his intelligence.

This habit of thought has throughout his existence led him from one distinct period to another, each clearly defined in his mind, and its conclusion marked by the writing of a large-scale work of which the title, or the text, or the action, provides for a general 'clearing'. Thus he could feel sure where he stood at any moment, and by the connexion of note and word determine for us all where 'we' had 'arrived' according to his estimate. Much of this was vaguely dreaded by a number of his hearers, and they liked his music all the less for it. Even then, that was mainly a coincidence, for before such instincts came into play many musicians had their own reasons for not taking to his music kindly.

In the first place it was widely distrusted as 'pianist's music'. I cannot avoid a digression here, since this prejudice has stood so immovably in Busoni's way. When, how, and why did this suspicion of pianists' compositions begin? Liszt suffered under it, although it was then relatively new. The older composers were usually celebrated performers, and it is not immediately clear why now, to a Busoni, a thing should be a handicap which rather smoothed the path for Mozart or Beethoven. The explanation probably is that they did not in the first instance become known by such sensational 'campaigns' as built the reputation of the nineteenth-century virtuosi who imitated Liszt and Paganini. These, however, were not only the last in the great Bach-Mozart and Corelli-Tartini traditions, but at the same time the first of a line in which neither was ever surpassed. A public that had become acquainted with the compositions of heavily advertised prodigies like Thalberg, Rubinstein, Miszka Hauser, or Vieuxtemps, and had a fairly good idea of what their performing horses were worth, made the double mistake of thinking that probably those of

'HE WHO IS NOT WITH US . . .'

Liszt and Paganini had not been much better, and that those of their modern successors would be, if anything, even more futile. Especially was this the prevailing obsession in virtuous Germany, where a Joachim had long forgotten how he used to perform Ernst's 'Otello Variations', but did remember all that Robert or Clara ever said. Joachim's heart was still with the old dilettanti, yet already he could speak with the new ones, and in the name of both refer slightingly to Busoni as 'just another virtuoso!'

In face of such ready-made mischief it was difficult for Busoni to get a hearing for his works. When he did get it there was another difficulty to overcome. The judges wished to know whether he must be taken as a German composer, or as an Italian, or as a frank hybrid. As critics who liked to keep method and order in their ideas, they felt annoyed when they could not quite make out whether he was a pure-blooded modern, or a traditionalist. If, in spite of these inauspicious conditions, his music was listened to at all, it still had to overcome inherent qualities that distinctly militated against acceptance. It was, for instance, accepted with frigidity when it was not refused outright for the 'something didactic in it' that even the least-informed quickly spotted, but very few knew how to value.

For Busoni himself there was never any choice; he *must* compose: from his earliest days he had been thinking in music, and there is no question of the insistent urge or of his deep sincerity. His music, unfortunately, seldom displays the disarming spontaneity which in many composers replaces more profound qualities, but he certainly made up for it by other, rarer powers. Mostly, however, these were of a kind too tardily appreciated by the musical public in general, who hate what they suspect and suspect what they cannot quickly grasp. But that does not take away from the impressiveness of his achievement, since sheer precision and force of intellect raised it to a level that admits none of the innocent virtues which other composers receive at birth.

He came as near as humanly possible to the deliberate creation of a living organism. His accomplishment can symbolically be likened to the production of the *homunculus* in Faust. But Goethe's synthetized human being disappears into the void; in Busoni's operatic version of the legend—and this is full of meaning—the magically evoked spirit becomes identified with Faust's own child, and rises from his dead body. Busoni hoped that his disciples might by his inspiration perform what he would have to leave undone.

'Time', in other words more frequent performance, may still prove what many students of his work believe—that his own 'Faust' has actually attained the miracle. Some of his admirers would have been happier to see a new departure in that work, and half expected it. As it happened, with his early death it was better that the work should have been a final autosynthesis. This made adequate completion by another hand less impossible, and increased the chances for the understanding of his last work, and thereby of the previous ones. It rounded off an idiom which had become exclusively his own. At the same time it was a conclusive, authoritative statement in the language he had produced with unremitting labour, and which by virtue of his own life-work had become circumscribedly traditional. In this double sense the whole of his production is unique, for it can be seen in the light of a tradition which to the initiated is identifiable as one he had made almost general by the wide applicability of its elements.

One must admit, however, the existence of a formidable obstacle. The public, to understand a single one of his important works with anything like completeness, must virtually set out to 'learn Busoni', as a Pole might learn English to read Massinger or Ford. One would have to know all modern music in addition to Busoni's own, to recognize why it is that passages of parallel sevenths, ninths, or elevenths, in *his* works have nothing in common with similar things in Strauss or Debussy. When people who looked at a page here or there of

ESOTERIC ALLUSIONS

his scores pointed with slipshod assurance to such alleged similarities, he was reasonably indignant, for he did not employ these devices to achieve the lurid colour-effects of 'Elektra', or to revive memories of organum, as in Debussy's piano pieces—they were acoustic additions to a purely designed polyphony, such as he first formulated in his second Sonatina. There the application was tentative, later they were used with consistency in other piano works. Finally, when they had become abstract dialectical terms for orchestral use, they appeared in his 'Faust' score, invested with the precise meaning they had acquired for the assiduous student of Busoni-lore. To him, by then, they should be simply logical and devoid of implications beyond what the Maestro's previous works had allowed. But how many composers can hope thus to obtain for themselves devoted personal followers who will intelligently study every page of their works? Mozart, realizing the immense fame of his 'Figaro' in Prague, would just risk quoting himself in a later opera expressly written for production in that city. Even then (I refer to the supper-music in 'Don Giovanni') he felt the need for sardonically pointing the quotation and let one of the stage-characters exclaim at the entry of the 'Non più andrai' theme: 'Oh, this is too stale!' (The German translation improves on the occasion with an elephantine 'I say, this is *Nothing* less *than* the Fi-garo of *Mozart*!') Yet Mozart could not doubt that whatever public he had were completely devoted to him, and lovingly studied every note of his they could get hold of.

Now Busoni did this sort of thing continually. He asked of his hearers sufficient familiarity with all his dramatic and symphonic compositions to elucidate any quotation on which he was relying for some important effect. With the few performances that even his more generally accepted compositions had, it would to outside observers appear exceedingly questionable that he ever received the benefits he claimed. He incessantly expanded his idiom and, ranging over all subjects, adjusted it for the inclusion of his latest stylistic discoveries.

In the course of these constant modifications he had to postulate hearers who kept pace with him, who studied every work as it appeared, and compared it with the preceding ones. Undeniably he had, more than any contemporary, a select following of resolute admirers who would travel across mountains and oceans to hear first performances of his works; but as the opportunities were relatively rare, it was still hard on the majority of the most absorbed disciples. And what aggravated the situation was that, although he might personally be flattered by seeing the familiar faces appear on every occasion when an important work was first performed, the most determined of his adherents were by no means always the most intelligent musically.

For the average musician he remained, and still is to-day, a composer who expresses himself in a kind of musical Esperanto. There must be many more than one cares to contemplate who, when they found that they were expected to acquire command of a new language solely to enable them to appreciate somewhat abstruse and austere works, felt that too much was being demanded of them, and abandoned the quest in despair.

This makes it easier to understand the otherwise friendly critics who complain that he asks too much of his hearer's understanding. Their case is that he first expects exceptional tributes of subjection, and that even when these are forthcoming he is not moved to unbend, but next demands of his docile listeners that they shall deal with numerous problems which might prove hard even for the adepts who, so to say, had their teeth specially filed to crack these nuts. A well-disposed novice to whom hints of such demands come, must feel like the zealous young missionary who learns that, apart from passing examinations, he must have his appendix removed before he can venture on his task *in partibus infidelium* where otherwise a sudden inflammation might lay him low. Some of the students of Busoni's music who approached him only later in life, who had not undergone the fascination of his personality when

ARISTOCRATIC MODESTY

they were young, resented the harshness of these exigencies. Especially when they saw that no sacrifice would infallibly ensure a smiling reception. One can imagine how a young theologian, after all the prophylactic injections and operations, feels somewhat disheartened when he finds the pontifex maximus not particularly encouraging. He may be badly wanting to get at the natives, but when he receives at every stage further instructions about abstract theological points, he may conceive a sneaking sympathy with the heathen.

This is regrettable because the implications are deceptive, and the persistent investigator will find them unjustified. Still, there is no denying that this is how the situation must have appeared to many an unsuspecting musician who could not know that the source of all the difficulty was really the aesthetic chastity of Busoni. Actually he was unfailingly grateful for genuine interest in his work and for serious, if critical, study of it. If sometimes he seemed detached and haughtily distant to naïvely insinuating youngsters it was because his spirit was strongly permeated with the mystery of music. This made him exclusive, for he wished to preserve it in the interest of the art he loved. He equally feared and loathed the familiarity of the slick professional and the ignorance of the amateur who would thoughtlessly challenge the mystery. The popularizing of music—what to-day with such excruciating aptness we call 'having music on tap'—was a thing he foresaw long ago with a prescience born of his dread of the appalling vulgarization of holy things which is perpetrated in the name of 'appreciation by the masses'.

He would have looked upon the conditions with which we have become painfully familiar as a realization of one of the cruellest of Villiers de L'Isle Adam's *Contes Cruels*. At one time he contemplated a musical setting of Villiers's 'Le Mystère'. He hoped that he could impart to other musicians something of his own apprehensions.

Busoni once earnestly pleaded with pianists to turn such relatively trivial occurrences as their recitals into a ritual. Every performance of music ought to be made a festive initiation to which listeners should go in a spirit of humility. What could be more out of balance with the redoubtable Spirit of the Time?

He was not himself aware of this. He mentioned a Schönberg rehearsal by some promising young musicians, in an article written in this semi-religious spirit. But 'as it fell out they all fell in'; that is to say, most of these bright young men have since given their time to convincing us that they are machines, that the world is a machine inside which there is a smaller machine called music, and that every one should be machinistically the happier for it.

For those who might be wavering between approval and denial Busoni made decision more difficult by the introduction of a personal problem on so questionable an occasion. He referred to the respect and the emotion with which he devoted a spare hour to the perusal of 'a beloved score'. Many of his readers were bewildered to see that this was done 'on Sunday mornings'. His Nordic, irreligious friends were pained by this bourgeois conventionality. They had no understanding of this and, therefore, no patience with hearkening to memories of the hour of Mass in the Catholic South, where religious observances have no plebeian associations. Even more unexpected seemed the choice of 'beloved scores'. One of them was the 'Zauberflöte'. That, of course, might pass. But the other one was 'Parsifal'. Youthful admirers who had pinned their faith to what Busoni had at times told of his likes and dislikes regarded this as blasphemous paradox. His personality appeared now as baffling as any of his music.

There was enough sense in the sections, the exposition and the development, but the bridge-passages seemed definitely occult to any but the nearest confidants, and of those only a few of the first grade.

That he should select 'Parsifal' as a suitable score for this shrinkingly intimate ritual, after having often succeeded in diverting from his allegiance some lifelong Wagnerian! The neophyte who, perhaps very much against his will, had been converted, believed that he had bought freedom of Busoni's spiritual domains. Must he conclude that just when he believed he had understood something of the reasons for Busoni's detestation of certain aspects of Wagner he must be disillusioned anew? And this time for what?

The dully luminous edges of the inveigling curvature of the 'Parsifal' polyphony held a strong appeal for Busoni. This could make him forget the sticky Kundry and the silver-paper knight-errantry of Wagner's bilious swan-song. But his musicianly weakness for the attractiveness of an otherwise rather unpleasant work was something not easily appraised without the kindly cynicism of intellectual mellowness. Younger men are quicker with their indignation than with their understanding, however generous they may be with their sympathies.

Having arrived at Wagner once more, I may quote a fragment of conversation:

MYSELF. I have been carefully studying the 'Tristan' Prelude to-day. . . .
BUSONI. And . . .
M. One must admit . . .
B. Ah, mustn't one . . .
M. Only, when one by one they all come in doing the same thing, —these crushing, crashing octaves . . .
B. Oh, but you must leave him that. That was his special acoustic discovery. One can understand his making the most of the sonority he got by it.

Such confidences about common preferences and distastes come nearer to the thoughts that really matter than pondered statements. Therefore I reproduce some more:

BUSONI. I am looking for the first time at a full score of 'Falstaff'.
MYSELF. Oh! Ah!
B. I am greatly disappointed.
M. ! ? !
B. Honestly—don't be upset—his brass writing is too . . .
M. Oh, please don't. Think of the richness . . .

B. Yes, but perhaps that reminds me too much of the Italian brass band of his day. That is what he imagined; that is what he wrote for.
M. Can't we give him the benefit of the doubt, and believe that he foresaw what sound we should hear later?
B. Let us—but what about the 'one-two-three', 'one-two-three'?
M. What about the agonizing brass of the 'Emperor' Concerto, and those recurring entries in imitation?
B. (*who has just played the work*) Let's not talk about it. But what did you think of the other work on the programme, I mean the 'Totentanz'?
M. I think Liszt . . .
B. Yes, I know all that; yet—one time I think he is more than capable, more capable than any one has need to be, and at other times that he is technically not quite competent. What *is* one to think?
M. That is not what people like or dislike him for. See how they are all crazy about Puccini now; here is a modicum of incompetence for you all the time, and yet . . .
B. All the same, last season when I was in Milan I walked in at the opera and I heard 'Butterfly'—and it was all so well put on, and so well done; I thought it was really quite charming.
M. ! ! !

A number of years after this conversation I made up for my peevish reply by some observations about the cleverness of Puccini's stage technique. I said I had learned that the wise economy with which Puccini obtains his greatest effects is, in a sense, at least as respectable as any other form of technical command.

MYSELF. . . . so that when I think of this now, I feel ashamed of myself. When I heard his 'Tryptico' I was greatly impressed.
BUSONI. That introduction of 'Il Tabarro' is worked with so much care, and with such excellent symphonic concision, that I am prepared for much from him now. Here I see real command. It is the work of a master.
M. Is it not a pity that he should have spent so much of his time on the appalling things that made him the darling of tenors and impresarios?
B. I have read your witticisms about the 'Fanciulla', and I have

ARTISTIC HONESTY

heard of a few more. As regards the work itself I daresay you are right. But I am not so sure about the 'waste'. The 'Fanciulla'.... Ahah!... del.... 'Waste'! There's an English pun for you!—I believe, myself, he could only learn in the way he did. Every mistake was a lesson.

M. I admit regretfully that I would have been capable of the pun. About the mistakes: think what profitable mistakes to make! I wish they would occur to us.

B. They could not; because we can't. But even although we may not be able to learn from him, he has shown us how a man learns from himself. I expect almost anything from him now.

One can understand from this how it came about that various people gathered very different impressions from Busoni's sayings. An observation about Puccini having prostituted himself, and become a business man, survived in the recollection of many friends his readjusted opinion. Others, again, were so haphazardly informed as to think him inconsistent. He was consistent enough. Only he was too much of an artist for the diplomat's studied discretion. He never troubled to hide himself when most people would. I discovered this in frequent honest admissions from which a lesser man would have shrunk. I will cite one significant instance. Busoni understood my interest in Meyerbeer, and he told me that he had studied his scores seriously, but without great profit. 'I had to forget much I had learned from him.' When I suggested that, via Berlioz, it had left him something, he admitted the possibility.

'However,' he insisted, 'Berlioz is not the last word either, as I fear you think.' I disclaimed the belief, while reasserting admiration for this composer, whom I described as of the most original musical genius, one of the greatest thinkers, and, in a sense, the most sensitive musical poet of his century.

BUSONI. There you are! That 'the greatest this, the greatest that' always infuriates me. I have noticed before that you have acquired English habits. I hear people talking here every moment about 'the finest poet', or of a man 'without a peer'. 'The bard! The champion! The Grand Old Man!' I suppose Berlioz too caught some of the spirit. He was given to 'l'Anglicisme', a forerunner of 'l'Anglomanie'. He was caught by Byron, as well as by Shakespeare, in his most impressionable years.

By the way, here is another curious thing; how is that? when you speak to English people about Shelley, they invariably say, 'Do you know Keats?' Have you noticed it?

I explained that I imagined it must be because there is a widespread conviction in England that Keats was a great poet. And that this was among people who think Shelley nothing of the kind. That perhaps this was a tactful way of drawing his attention to such relative valuations, when one recalled the continental superstition that Shelley (with the possible exception of Byron) was the only English poet after Shakespeare who mattered. From this we came to speak of the relativity of fame, and of Berlioz's preferences. I asked what he thought of Spontini.

BUSONI. I don't know him at all. There are composers like that of whom I know nothing. I know nothing of Gluck, 'qu'à l'instar de votre maître Berlioz vous admirez tant'—I don't know anything of Handel.
MYSELF. 'Ce tonneau de porc et de bière. . . .'
B. Who said that?
M. Berlioz.
B. Not in England I hope. (*Rather doubtfully*) I suppose *he* knew his music? Wasn't he here once for a Festival?

Berlioz was, of course, once employed in an 'official-only' capacity here, to examine and report on musical instruments, but he heard, I believe, at one of the 'Concerts Monstre Crystal Palace' some Handel for 'massed choirs and bands'.

Busoni's notions of English life and literature were, on the whole, unequal. Or, to say the least, they were curiously mixed. I fear Professor Dent does him an injustice when he describes him as being amazed at the absence of great-man solemnity in Shaw. He knew enough about Shaw and about Shaw's deliberate levity to be prepared for anything. Where he shared the continental point of view was in regarding Shaw

PUBLIC BORES

as primarily a creative artist, as Hauptmann might be, instead of Irish-critic-and-facetious-Busybody-in-Chief at the Capital.

Busoni was too much an artist before all else to visualize Shaw's journalistic career, and the importance it had for him to put everybody right at his own job before he found leisure for his work as a poet or a playwright. Much in the same way, he did not see Wilde as a social figure. He saw chiefly the tragedy of the artist who was irrelevantly persecuted for his indiscretions. Against this his judgements of Sterne and Smollett, of Fielding and Thackeray, Sheridan and Meredith, were sound. And he had none of the continental superstitions and misapprehensions about Dickens. He had understood well enough how loose was the connexion between Dickens's sentimental attitude and his topographical descriptions. In spite of his Hoffmannesque leanings, he never made the mistake of thinking of London as a city wrapped in gloom, where fantastic figures jostle each other in an everlasting fog. On spring visits he had learned to love London, although he had seen quite enough of November fogs and drizzle. His instinct led him, on the whole reliably, whatever the obvious drawbacks reliance on intuition entails. Usually it was buttressed by precise information, but in its absence he did not hesitate to trust his feelings.

Speaking of Spontini and Gluck (the conversation recorded) Busoni said: 'There are some men like that, about whose work I have never troubled. I am sure they must be bad. I wouldn't read more than the few lines I know of Huysmans for anything. Alphonse Daudet is another.'

MYSELF. But surely you would appreciate Tartarin? Don't you know him? I think he is a figure to be counted among the great comic creations.
BUSONI. I daresay you are right, but you should leave me my prejudices. One cannot get along without them.
M. You mean, as Goethe said, that it is impossible for one man to take in everything; that there are some matters which one must discard altogether? He singled out Buddhist art and

folk-lore . . . 'all these elephants' trunks. . . . I only see the monstrosity and loathe the whole business from the bottom of my heart', or something like that?
B. I quite agree. I often feel it strongly.
M. Are you not afraid that instinct may lead you astray now and then when it comes to positive appreciation?
B. Ah, I see you are coming back to our discussion on Bulwer Lytton.

This indeed I was doing. He had told me that, reading Lytton, he came to the conclusion that here was a wise and deeply humane figure. He was taken aback when I asked him whether he realized that Lytton for years had been regarded as the champion wiseacre of Great Britain, and that he had made himself so tiresome that mention of his wisdom to-day would call forth derision.

BUSONI. My recent discovery cannot be influenced by opinions formed years ago.
MYSELF. This reminds me of your own praises of the popular illustrations of Doré. Those of the 'Contes Drôlatiques' are masterly. What about those of Tennyson, or Dante, or the Bible? They were hugely popular with the worst judges.

There lies a profound danger in the somewhat exotic appreciation or condemnation at which an erudite arrives when he is insufficiently familiar with the general trend of ideals and prejudices of the country that produced or adopted an artist. A telling example is a blunder of the very learned professor who provides information on music for the readers of the *Encyclopædia Britannica*. He refers to Berlioz as 'a typical Gascon'. As one might refer to Hardy as a 'typical North-countryman', or Shaw as a 'typical East Anglian'. Busoni's intuition and the orderliness of his mind protected him against such slips. He was the first to laugh at stolid desipience wherever it originated. If he kept away from certain forms of information it was because he considered it necessary to retain a clear view of inevitable limitations. His special study of the works of a restricted number of artists had been so profound that it enabled him to approach others, less familiar to him, with an understanding never obtained by scholars whose investigations proceed gingerly from man to man and from period to period, in the faith that detailed knowledge will, by its bulk, make up for the lack of penetration. He was altogether so unprepared for the dishonesty which supports some reputations built on the finicky collecting and sorting of dates and facts, that he would hesitate to deny pretended scientists credit for their dubious cleverness or chimerical information. A scholar might make observations such as the one about Berlioz, yet Busoni would not grudge him his academic honours. He kindly presumed that these were deserved for glib discourses on Caccini and Peri, or Christoph Bach, Kuhnau, Stamitz, or 'The Relations of the Early Formalists and the Traditionalists in the Light of Experimental Chromaticism', and similar useful dissertation subjects. But it was sheer goodness of heart. If one hinted at the doubtfulness of this type of knowledge, or at the difficulty of control over writers who assume the most authoritative tone when they deal with the most hypothetical material, he revealed his slumbering, deep irritation with the bookish wisdom of their compilations.

Professor Riemann had to write that bird-song 'must be counted among artistic achievements, since its consciousness has been proved' before Busoni could bring himself to admit that he had always suspected Riemann's science. His own innate honesty made it difficult for him to recognize certain forms of scientific and historic sharp-practice, unless the evidence was too clearly damning. He once said:

BUSONI. One must admit that the historical studies of German musicians yield fine results. When, shortly after the War, I wanted some Monteverdi for a concert in Berlin of old Italian music, they at once produced some of his scores for me.
MYSELF. Were you astonished? I am certain that any of the London colleges would have done as much.
B. Do you really tell me that they would have that ready? They surely never look at it?

M. I am not sure whether they look at it, but I am fairly sure that they would find you most of the things you could have dug out in Berlin. And I am prepared to trust the motives of the people there and here about equally, to put it sweetly.

He took this as badly as I meant it, but I believe he would have preferred to think that the German professors at least had conscientiously studied works which elsewhere had been forgotten. When Sir Thomas Beecham[1] first appeared in Berlin, Busoni, who was indisposed, asked me about the concert which I had attended as 'our own correspondent':

BUSONI. *What* did you say was that overture?
MYSELF. 'Il Re Teodoro.'
B. Scusa! Il Re ...? ... chi ...?
M. 'Teodoro.' Paisiello, you know.
B. Old Pa-i-si-el-lo? Where on earth did he get him from?
M. Well, I suppose he picked him up in the library.
B. D'you mean to say that one actually sits down in a library looking for unfamiliar pieces in the hope that something good will turn up?
M. That is exactly what Beecham would do, I dare say.
B. Well, I ...

Busoni himself would not look on Paisiello as an historical figure, kept on dust for the roving antiquarian. For him, as musician *per se*, this was 'old Paisiello', a hoary worthy of San Carlo, forgotten by all but some cranky fanatic of dead opera. (If not dead then outlived. One thinks of Verdi and the centenarian connoisseur in Werfel's romance.) He might expect some stricken-in-years Neapolitan to produce Paisiello, remembering a grandfather's wild laudations. He might himself have loved the music perhaps, but he would not go out of his way to get to know it. It had its day, and he never was in living contact with it. It seemed distinctly odd to him that Beecham, with the whole of modern literature at hand, should use his

[1] *Query.* How did he conduct? *Answer.* Not quite as good as Toscanini. Q. Toscanini is a genius; had you expected so much? A. I have heard that Beecham criticizes him. Q. Delius likes Beecham, doesn't he?—*conclusively*—That is something at least. H'm! Toscanini! I met Beecham once, you know? ... Ah! Let's change the subject; I don't feel like arguing just now.

time to excavate a piece whose existence had left him unembarrassed before.

This was characteristic of Busoni. He would have a first edition of Chateaubriand bound with aggressively modern endpapers. His interest was not antiquarian. However curious and quaint a thing might appear to others, if he took notice of it, it was to him living all the time. Discussing an episode of Berlioz's life I mentioned Scudo, to hear Busoni say, 'what made *you* ever come across Scudo? That was a critic my mother used to be worried about!' That Scudo as a 'critical phenomenon' could be an object for study seemed exceedingly strange to him. This explains to a great extent how he could write transcriptions of old works that shocked his contemporaries. For him they were not 'old'—in the sense of 'worn out'—works, even though they may have first appeared in the seventeenth century. He was perfectly familiar with them. They were part of his daily existence. The word 'hackneyed' had no meaning for him. Either a work was alive, and then it was always fresh again, or it was dead, and then there was no need to think about it. Exhumation did not fascinate him. One might say that he could only understand ancestor-worship if it were kept impersonal. His adaptation of a Bach Fugue with whole-tone scales and chords built on fourths was devoid of perversity. It was a treatment that came to him naturally. On the other hand, the antiquarian attitude which occupies itself with a work chiefly for its historical value struck him as unnatural. Those works which he could not immediately conceive as suitable for incorporation in his own repertoire he would reject altogether. Modern works, however, if they interested him, even if he had no great personal liking for them, he would wish to make heard. He did not rest before he had presented, either under his personal direction, or if possible under that of the composer, new pieces by Bartòk, Delius, D'Indy, or Sibelius, some of which certainly caused no echo of sentiment in his own spirit.

His followers did not find their task made easier by this

absence of a sense of 'propriety' of opinion on his part. The taste in bookbinding I cited was not an isolated instance of his unusual prepossessions. He astounded many friendly musicians with the assertion that Caruso would have been the ideal Bach singer. The German 'chamber-singer' he deemed to be the last to be entrusted with the cantilena of the Passion music.

Here we meet the old trouble once more: friends who believed that this warm praise of an Italian singer indicated where his tastes lay were astonished when they discovered how conditional was his appreciation of Italian opera. He admired Bellini and Donizetti for a few things, but he was unrepentantly censorious as regards the rest.

BUSONI. You think, too, that real melody is of the type of 'Casta Diva', like the slow movement of the 'Sonate Pathétique'? Beethoven adheres to the model in his melodies whenever he lets himself go. Look at the C minor Concerto.

MYSELF. Certainly. But I believe one might almost say that Bellini is the only composer who ever wrote extended melodic structures which are on the level of the finest poetry, for logical coherence and unforced development. In that respect he is probably without a rival.

B. Forgive me if I say that the greater part of his operas is painfully disappointing to me. Can you quite suppress a shudder at the last part of 'Casta Diva' or at whole stretches of 'Il Pirata'?

M. Why should I look at the dark spots? Besides, I was not speaking of the works as a whole. We were agreed about the quality of the melodies. Donizetti is another who has produced a few ramshackle works, and yet he can at times rise to the same heights as Bellini. Wouldn't you call 'Lucia' an admirable work? A genuine master-work?

B. I cannot recall a complete performance in detail. But of what I remember there is not much that has particularly struck me. At least not in that way.

M. What about the sextet?

B. Yes, that is one of those miracles that leave one speechless. If only he had worked some more of them!

M. Can't you believe that they must exist, but that we fail to recognize them? I mean that the capacity for the appreciation of some music is lost, rather like the palate for lampreys or peacock.

B. Do you imagine that if only we tried we might delight again in nightingales' tongues?

M. Hardly that. I was thinking more of aesthetic innocence than of outmoded sophistication. We don't get the right singers for Bellini and Donizetti now. The few that could sing the parts feel foolish if they don't attempt to modernize them. I heard a famous baritone in the 'Sonnambula' adapting all the roulades and cadenzas. I know he could sing them after a fashion, but he considered them outmoded and childish, so he smoothed them out into dramatic flourishes à la Strauss.

B. Did the conductor let him?

M. The work was only put on to please Tetrazzini, and the conductor probably did not think it mattered much what the singers did with the music.

B. There you are! *He* had not enough historical perspective. He would probably have had no taste even for the tongue of a Swedish Nightingale.

M. The most satisfactory performance of 'Lucia' I have heard was by the Children's Opera Company of Milan. The 'tenor' was twelve and the soprano was fourteen. They were excellent, and the chorus sang well, and acted better than any chorus of grown-ups I have ever seen. Just the right amount of stylization, without self-consciousness. And just the right amount of stage passion to be convincing, without realism. Altogether it was a very moving performance. It even inspired the orchestra, who for once listened to what they were playing.

B. You were lucky then in hearing the work more or less as it must have appeared to the audiences of Donizetti's own time.

M. It was true to life in so far as it was true to opera. I would always search for the true meaning of apparently dull passages in the work of a composer whose music had once been so clearly revealed to me.

B. But doesn't that become largely a matter of faith? Mustn't one begin by sacrificing a good part of one's intuitive critical instinct? I cannot be reconciled to a faith which asks that surrender. I cannot help it, a thing must be completely alive for me, and now. Else I have no use for it, certainly no patience with it.

M. You do not feel like hero-worship?

B. I am not sure that I quite understand what it means. So much I do know, that if it means swallowing all the imbecilities of a man who has once impressed you, then I can't oblige. It seems to me a cultivated weakness; one must deliberately ignore faults that otherwise one would not bear for a moment.

M. I'd rather avoid personalities, but I agree with you when you speak of the dread of being kept in thrall by enthusiasms roused in youth or that rest on the impression some master-work once caused. When it comes to pinning one's faith to the direction suggested by the best of one man's work, and expecting salvation from blind trust, I must say that I see how dangerous it could be.

B. I suppose you are thinking of the people who want to 'go back' to Bellini. One step farther than the rococo-bitten old fogies who preach going 'back to Mozart'.

M. They remind me of the old women with too-much-of-a-past who, according to the French proverb, sit right under the pulpit. It is true that they usually bring their bounty to the church, but one does not care to visualize any of the masters one loves receiving that sort of veneration. Think how fearful it is to contemplate that there could one day be people who might want to 'go back' to ourselves!

B. Speaking for myself, I hope I may be spared it. I believe one should attempt to put into one's own music all that is assimilable of the composers one admires most and loves best. That is a sensible procedure, and a better tribute than uncritical veneration. Surely better than to ape a style and then set this up as the exclusive model for others.

Busoni tried to live up to this precept. It did not necessitate a high opinion of every composer in whose works he had found something that could be profitably used.

The same attitude prevented him from rating his own achievement higher when it received striking recognition. He did not have any great love for the Liceo of Bologna because they struck a medal in his honour. It was encouraging, but he did not regard it as a compliment redounding to the credit of those who had paid it.

Similar misgivings caused his perpetual anxiety lest music in which at some moment he was interested should lead him into an impasse. At a period when he was playing more Chopin than usual, he spoke doubtfully about the 'Ballades', of which he had given a bewitching interpretation.

MYSELF. I was completely fascinated.

BUSONI. Oh yes, thank you, I quite believe that; but what I want to know is whether you see anything in these pieces beyond their surface charm, their romantic appeal.

M. I am afraid I see nothing but waltzes.

B. That is exactly what I find myself. All Chopin's music is waltzes, *and* waltzes.

M. I don't think that is the worst. But they are always the same waltzes. It must have struck you that Chopin invariably repeats his expositions. His only idea of form is a further repetition on a larger scale of what he has already said twice.

B. That is one of his faults. I try to make the best of his music, yet I cannot bring myself to believe in it. There remains something one cannot explain. I mean what for short we call Chopin's 'originality'.

M. Is not that largely his manner with the piano?—of using his hands? I am thinking of the originality of his harmony, which is often mechanically produced by the movements of the hands on the keyboard. Curiously enough, much of it anticipates Wagner, I suppose via Liszt. Do you know that Liszt said: 'Even Meyerbeer, that father of the fathers of all harmony, could for hours listen to Chopin'?

B. Once a man is famous, every one who ever met him reports pithy and startling sayings relating to him. But I remember now. It was Heine, wasn't it, who said this?

M. It was, but this brings us no nearer to a solution of the mystery of originality.

B. Originality is a strange thing. Ponder it as you will, it is deceptive, fugitive. An intractable, elusive quality. A creative artist should not be consciously occupied with it. The real originality of music is something that cannot be grasped until the whole of a man's work is comprehensively studied. Obvious originality is the effect of an idiosyncrasy which appears in the course of a few bars. That we soon become impatient of. When Grieg first attracted attention, he was discussed in the exact words that were later applied to Debussy.[1]

[1] This conversation took place several years ago.

M. You refer to national characteristics?

B. If it had been only that! No—one was told that he was wholly and entirely original. That his way with music, as much as his writing for the piano, was without precedent. All the things we heard again about Debussy! Finesse, distinction, subtlety, intellectual penetration, new colouring, new shades, new forms, fresh outlook, personal formula, nothing was too good, if good enough.

M. I seem to have heard something like that about Scriabin.

B. Don't speak to me of Scriabin! 'Poème de L'Extase'! If the man is so obsessed with his neurasthenia, or whatever other obscure troubles, the least he can do is to spare us the picture. If instead he colours it with theosophy, as in that other ludicrous symphonic concoction of his, and we get tinted lights added, and the pretence that his melting harmony has some profound ethical and mystical meaning, he simply becomes nauseating. It is an impudent imposition on a presumed public of half-wits, a mystico-erotic appeal to softening brains.

M. I hope you don't make Russian music responsible for the miseries and the sloppiness that Scriabin inherited from Tchaikovsky?

B. I won't give an opinion on what are now collectively called 'Russian composers'. I was looking at a score of Stravinsky the other day. I could not in the least make out what it is all young people at present make such a tremendous pother about.

M. One of our modernist friends was most enthusiastic about the 'delightful barrel-organ effects' of Stravinsky.

B. To me it seems all barrel-organ. Oh! these Russians! They remind me too much of my Russian experiences.

M. (*quoting Busoni as above*) 'It is everlastingly raining, and all the people have fever. . . .'?

B. No, no. That is distressing enough, but I was not thinking of that just now. I was thinking of my personal experiences in the old days in Moscow. Every recollection of them brings with it memories of scented cigarettes and of silk coat-collars sown with dandruff. Honestly, if you don't mind, I would rather leave the subject alone. It is most unattractive to me.

M. You are being very 'unzeitgemäss'. Only a few days ago one of the leading lights of modernism, our American friend who out-dadas Dada, prophesied to me that 'everything is going to be Russian now'. I strongly suspect you always suffered from a tendency to fall out of step with the troops marching to their fashionable devotions.

Undoubtedly part of Busoni's disagreement with his contemporaries might be traced to this disability. He was indifferent to the fashions which send bright-young-men scurrying every season after a new *ignis fatuus*. Whether in his works or his opinions, his independence defeated the calculations of many disciples. They were eager to adjust their views by his, but incapable of his intellectual detachment. They could not, as he did, decide personally without fear or rancour. Therefore they could the less understand his apparent recklessness. Occasionally his judgements were incomprehensible to them, and they criticized him for actions which they could not see in proportion. A German scholar of modest fame who, somewhat late in life, had taken to composition, once showed him a pretentiously incompetent score. Some of the young enthusiasts present were awaiting his criticisms with malicious glee. They were discomfited to hear him describe the work as balanced and conscientiously designed, without underlining the sarcasm enclosed in these gratifying phrases. Long afterwards some of the disillusioned witnesses still called this a betrayal of the Holy Truth. They needed many more years before they could understand Busoni's wise tolerance. He had explained it at the first opportunity, but they had not yet attained the mature kindness which teaches that unswerving integrity is not under all circumstances demanded. Here was a man, past middle age, who had never seriously worked at composition, but who was mentally completely formed, one without a spark of talent that by criticism or help could be fanned into the semblance of a flame. A frank opinion on his work could only have hurt him, and done no conceivable good. Busoni could afford to be as utterly indifferent to his fate as he was wholeheartedly interested in the efforts of any composer, old or young, in whom he detected the slightest suggestion of promise.

He never grudged his time to such work. He did not object

to honest striving in whatever direction because it was different from his own. No more did he resent antagonistic opinions offered with an appearance of conviction. Only, he would sometimes find himself confronted with views or arguments that to him sounded so fantastic that he had difficulty in accepting the sincerity of their exponent. Here is a snatch of conversation with a French critic:

'Romain Rolland? You are not going to maintain that, apart from his amateurish judgements on music, he is a writer of consequence?'

'But! The greatest of our time,' the Frenchman made bold to say. 'I simply don't believe that you mean it,' quoth Busoni, and then, rather peevishly: 'before you have finished, you will tell me . . .'—signs of growing anger—'that he is . . . greater . . .'—after an ominous pause of cold fury—'. . . greater than Victor Hugo!!'

The apostate admitted imperturbably that this was precisely what he meant: 'Parfaitement, monsieur!' Busoni, who had a great regard for Hugo's rhetorical humanism and superb attitudinizing, turned away from the critic in a stage-effort to hide his scorching indignation, and whispered:

BUSONI. He also thinks Strauss is the greatest genius! Now you know!

MYSELF. You think by way of Jean Christophe he got all mixed up about Rolland, and about being 'au-dessus de la mêlée', and German music? Anyhow, he shares the respect for Strauss with Weingartner, who when he sat with Strauss in a box at the première of 'Salome' told him that he was frightened of him!

B. Rataplan! Strauss *must* have been tickled! If the story is true. Probably it is not; good anecdotes never are. But 'Salome' *is* a throw of genius. You were right about that from the first. I am thinking of that old article you sent me.

M. Do you remember your American tour, when you heard 'Don Quixote' at every concert?

B. Am I likely to forget an American tour? But I know what you mean. Yes, I ended by admiring the work, and I confess that it was rather an unexpected result.

THE DEVIL A MONK

M. You are stating it blandly, now. Compare this to when you heard a work of Elgar again, a little while ago; and you found it had become unbearable.

B. What makes you suddenly name Elgar?

M. Don't you remember that yesterday we spoke of the way composers who can 'write for the brass' have of letting one know it?

B. Strauss certainly never permits you to forget it. He must find it hard to leave it alone. Elgar has picked up the habit. His descending brass is a weariness to the flesh!

M. Have you seen that Strauss in his edition of Berlioz's 'Traité' warns composers against such dangerous seductions?

B. The Devil in the pulpit! What is the edition like otherwise?

M. He advises young composers to consult old string-players about quartets before they proceed to 'Grosses Orchester', and to seek their approval. He warns them against 'effects': violin-solos, harp glissandos, muted trumpets and all!

B. I like *that*! What wisdom! If only he would live up to it! Does he not put on his title-pages 'für grosses Orchester'? Is there any literary quality in his emendations of Berlioz's text?

M. Here are some plums: he calls students 'werte Herren Kollegen von der Notenfeder', and, when Berlioz concludes his lyrical description of the soul of the clarinet with his 'O, Weber!!!', Strauss adds: 'These may all be very fine feelings, but it is rather one-sided . . .', and so on.

B. God help us! A little more sensitiveness could not hurt these gentry. This is what one expects of our composers, with their constant 'climaxes'.

He fails to recognize poetic intensity in a passage where he should respect it.

Oh, if they had the sense and heart to understand that the greatest 'climax' ought to be a tense whisper, a shrinking intensification of emotion, a closer intimacy!

M. Is that by any chance what you would expect of Elgar? If there is anything beyond 'brass' that he got from Strauss, it is the musical exhibitionism which wounds you so much.

B. I am told he has been writing Imperial music that leaves the most blatant Kipling in the shade!

M. He probably had his reasons. But, musically speaking, he

knew no better; one might say, as of Franck, that his worst crudities at least come straight from the heart.

B. I may as years passed have been disappointed in Franck, but he never hurt me as much as Elgar, and certainly never in the same way.

M. You performed Elgar once. He was almost unknown then. Don't you feel it is a loss if now you cannot abide him?

B. I am sorry. I can't help it; there is something in Elgar that gets on my nerves. I want to flee after a few bars.

M. Some people are so persistently sweet and polite that one wants to run! If one finds them at one's elbow wherever one turns, one becomes inexpressibly embarrassed.

B. Don't I know it! One feels as uncomfortable as a schoolboy with a master who is altogether too human and fatherly. But one must concede that after Strauss there is no greater virtuoso with the modern orchestra than Elgar. The 'right-and-proper' way with the 'stock-orchestra', that is.

M. As 'THE' Schoolboy tells us, '*that* is a trick that can be learnt'. Do you believe it?

B. It shows you how little THE Schoolboy knows. I need not tell you that it cannot be done. Think of our experience in Newcastle,[1] when we looked at the scores. Elgar came up to expectations, but remember the disappointment when we heard Bantock un-Ltd! I thought it would never end, and not even then.

M. You were risking the worst, sitting in the orchestra. Once there, you had to swallow the whole performance. Local colour is not easily tolerated in such massive doses.

B. Ghrrrr! Parallel fifths, and harps and flutes! I could not help thinking of Leipzig. I was a youth; I had submitted some work to Reinecke. He diffidently stated that what he wanted of music was 'that it should give him pleasure'. But none was to be had from mine. He had the face of a good-hearted baboon, but not the mind: Herr Boosesoahneeh, tcha, you must think of your hearers, tcha. I, now, have been writing, tcha . . . lately . . . tcha, a Duet for Flute and Harp . . . and . . . I had the pleasure of having it performed, tcha, in Zwickau.

M. It makes me shiver to think of what you must have gone

---

[1] The 1909 Festival, when Busoni's Concerto, Elgar's 'Kingdom', and Bantock's 'Omar Khayyám' were given.

through in Germany, trying to assert yourself against such conceptions of artistic duties.

B. That is not sympathy wasted! Oh! these Germans, with their '*Our* Bach', '*Our* Beethoven'! blessing and cursing in the name of Our-Great-Men with High-Priestly solemnity. At the same time speaking of them with offensive familiarity and quasi-parental pride. As if they had a share in the merits. But there are Reineckes everywhere; you wait, you have not settled in the land of your fathers; your experiences may prove different in kind, but they will prove as painful.

Busoni had a terrifying uphill struggle all the time. When in Berlin he had already become what to his circle there seemed a world-figure, he was still regarded by the wider musical public with 'armed indifference'. Not long before the War a number of his works were presented in Berlin in a series of concerts. It included his Piano Concerto, which is really a 'dramatic symphony' in the Berliozian sense, an impressive achievement, of the highest importance to himself and his friends, as it will be to others one day. As a further stock-taking—to which, as we have seen, he was irrevocably addicted by his passion for analysis and survey—he wrote for a highly reputed Berlin periodical, a 'Selbst-Rezension'. The editor regarded this as an exceptionally interesting contribution: a caustic self-portrait by an eminent and undeniably original artist. It comprised a reasoned criticism of his own works, a review entirely free from the gossiping conceit, the flippant dogmatism, and the solemn garrulousness of the lesser musician. Busoni here honestly attempted to assess the abstract value of his own production by resolute probing and searching dissection. He sought to establish its position in the historical order. It was not only read with absorbed devotion by disciples and artists, but it commanded profound and respectful attention among the intellectually curious in countries where German publications penetrate and where music is considered of importance. None the less, when he asked me to make a few translations, and see that these appeared in some further continental capitals and in England, I found it impossible to rouse sufficient interest. I took care to choose likely editors and plead the cause in person. My advocacy did not succeed in making anybody amenable. They would not risk something so 'out-of-the-way', it had no interest for their readers, whose tastes and inclinations they had 'studied and experienced long and well enough to know'. This at a time when to critics of acknowledged position Busoni was an indubitably great figure; when already he could see his own earlier work dispassionately and impersonally in the light of his later achievements. He had been uninterruptedly before the public of every European country and of America for nearly forty years.

In almost every continental music centre there existed a colony of fanatical believers in his art. In Berlin he was the leader of an intellectual community largely attracted there by his presence. He might be proud of this; certainly Berlin ought to have been proud of him. But still some of the tradition-bound natives regarded him as an exotic, poisonous intruder. And a section of the technical press made itself the willing mouthpiece of this despicable, jealousy-haunted antipathy. Busoni-baiting was a popular pastime with the dug-in greybeards, troglodyte guardians of the sacrosanct parish pump who lived there comfortably on their comfortable beliefs. He disturbed them in their dreamy lethargy; he was the offensive foreign body to expel which unceasing efforts were being made. Ancient critics who had harmfully doddered through the seventies could after all these years still stir from their quasi-fossil state in this cause. Thus the laboratory-frog with its brain removed, mechanically lifts a paw to rub the spot on its epidermis where a touch of acid has been applied.

One of the best known specialists in Germany would regularly devote idle moments to *feuilletons* abusing Busoni and his works. Busoni suffered it all with unruffled dignity and an imperturbable application to the embodiment of his poetic vision.

English critics never had such special reasons for personal

CADENZAPHOBIA

hostility. Many of them, indeed, had only remote notions of his compositions. Yet, however gladly they welcomed the brilliant virtuoso, they shared the suspicion of a composing pianist. His cadenzas, arrangements, transcriptions, paraphrases, and adaptations constituted so much material for unkind comments. The announcement of a programme would call forth something like, 'One may well ask whether . . . for all Mr. Busoni's undoubted capabilities . . . these composers had not been better left alone', &c.

Without starting here an apology for cadenzas, one might briefly inquire why, in a world that accepts without question the bookplate on which space for the owner's signature is decoratively provided by the artist, a musical device should not be tolerated in which the composer leaves a similar space, and why the performer should be condemned for putting it to its intended use.

Busoni's adaptations of forgotten Bach or Mozart pieces, which made their successful reappearance in the concert hall possible, should not need any defence. Nor should his brilliant transcriptions of Paganini Caprices, unless it be still necessary to defend the composer. Those critics who write about Paganini's music as if it were on a level with the poorest stuff of the poorest fiddler, only betray their total ignorance of the works. They are not all dead yet (at least, not so dead as they ought to be, so that they can be libelled as they ought to be), but when that delectable moment arrives, their incompetence, perhaps forgiven then, will at least serve to show up their successors in the same line for the poor fishes they are.

The contemporary student can watch the mechanical critic at his daily grind and pity his hard task together with the dismal effects of costive ratiocination. Would there were also a daily dose to move those tardy notions.

When Caruso was the recipient of public hero-worship, many critics of the superior and very superior grades cravenly fought shy of joining the chorus of adulation. They were hesitantly ogling Future's tribunal, compliantly prepared to depreciate him in favour of the unspeakable German 'Heldentenor' who on the Wagnerian stage exposes a big, pallid, flabby body obtruding from a jungle doormat. Others, whose heart advised them better, yet affected to prefer the bespectacled, script-sniffing professor who, with irreproachable good and dull taste, displays on the platform his disabilities as a musician together with his highly schooled deficiencies as a singer.[1] No wonder that with the obstinate survival of these officially encouraged and approved, so-educated bunglers, Bach Arias have been musically slandered with irreproachable intentions. One is convinced that if Bach were to challenge the shades of the fastidious academics who have made him appear more than half dead, they would in the best pedagogic tradition explain to him that it was all done for his own best.

But I strongly suspect that Bach would not have objected to the Italianate interpretation which Busoni preferred. The evidence of his style alone is conclusive for the musician who does not feel that tradition requires distortion. That drag-the-last-bars, pound-out-the-subject, be-classic-and-let-who-will-be-clever attitude is responsible for the pompous caricature of 'the Thomas Cantor—look-out-fellows-here-comes-the-Head!' which platform fiends have made excruciatingly familiar.

How Bach, the most graceful, nimble-witted, generous-hearted, gay dreamer, the most universally minded of composers, would have detested the plesiosaurian interpretation that with the concert public passes as correct! Busoni's grasp of detail, and his boldly song-like annunciation of the structure, were based on a better and fuller knowledge. And if it was dictated by his fiery Italian heart, it was weighed and approved by his piercing intellect.

What if a talented singer is directed by his intuition most of the time? This is immaterial to my argument. He imparts the sane conviction his temperament dictates, to the vocal line, be it that of Donizetti or Bach. The character of Bach's line de-

[1] 'All characters are purely imaginary.' No damages for damage.

QUI TOLLIS . . .

mands such treatment. The sweetest refinement and the most primitive surrender are not out of place here. However majestic the melodies, they can only gain by it: unless the spiritual completeness of Bach is forgotten.

Think of our Central European vocal heavyweights, or worse, their over-refined, emasculate counterparts! Can one hear them busy with Mozart or Verdi without a shudder? So far from suffering them gladly, one does not mind being damned for an Italian-opera-monger like any Soho barber or waiter. Were it only for the voluptuous pleasure of hearing the disdained three final high notes done well.

Good singers are so rare that it is all the more vexatious if we stand in their way with stern prescripts about what they should be allowed to do and what not.

Busoni was not only free from the cant of distrust of Star Performers; he was equally free from the cant of respect for the accepted conventions, whether in creative or reproductive work.

He did not pretend to improve the old works which he touched. When he gave his personal, intellectually unfettered interpretation of the old master-works, he cleansed them of the layers of grease and dust which a thousand traditionalists' hands had left on them. He was not deceived by the 'mellowed tints' of old varnish hiding the freshness of the original colours. When the colour of an old canvas is freed from this disguise, it does not at once please all eyes. It appears lurid to many people whose sensibilities have become too tender with protracted gazing on deliquescent shades. For their dissolving perceptions all stark forms are reduced to the chaotic sliminess of a snail in brine.

Busoni scandalized such sentiment-wallowers with his precise delineations of the music of Bach, Mozart, and Chopin. He reconstructed it in pristine freshness. They had learned to call the accepted interpretations 'restrained'. The accepted interpretations are, in fact, all too restrained, simply because over-refined players find themselves so much more at ease in half-tints. These involve no strain on their demulcent faculties. No wonder that sweet-souled, cloudy-minded musicians were frightened out of their complacency when they were shown 'their' classics in such clear lines and in as bright a range of colours as the National Gallery El Greco revealed after a healthy course of cleaning. Busoni's readings were so many successful restorations. His was the expert's handling of dulled brown-and-gold Old Masters. One is prepared to believe that the people who prefer a convenient 'patina' are genuine in their detestation of such liberty and untrammelled conviction. Gentle music lovers are inclined to the belief that crude contrasts and loud accents have been the invention of the serpent that spoilt the idyll. Appropriately in their eyes, the serpent itself has wallowed in so much dust as to have become quite softened in- and outside to all appearances. All ancient music, to all aged musicians, has that lovely shade of old gold and half-light. There they find that purity and simplicity which their hardened arteries make them expect and their tired eyes crave. There they find that classical repose, the unity, the perfect balance and alleged inevitableness, which they fondly believe to have been the privilege of 'ancients', whenever these may have lived.

Busoni rode over all such senile nursery ideals rough-shod. The self-satisfied pedagogues and governesses who 'adore the classics', all the crushed and timid souls who find unfailing consolation in their thimbleful of art-as-I-have-learnt-to-understand-and-love-it, were left aghast at his ruthless, remorseless, pitilessly logical exposition which seemed exposure, and a treatment of the sound of the piano that hurt them by its uncompromising truth and intensity. Where a composer had been frankly vulgar at an appropriate moment, Busoni made no effort to smooth over the 'painful fact'. On the contrary, he would, without stressing the vulgarity, let the bridle slip from the phrase, and 'give it its head', as far as compatible with the general pace.

He likened the concert tradition moulded on so-called

SICK OF THE JUST

authorized readings to a death-mask handled until it had become unrecognizable. He had been a practitioner of the Arts too long not to know that even the Ancient Greeks, 'those perpetual models', did not delight in the mild contemplation of sedate, sightless-eyed, 'classical' semi-goddesses; that on the contrary they came with lustful eyes to a brutal feast of forms and colours, and that those marble abstractions to which our prim spinsters now give their fig-leaved approval are only pallid wraiths of once apoplectically blood-filled males and females.

The exuberantly alive, aggressively colourful originals would scandalize the vast majority of the people who in blissful innocence call themselves lovers of classical art.

Apart from his individual understanding, Busoni was in these matters a representative Latin. The Latins' respect is naturally mixed with familiarity. They converse aloud in the cathedrals they have built. They feel at home there, so much so that they bring their dogs and their vices with them. Even if they are not believers, they are not shamefacedly conscious of their unbelief. They need not show a guilty lack of faith by walking on tiptoe and whispering. This is left to the northern tourist, who in his mistaken delicacy fears every moment that he may be offending supposed local susceptibilities.

The Greeks did not listen to Sophocles with awe, or anything like it; Alcibiades was a significant character. When they killed Socrates, it was to teach themselves a lesson. They wanted to remind themselves of all there was behind his dignified obstreperousness. Wise men knew the danger of becoming cynical by taking things too seriously. Socrates himself did not complain at his sentence. He could see the justice of it. He left his final defence to others, not because he could bide his time, but simply because he himself best understood the social deficiencies of his case. Plato, a combination of past and future, a Saint Paul cum Proust, saw the publicity value of what had not yet become a movement. Besides, he was chiefly occupied with the classification of ideas. Sentiment was no more his last word than it had been the first. But the head mistress of a ladies' finishing school is the one who cannot get over the scandal of the whole affair, the oh-the-injustice and oh-the-pity-of-it-all.

Busoni may, through his stay in the country of Winckelmann and aesthetic paederasty, have approached the danger of the Socratic pit at one time. The earnestness of his spirit drove him perilously near to the edge. But his unfaltering conviction always brought him back to the old inspiration of aesthetic clarity. He must have passed through an intervening period of introspection that saved him from the lure of a graceful dogma which might efface the memories of aristocratic measure. His interests, fortunately, were too strongly human to let him succumb to the polished graces of dilettantism. He was too warm-blooded and too intensively alive ever to regard aesthetic questions as material for abstracted meditation. His feet were firmly planted on the earth and he resisted all temptation to escape mental strife by the cultivation of a sterile, bookish aestheticism, or in the sweet stupor of a recondite intellectual partisanship.

Possibly in this respect his residence in Germany did some good. He looked into the depths of shallowness and of ponderousness, and he plumbed the abyss of frivolity, to borrow Nietzschean phrases. He too, by auscultation and percussion, found hollowness and emptiness beneath the shining exterior —'überall aufgeblähte Eingeweide!' Perhaps only thus could his restless and inquiring spirit become unencumbered. Without contempt he had freed himself of the passéism that was the bane growing in the garden of his heritage, even as he was saved from its natural correlative, Marinetti's futurism, with its 'one potsherd of to-day means more to us than the Victory of Samothrace'.

His prolonged and far from welcome presence in a country that had so little use for his views, and which so harshly criticized his intentions, acted as a hardening in the furnace. Without that he would perhaps have remained too vulnerable, he would not have acquired the glazed surface from which blows glance off. His mental adjustment reminds us occasionally of the spiritual virginity of the English Bench. He had in common with some of its brilliant occupants that painstaking unworldliness which reproves the frivolities of mankind. 'I don't know Handel', 'I have never read Daudet', bring to our ears the authentic tone that resounds in the oak-panelled rooms where a judicial voice inquires: 'Who is George Robey?' Here is the true sylvan, bee-buzzing, honey-laden atmosphere of the Golden Age.

But this world also contains spirits breathing our restless, scream-propelled air, scattering all the patient inanity of snug scholars with a lusty 'What is the Greeks?'

Busoni had been made to suffer under such queries as often as ever he made others do. He repaid but a fraction, and without real malice, when he dismayed his interlocutors with thorny conundrums. The people to whom he addressed them may have been perturbed, but they should have counted themselves lucky if by subjection to the ordeal they were helping a greater man to sort out his thoughts.

If by half-pleasure or pain one contributes to the needs of creative genius one ought to be grateful with the simple gratitude of the lover who could say: 'these lips have been touched by Ninon's.' Companions of a great artist must realize their humble duties and responsibilities together with the inestimable advantages conferred on them by proximity. It was a memorable and a noble thing for the 'common mummer' who heard of Marie-Louise's liaison with her ridiculous general, to say: 'If the great man had done *me* the honour of... kissing me, I would have been proud enough to preserve myself intact afterwards.'

One cannot wonder if Busoni, conscious of his worth and antecedents, was impatient when German critics, by calling him a 'German Debussy', tried to saddle him with all the narrowness of musical and spiritual outlook which he most feared and detested. In his own words he 'attempted to widen his musical speech to a universality that could contain whatever presented itself to his imagination'. He saw himself as a polyglot where Debussy was a dialect composer; some phrase or figure which their works might show in common, had for himself a totally different significance. What in his music was a single term in a vast and varied vocabulary, was in a Debussy the sign which spread over his whole production like an all-pervading perfume. Busoni was quite impersonally offended by such inconsequent approximations.

This shrinking from comparison with a smaller figure was in itself characteristic, apart from being justified by his achievement. How far it was exaggerated by the excessive adulation of disciples who overstated the case Busoni had made out for himself, would not be easy to say.

There was a slightly embarrassing incident when, shortly after the War, Epstein was anxious to do a head of Busoni. Instead of arrangements being completed in a few minutes, as Epstein, with a certain right, expected, there were interminable preliminaries conducted through self-important messengers who volunteered their preposterous services. When by their offices Epstein was eventually given to understand that having heard the master play, and having had some table talk with him, could not ensure sufficient understanding for the purpose, he became frankly exasperated. It had been solemnly explained to him that he should first travel to Berlin to study his model in his own surroundings, and learn to apprehend his full importance from the respect paid him there by other men of eminence.

Busoni here was the victim of an adoring circle that stood between him and a common-sense arrangement which could easily have been made. But Epstein not unreasonably felt like a dog balancing a biscuit on his nose and being all the time told not to snap it up; so he simply dropped it in despair at the unfamiliar role. I refer to this incident only to show how the idiotic solemnities of Busoni's peripatetic clique of Byzantine courtiers interfered with a rational appreciation of his activities. Many potential admirers were frightened away by them. Had they only known Busoni himself they would have approached his music without the prejudice these perambulating noodles provoked. Busoni himself was never so forbidding as some of his commentators are wont to make out. They have written so much about his intellect, about his austerity, about his serenity, about 'sentiments built by him out of his intellectual recognition of their formal necessity in composition' (*sic*), that many people, although sympathetically inclined, felt that they only wanted to like or dislike a composer's music, and therefore met his with overmuch hesitation and suspicion. Busoni himself was most appreciative of any immediate sentimental approach to his work. When I once told him that a rather wavering friend had been greatly impressed as well as moved by a minor work of his, he at once expressed his gratification, saying that he considered this a definite proof of achievement. 'It means that I have succeeded,' were his words: 'only this finally matters.'

BUSONI. All we do with those brains we are so proud of means little compared to the feeling which at once recognizes the note of truth in a work. Our intellectual flatterers profess to see in it a thousand things that we may, or may not, have put there. They describe them to us! Should we be pleased? It does not tell us anything about ourselves, anyhow. But this mysterious, sudden surrender of a listener who is guided by emotion alone is our greatest reward. We have touched the heart and senses of those whose judgement we most cherish.

MYSELF. You would rather see one moist eye than conquer the seething brains of a dozen 'cerebral pathfinders'?

B. Can they be separated? I often wonder. I must tell you something amusing about 'feeling' and 'interpretation', seen as separate and independent entities.

I went to visit a German factory where they faked 'interpreted' pianola rolls. My guide explained something of the procedure with quite unsophisticated pride in its cleverness. Some schoolmaster would determine the 'right' tempi, and give all further technical indications. These were used for the construction of one coloured line on the roll. But there was more to come! That was a separate task! In the next department I guilelessly inquired: 'What may these young ladies be doing?' and one of them promptly replied: 'Please, sir, we put in the feeling!' By nondescript methods the sentimental contents of the music were defined for the girls in a brief résumé from which they constructed a second coloured graph. The player of the roll could never remain in doubt about the genuine 'feeling'.

M. Would the graphs ever flow into a single one for the 'true rendering'? Is your idea that, whether in interpretation or in appreciation, the two are 'one and indivisible' like the Third Republic?

B. It is! Not as if intellectual grasp comprises all the mysteries of sentiment. I believe on the contrary that the fullest understanding born from the heart reveals every mystery of technical structure, all the intricacies of organic build.

M. That is going very far. Very much farther than would be expected of you of all people. Isn't that so?

B. I said 'the fullest understanding'. The emotion of a moment does not suffice. I refer to that deep, lasting feeling which only arises when the intellect functions automatically. It cannot exist apart from that. A feeling so profound and comprehensive as I presume only comes to those whose intellect can intuitively penetrate every technical point.

M. As the solution of a mathematical problem may present itself to one's instincts, even in a dream; always provided that one is a trained mathematician.

B. Does that happen? That would prove my assumptions.

M. Beyond a doubt. Besides, are not most great scientific discoveries and inventions arrived at in some such way?

B. I see what you are driving at. I agree. They probably are. But what about Pascal and his geometry?

M. What about Mozart and his music? There are evidently some unaccountable prodigies of whom one can only assume that they are born with all human knowledge deposited in their brains. They do not only display their intuition sooner than others who must learn facts first, but their precocious understanding is inexplicable unless one believes that they started from a higher plane of cerebral formation. They are like children coming into the world with a complete set of teeth. . . .

B. Fully formed? Pallas Athene? Pantagruel?

M. If you like. If we don't mind being guilty of levity in such serious matters, I might say, more like a civilized dog coming into the world with a collar round its neck, and the name and address of its prospective master on it.
B. True, true! But considering where our facetiousness is leading us, let us be serious. All you have said goes to prove the correctness of my first submission.
M. True feeling counts for more than tons of brains?
B. I am convinced that it is the final truth.

I dwell on this aspect at some length because it may come as a surprise to many people who have been in the habit of regarding Busoni as an intellectual first and last. Also because in view of his mild didacticism this generous praise of sentiment might seem an unexpected deviation. Any censure taking this as a point of departure would be mistaken. His heart yearned for a simple response to the unsophisticated language of emotion, even if possibly it was not by nature vouchsafed him, for he never lost sight of its desirability and of its great importance.

His respectful attention was freely offered to composers who were confessedly in search of a consciously designed new idiom. On condition, however, that like Schönberg they could prove their abundant mastery of the *métier*. Or their power of saying a simple thing simply. If convincing proof of this was not available, he had very little patience with obtrusive originality, but an all the more alert suspicion. And although he would be the last to believe that sincerity alone could make up for any failing whatever, he demanded sincerity of every composer as a *sine qua non* when it came to music that did not openly announce itself as heartless.

The light-hearted wit in his own music forms the bridge over which the unreflective music of the instinctive and the pondered idiom of the intellectual meet. But he had to bear the continued distrust provoked by the complexity of his thought, for allusiveness is naturally distrusted by slower thinkers.

'People believe that I am full of malice: I assure you that I am a very kind-hearted man.'

BUSONI

My own action once served to bring home to him the roots and the consequences of such misunderstandings. We were together visiting a South German town. Busoni had promised to show me some interesting buildings. In the course of our walk he entered a dark court and then mounted a wide, dimly-lit stone staircase. I followed without question. We arrived at what unexpectedly proved a restaurant on the first floor. On the landing he turned round to say:

BUSONI. You are a queer fellow!
MYSELF. What makes you think so?
B. You never asked where I was going. . . .
M. Well, are we not 'out for a walk' together?
B. We are; in fact I took you here for a glass of wine. . . .
M. It did not look in the least like a place where that could be found; it looked to me more like a coiners' den, but I would naturally follow where you go.
B. I suppose it does seem natural to you! I would have wanted to know what came next.
M. Speak of reversed roles! I once felt you did something quite as odd.
B. And when may that have been?
M. You remember when you wanted us to hear Liszt's 'Figaro' which you had just discovered. You asked me to turn the pages. The manuscript was illegible, and you played your own additions that were not marked on it. Not unnaturally, I soon lost my way. Yet by never a whisper or a nod did you tell me when to turn next.
B. But I played the whole work to a finish!
M. I admired that as much as I could while feeling so disgruntled. You must realize that you made me feel foolish. It was unkind. . . .
B. But you said nothing.
M. I should have had to interrupt you. No, on that occasion it was I who was expecting a word or a sign. And more reasonably, I think.
B. And you didn't get it! Now I suppose that this time again you think it was for me to speak first?
M. Not this time. There was nothing here like one page hiding all the following ones. I should soon enough discover where you

'AS NEVER WAS BY MORTAL FINGERS STROOK'

were leading me. Very much as if I listened—without any impediment—to some of your music. I should not begin arguing before I had seen what you were getting at.

B. Unfortunately that is what I find people nearly always do. So perhaps your way is best after all. What could not one do if listeners had the patience to reserve critical observations!

M. Since we are here, let us go in and have the wine.

(*Seated with the bottle.*) You were lamenting that much you could do is left undone. You said people should refrain from mentally formulating their criticisms while you addressed them. That they should surrender for the moment, until they knew where you were leading them. Did I get it right?

B. That is more or less what I had in mind.

M. Did you refer to remembered disillusions? Or are you thinking of the future, and of works as yet unwritten?

B. Of both, but chiefly of so much music I should like to write for which I do not yet trust myself. Perhaps I ought to say, for which I don't trust my public yet—unless I were to adapt my writing to their habits. I should love to set some of those wondrous speeches of Don Quixote. His address to the goatherds in the first book, for instance. There I feel I could achieve something of real worth.

M. It seems an exceptionally suitable subject. It is a great pity that you hesitate.

B. I should want to say so infinitely much that I hardly trust the power of music to convey all that presses itself on my imagination.

M. It is strange that you should distrust your powers for the task—even counting the limitations of music. As strange as that you distrust my rational mentality when you think I behave in an unexpected way. Honestly, I think it is 'queer' when you say there is something of mystery about me. In the incident I recalled, I showed my confidence in you, as I always should where music is concerned. And that, after all, is what you desire.

B. What you say sounds flattering. I ought to be pleased. Perhaps most people speak too soon in daily affairs too, and spoil me for the appreciation of your silences.

M. You would not want me to argue more, or sooner, music or no music?

B. Mercy! Don't I know that you can beat anybody in debate?

Besides, out of my own mouth you have already convinced me.

M. Granted my debating prowess, why not take it as a compliment if I follow your lead without a word, or listen to your words or your music without itching to interrupt?

B. Well, perhaps I was slow to see my mistake. Perhaps I did not like having to admit it. Anyhow, you were right. You usually are.

M. Please! Don't make it too good! You only make me blush. Let us rather empty our glasses and drink to the Don Quixote speeches.

(They were, alas, never composed, and the more's the pity, for Busoni should have succeeded with their mixture of the fantastic, the burlesque, and mellow wisdom better than any one.)

B. Don't be too sanguine. You will have enough composer's miseries to come to the conclusion that sometimes it is better to leave cherished projects unexecuted.

M. From choice or from need? Are you thinking of the jealous lover hiding his mistress, or of Berlioz abandoning a symphony after he had calculated the cost?

B. Both, I am afraid. You ought to make yourself quite independent of composition for your existence. You should, like Rousseau, copy music for instance.

M. What on earth brings you to this? You know very well that he did not make anything like a living out of it. Besides, there were no trade-unions in his way. I have tried, and found it difficult to enter that closely guarded domain.

B. (*reproachfully*) You have been sending in a work for a competition! Did you imagine that any jury would give *you* a prize? Is it likely?

M. Oh, that is what you were driving at all the time. Do reflect; I must at least make an honest attempt. You once got a prize yourself, you know.

B. You don't suppose that I was one-tenth as much of a formed composer then as you are now? A single page of your music will frighten any one who is ever acceptable as a member of a jury.

M. But you cannot deny that you are on juries yourself? Wouldn't you give me a chance?

B. I could not; I should recognize the first bar.

M. Worse luck! We are turning in a vicious circle. I had hoped

THE SAMARITAN

that some dishonesty on a jury might bring me a chance some day.
B. It will! When it is too late! When you don't need it any more for your name. Even then, materially, it won't help you much. And don't forget that a sentimental jury will have other friends. You have nothing to expect from that, I repeat. No, you ought to make a living from something that has nothing to do with music. Then you could afford to write whatever pleased you.
M. Ouch! Don't you know that I shall be looked upon as an amateur and an interloper, and shunned by all musicians?
B. Publishers used to accept my works because of my fame as a pianist. But that fame stands in my way with the public.
M. Because they think you ought to be *only* a pianist. What would they think of 'only an amateur'? *You* despise amateurs.
B. If you were taken for one, that would not make you one. Still, I admit the objection. I see no way out for you. I should like to give you an income for a number of years so that you could work with complete freedom. Only, honestly, I have been carefully calculating—I cannot manage it. People think I am a wealthy man: I am nothing of the sort. However much I should like to, I simply have not the money.

There are not many composers who would think of such assistance to a confrère, and if Busoni, in this case, was not in a position to do what his feeling prompted, it was because he always had most lavishly given away money, right and left, to pupils and struggling musicians, and sacrificed much of his time to teaching them[1] and performing their works.

If he ever complained of anything, it was that his example had not borne fruit, that younger men, when their successes had made them financially competent, were not in their turn ready to give of what they had acquired, to others less fortunate, whose work might enrich music if not themselves.

He could never understand selfishness, whether reasoning or unreasoning, and one could not point to a nobler trait in his character, or to one that showed better how loyal and true-hearted an artist he was.

His duty, he felt, was to art, and in every sense. He had very

---

[1] It will be remembered that he never accepted remuneration.

little regard for the bourgeois solidity which preaches that a man's first duty is 'to himself and his family'. He distrusted the ostensible sacrifices of the staid artist to the social and domestic virtues, for he suspected that they were only a cloak for an overruling desire of personal comfort.

Busoni sincerely believed that if musicians would exist on so modest an income as Rousseau's copying may have produced, the colossal rest of their earnings ought to be used for the one purpose of furthering music in every way. He was much moved by the idea of Spinoza polishing his lenses—especially when he heard that orthodox Jewry regards with disfavour the systematic earning of income by poetic and philosophical talent. The conversation I have recorded reveals, however, that he was not blind to the insuperable difficulties realization of this ideal meets in a modern community. Rousseau, while hoping for the perfect state to arrive after his tenets had taken root, clung temporarily, if presumably with theoretical reluctance, to other sources that offered themselves for his sustenance.

If there is a lesson to be learnt from the real and seeming contradictions I have enumerated, it is how difficult is the position of a thoughtful, disinterested artist to-day. That Busoni should have suffered in this cause as he did, without ever being aware of his martyrdom, is the most convincing proof of his single-minded subjection to the ideal he served. It was actually left to his biographers to discover how tragic his existence had been. It certainly did not occur to him, unless perhaps in the final months, to ascribe the appalling mental and material stresses of his life, and the breakdown of his health, to the clash between his own ambitions and the smug assumptions of the world. He never envied the better lot of some of his contemporaries; he believed they paid for comfort with renunciations that would have caused him greater unhappiness than any discomfort could. It would not enter his mind that these others were unjustly favoured, that he did not gain nearly enough of the success and its concomitant rewards

'THIS LIKE THY GLORY . . .'

his talents deserved. So far was he from self-pity that he took it as the natural lot of the honest artist, to quote Vasari, early to learn to suffer cold, hunger, thirst, and other discomforts. 'Those deceive themselves altogether who suppose that while taking their ease, and surrounded by all the enjoyments of the world, they may attain to honourable distinction—for it is not by sleeping, but by waking, watching, and labouring continually that proficiency is attained.'

What could be more lovable and admirable in so great an artist as Busoni, than that simply and unaffectedly he lived according to this standard, without ever being so far aware of it as to take pride in what few others can or dare endure?

We should feel grateful for such an inspiring example. The more, where it was provided by a man who, always on the plane of highest ambition, was distinguished for his untiring endeavour as much as for his matchless accomplishment.

· ❦ *Three* ❧·

MUSIC AND WIT

MANY OF THE FACES THAT STARE AT US FROM THE PAGES OF our 'History of Music' are draped in wigs. 'The old peruke', Bach's successors—his own sons among them—used to call him. Yet there was more than one reason for the fashion. A wig achieves, at the other end, the same that stilts do. But there were other, if half-forgotten, functions for it. A wig was useful as well as ornamental. To-day we regard it almost exclusively as a symbol. That is how some writers come to pity Mozart; they feel sad about the 'indignities' time and circumstances imposed on him. But Mozart looks too human for any disguise to hide his real being, which was divine as we know now.

We tolerate Handel's periwig because it suits his florid countenance as well as his productions. And perhaps because we know that without it he looks too much of a brute. Yet Wagner could still say that Bach cannot have been as truly human as Beethoven: '... as the Sphinx with a human face attempts to free itself from the body of the Beast, so Bach's noble human head seeks to emerge from its wig.'

It has been creditably reported that Mozart was proud of his own silky golden curls, but never that he felt uneasy under the artificial, powdered ones. Evidently he despised his wig no more than the clothes which were in harmony with it. The scant reliable literature does not support any belief that he felt the figurative pressure of his peruke any more than the humiliation of what commiserating biographers have called his livery. The descriptions of his wardrobe, and of his interest in it, nowhere suggest humiliation. The democratic pretensions on his behalf are beside the point; too much sentiment has been wasted here. There is ample reason to believe that composers cherish distinguishing marks sufficiently to mourn their loss.

It is instructive to compare the habits of creative and executant musicians. The executant has retained as long as he could sartorial customs that set him apart. He even stuck to a frock-coat after it had been abandoned by the superannuated provincial best man.

Since composers need not show themselves on the platform, the fancy is not too far-fetched that they found an escape from reality in such loyalties. They held on to spiritual habits if not to material. They always have fads which reveal a symbolic substitution. Wagner stroked his velvets and silks, as Gluck drank his champagne; and, if legend may be trusted, Haydn and Spontini, amongst others, never set down a note before they had dressed in ceremonial robes. Those that discarded old habits remained committed to old dreams. They secretly yearned for the departed glories of apparel. When executants had almost toed the social line, the creative musician still dreaded the lack of distinctiveness. Beethoven's proletarian successors, deprived of the long coat and the tall hat which he (an aristocrat among the spiritual plebs, and the first democrat among the aristocracy) paraded in the Prater, still donned them in the spirit.

They acted with appropriate obedience to a need of the composer's soul. Composers may be devilish revolutionary in their music, and obey hoary conventions in their personal practices. Your democratic composer ostensibly despises patrons. Your truly human composer may despise the preposterous public for which he professes to write. But not before having once believed that it consisted of reasonable people. Both submit to the ideal expectations of a ghostly public which, in their day-dreams, they see supervising their labours.

The one must have flowing locks when the suburban fashion is a weekly trim. The other shaves his head like an Egyptian priest or a Prussian officer, when temperamental people let their mop grow. The motives are identical. And they affect the spiritual focus. Physical habits are intertwined with mental needs. They retain their hold on the man at his desk.

His faith in conventions may be obscure but it does guide him where appearances are concerned. Consciously or instinctively, composers seek to sanctify their customs by making them conform to reputed ideals. It is not because they cannot see the comic aspect. Most musicians value full-blooded and hearty fun.

The weakness that sometimes darkens so pleasing a disposition is one more of manners than of the soul.

Composers, even more than executants, have it early hammered into their impressionable minds that music is a serious affair. They suspect a weak moment when they are tickled by a joke. Yet no Rose-Red-and-Snow-White-washing biographers can hide the fact that the greatest composers were invariably good fellows. In spite of Jahn himself we know that Mozart was far from being all angelic child and silk pants. The more we see him on a level with the gods the more we see in him everything that the mortal envelope can contain. Mozart was affectionate and masculine; equally attractive to males and females by his charm and his power. While still adolescent he appeared venerable because his achievement raised him high above all others. Not many composers have been so successful socially, although generally they are avid of the approbation of their friends in moments of light-hearted intercourse. Most great musicians are reputed tellers of good tales and felicitous actors of anecdote. In private they submit without restraint to the more irresponsible attractions of life.

This concerns the way of looking at things When it comes to the way of doing things, however, we find musicians often making solemn faces, and not every one knows that this does not necessarily denote inborn gravity. Composers are mostly anxious to keep the two sides apart; they would regard it as a calamity if potential patrons were to intermingle their impressions. They have no wish to appear half man, half child; they prefer to be seen as man half the time, for the rest as exclusively composer. Not as centaurs, where one part imperceptibly turns into the other. They would rather be regarded as dual personalities. The illusion is confirmed by a great wealth of contradictory anecdote. We know Handel the business man and Handel the composer. We know Beethoven the ostentatious democrat who dragged his hat over his eyes when he passed the highly placed personages whom Goethe ceremoniously greeted, and the Ludwig von Beethoven— 'one of us' as the Viennese aristocrats said—who insists on the disdainful refinement of his quieter musical utterances. There is Berlioz, the romantic revolutionary of the 1830 July days, conducting the singing crowds in the 'Marseillaise', and Berlioz the retiring classicist of 'Les Troyens', who even as a child wept over Dido. Or again, Berlioz the man of the world, who invited his friends' support to rid himself of Mlle Recio, and Berlioz the Peter Pan, who wrote love-letters to the Stella of his early 'teens when she had become a dignified, silver-haired grandmother. Wagner, as usual, supplies the most extravagant instance. Although he presents neither the humanity nor the divinity of a Mozart, he can alternatively be seen as the accomplished cad and unflinching sponger, the loud-voiced drama-merchant and shameless exhibitionist, and as Wagner the exquisite dreamer of the Waldweben, with his love of little birds and his generous tears over the orphan's tragedy.

A composer's adherents are not expected to unravel the occult strands of his diversified motives. They are least welcome when, probing into this dualism, they would explain his music by the light of what its maker's life reveals of too-human inclinations.

The composer who feels most consequential about his daily deeds may be most deliciously inconsequential in his music. And the one who permits irresponsibility in his music need not relax whatever ethical strictness he considers necessary in his behaviour.

Dilettanti who understand neither music nor life suffer

from the conviction that the artist must establish perfect balance between the two. Some people, however, are in love with music without being sentimental about musicians. They judge with considerable severity where their adored art is concerned, and they resent the most distant hint of foolery.

Music is a cherished consolation of bruised souls and uneasy consciences, a popular antidote for undigested tragedy. Any one who has lost dear friends, who struggles with unrelieved poverty, or feels hurt by the world's triviality, by uncongenial surroundings and contact with life's crudities, looks upon music as his ordained and inalienable domain. From such private sentimentality to universal, transitive sentimentality is a short step, and a natural human weakness makes music-lovers indiscriminately assume that the stresses which they undergo must have been similarly felt by the makers of that music to which they look for release. That is why tears are being shed over 'poor' Schubert, why well-meaning indignation, somewhat belatedly for individual cases, but probably all the more sincere for that, has created a poison belt of sloppiness round the musician's vocation. He pathetically tries to penetrate this without losing too much of the poetic dignity to which his presumed remoteness entitles him. That is, as long as he remains proud, and poor, and aloof—poetically hungry while full of hope, but assured of salvation if only he does not seek it. If it were not for this, composers would follow their natural bent with greater courage. They would not be so diffident about raising a candid laugh. As it is, they encourage the superstition that only subtle irony or the fugitive touch of sardonic humour can pass as a component of 'abstract music'. However good a companion and exhilarating a wit he may be, a musician usually becomes portentously dignified when he chins his fiddle or takes up his ruled paper. He does not even wait to see how much liberty he will be allowed; he feels it incumbent upon him to keep that problem at a trombone's length.

Occasionally a popular executant can take risks. Once his

career is secure he can surrender to his sense of fun without damaging his reputation. After Pachmann had by genuine achievement established himself, he could afford to make gentle clowning a fine art. But it had to be carried to a point where it practically equalled his other performances, otherwise the risk would be too great. It demands a special talent to introduce the graces of the comic stage to the concert platform.

But now picture a composer at his desk or his piano—or his harmonium (it has happened!)—can one still imagine him as an entertaining companion? Usually he feels that humanity is waiting for another work which may add to the weekly and daily thrills of inveterate concert addicts. He is overcome by his Sunday-best sensation. It is about the only impressive consciousness left to him in these insufficiently ornate days. There was a time when he could have adjusted his peruke. Later, he could still have put in front of him the jewelled sabres presented by grateful cities and universities. What is he to do when the resources of these decorative epochs are exhausted, when gilt medals and honorary degrees are all he can hope for? Unless he is one of those Good-Biz monsters who find inspiration in their banker's pass-book on the piano-lectern, he must console himself with thoughts of past loveliness.

The composer who dreams of the 'great line of masters' feels his duties weighing most heavily when he asks himself: 'Can I maintain the Form?' or, 'Shall I reach my Tenth Symphony?' or—here bulges the Monster Itself—'Is the Vehicle I chose commensurate with the Elevation of My Thoughts?' or the anguishing parallel: 'Does the Elevation of my Thoughts soar to the Height of Eminence of the Vehicle to which I am committed?'

Before composers discovered the advantages of becoming hard-headed commercial rhinoceroses, they were satisfied with the bourgeois spirit of the post-Beethoven period. However innocent this was in its inception, it has been responsible for much shatteringly dull and pretentious formality. The nine-symphonies obsession has killed more than one composer. Writing symphonies became so responsible an occupation that no one who took it up could without shame surrender to light-heartedness, whatever his natural inclination. Ebullient spirits needed constant, strict control on such weighty occasions. The maker of symphonies sets out with oppressive responsibility. He addresses a public which has learned to grovel in adoration before the musical monuments he aspires to approach. He cannot afford to forget this when he gets busy with his first and his second subject.

We are none of us free from guilt; we have all contributed to the shaping of this gloom.

Every one of us has, at some time or other, been weak enough to search for serious intentions in music that was probably conceived with very different feelings. If we could reconstruct the composer's original state of mind, we should probably be often scandalized. What irreverent exuberance may not have served as a basis for phrases in which now we read nothing but aesthetic beatitude and moral uplift! In the days of silent films a famous French surgeon was shown at work, muttering over his patient. Naturally, audiences imagined that he was repeating to himself some principle of technique to be always remembered, or whispering an invocation to Aesculapius. Once, when the film was shown to a class of deaf-mutes, these expert lip-readers were contorted with laughter. They had seen him describing details of the operation in terms adapted from a notoriously indelicate music-hall song.

If there were similar means to reveal a composer's mind, with what indecorous hilarity would many a symphonic movement be greeted. One may have suspicions, but it is considered an undesirable subject. Most of the wily authors of thematical analyses and programme-notes of popular masterpieces are so saturated with the solemnity of their task that they cannot see how a musical utterance may have been conceived in a mood of drollery which to the composer alone did not seem blasphemous.

Would any one whose senses had not been distempered by the twilight atmosphere of the old-time academy believe that Bach always took his work as seriously as it is regarded by most Bach students? Is it altogether probable that his piece of programme music about the Beloved Brother's journey was much more than a joke? Had he stopped at the pain of parting and the pleasure of reunion one might admit that he employed legitimate elements of music in his ordinary manner. When, however, he introduces the efforts of friends to keep the bold adventurer from risking his body in the stage-coach, the enumeration of all the further dangers he may meet on his perilous excursion into foreign parts, the failure of their arguments, and the mental agony caused by anticipated troubles, it would be an injustice to Bach to call it anything but quite good fun.

The same can be said about Haydn who, in many of his symphonies, sonatas, and string quartets, shows of what high seriousness he is capable. At all times he used to relieve the atmosphere with occasional flashes of wit. Sometimes he gives an entire movement of rollicking humour. Naturally with advancing age he did not so often exhibit the same high spirits, but even then his work is full of quips witty enough to escape the charge of senility (which might legitimately be made against some of the serious sections). Most of his later works have all the male power of the early ones, and we cannot reasonably believe that the comic miniatures of the 'Seasons' or of the 'Creation' were produced in innocence. The leap of the tiger, the slow wallowings of the whale, the trotting deer, the crowing of the cocks, and the charmingly inconsequent way in which these pictures are presented outside thematic coherence, should convince unbiased listeners of Haydn's light-hearted purpose.

Beethoven's wit cannot, by his most fanatic admirers, be called exactly volatile. His joking is difficult, sometimes appallingly laborious. But the object and the manner could not possibly be mistaken. In his settings of poems which contain the sort of wit that appealed to him, he shows how his primitive jokes depend for their effect mainly on what in ordinary life would provide the occasion for simple horseplay. One of his stand-bys is the reiteration which prolongs the belly-shaking guffaws first provoked by such incongruities as a big nose or a big head on a little man, or bow-legs under a pretty woman. His witticisms classify themselves in his vocal compositions and thus can be identified in his instrumental work, where perhaps no more than a title or an occasional indication betrays the humorous intent. The title of his famous rondo, 'Die Wut über den verlorenen Groschen', was not a gratuitous afterthought. One could methodically dissect it and find all that Beethoven judged funny in the impatient search of a nervous miser for a small coin. Beethovenians do not feel like admitting this, but it need not diminish his greatness if the essence of the fun is that of the Mickey Mouse symphonies. No one less than Schumann was distressed in his genuine understanding of Beethoven's intentions; in spite of the respect due to a posthumous work, he described it as 'a perfectly ridiculous piece'. And Schumann was a pontifical authority amongst those Brahmins who never tire of pointing to the great mission of musicians. It is therefore all the more significant that Schumann in his later years failed to detect anything funny in Brahms at his most pompous, and that eventually he spent most of his waking hours in the asylum in enthralling discourses with his dear, departed Mendelssohn.

The indefatigable Professor Hugo Riemann tells us that 'The Master Brahms' did 'not disdain humour'. He quotes what are supposed to be witty passages in his 'Akademische Festouvertüre'. Perhaps Brahms found exquisite fun in the squeak of an overblown muted trumpet. Since the phrases he writes for it are anything but amusing in themselves, one might also adopt the interpretation of other commentators, i.e. that he was hinting at the 'Meistersinger', and knew he could leave to his university audience the choice of hearing these yaps and croaks as inherently witty, or as a biting caricature of the pleasantries of Wagner. Let us not forget that the work was his thanks to the Akademie for making him Doktor der Filosofie, *honoris causa*.

The popular conception of the musical classics is of conscious demi-gods enjoying in advance on earth the veneration which centuries were going to bestow—premature Olympians sniffing in imagination the odour of burnt-offerings not as yet alight but piled up for their expectant nostrils. If, however, one studies them unhampered by this warped entelechy, if instead one values their surpassing humaneness, one knows that their greatness must be measured by a different standard. The desire for unbridled jocularity is found commensurate with the spontaneity of a composer's talent. The works of the classics seldom fail to supply proof of this, even within the limits of one movement. Many pundits in their expounding concentrate on features which seem to exclude so much common humanity. Still, the facts are there for whoever will read between the staves and listen between the parts.

There are few worse misfortunes for the true understanding of music than the absence of a fully reliable biography of Mozart. Even so, enough is known to reveal the traits that combine to make a complete man, and to suggest that his quick laughter and the pervading tang of his mordant irony are important elements of his character. If, with a semblance of justification, they are denied by the students of his symphonies, they cannot possibly be by any one who knows the operas intimately. Some disgruntled critics admit such characteristics only to disparage them, to praise his symphonies above his operas, and to classify the operas themselves according to their greater or lesser seriousness. Has not Wagner, whose theories of music were forbiddingly earnest (although here again, fortunately, his bite was sweet compared to his bark), published his melancholy discovery that Mozart's relation to music was 'at bottom frivolous'? He did not hesitate to say in support of this contention that Mozart's music to 'serious' texts was superior to music like that of 'Così fan tutte'. He called Mozart all the more worthy of love and veneration for that very failing which revealed his ethical purity (else, 'how shamefully would that have dishonoured music').

I have a wicked faith that holds Mozart capable of anything, and although I would not for a moment question that he was possessed of the highest moral qualities, I am sure that he had a few others besides that were not less profound and admirable for being not precisely moral.

I do not think I am mistaken if I say that to-day the best-informed critics and most assiduous Mozart-lovers are inclined to rank 'Così fan tutte' with his greatest achievements.

Yet, generally speaking, the old prejudice persists as the chief reason why some of the operas are unjustly rated higher than those in which ironical intentions are too clearly evident. His 'Seraglio' is full of good-natured satire from beginning to end, but his powerful individuality and his matchless originality raise it high above the plane of mere parody. His dramatic style is everywhere partly dependent on his wit. Even in 'Don Giovanni'—not to mention the 'Zauberflöte'—there are all the comic ingredients, from gentle, harmless mockery to bland yet purposeful cynicism. His unerring dramatic instinct prescribed this admixture. It is a common factor in all his operas. They remain essentially lyrical works for the stage, in which the sarcasm and cynicism enter as components, redeemed by the kindly tolerant smile which irradiates the grave countenance. His exquisite sense of balance never deserts him. The laugh in his mock-solemn lines, and in his elegant formality, everywhere interpenetrates the serious spirit of adjacent sections, without ever producing the stress of conscious effort, however intricate the dramatic relationship grows.

Most of Mozart's biographers have failed to do justice to this side of him, if they observed it at all. One could not expect that of aesthetes disciplined in the stern Teutonic school. They have been too long and too openly committed to the belief that ponderousness and gravity are signs of profundity. Their own reserve and dignity preclude every suspicion of their ultimate seriousness, and it were fatal had they to disclose, supposing they could know, that the revered masters could be deficient in decorum. How is the teacher to conserve his own dignity when his students find out that Bach or Mozart or any of the idols on whom professors profess to model themselves were not, as the latter, filled with a due sense of the solemnity of their occupation? Young musicians have to discover for themselves facts their elders should have pointed out. They are encouraged in the irrational faith that size and depth have an ascertainable relation in aesthetic values, that a gay piece cannot convey profound feeling, that a short piece cannot convey a valuable message. Students must believe that the cogitations of a composer of any probity naturally require three or four movements whose length varies with their significance. Although concision is abstractly praised, it is persistently questioned that important ideas or sentiments can be satisfactorily communicated in less than the hundreds of bars of the 'sonata-form' sections of a symphony.

The first requisite of a good joke is that it should be brief. It need not on that account lack profundity. The wisdom of facetiae demands condensed statement as emphatically as the most intense speculation. Long development may sacrifice none of the precision or pertinence of deep thoughts; but it is never a requisite condition. Some of the profoundest observations on grave subjects have been expressed aphoristically by Pascal, Rochefoucauld, or Vauvenargues, not to forget Spinoza, none of them frivolous gossips. Here were thinkers who pierced through to the innermost core of all matter, and yet all irretrievably committed to the methodical employment of the simplest forms and terminology.

Whatever doctrinaires may uphold, even a symphony need not preponderantly exhibit an austere disposition. No more need an aphorism be trivial. People easily suspect that a brilliant thought pithily stated is a flash in the pan. When restated on a vast scale, the profound wit contained in the small dimensions might become tenuous to the point of extinction. But we must be careful not to confuse the exigencies of a form with the potentialities of an idea, or of a theme. The large forms do not by their nature exclude the admixture of humour any more than the brief statement excludes austerity. 'Jesting Pilate' was desperately earnest, and the preoccupation of the Evangelists with what they considered the most urgent parts of their message does not conceal that in Jesus's thoughts and actions a wise and gentle humour takes its legitimate place.

Mozart copiously provides examples of the depths that can be plumbed in the brief moments of a single musical phrase which depends on mirthful observation or droll comment. The playful irony of the 'Mille e Tre', and the sarcastic teasing of 'Non più andrai' with its enchanting caricature of martial pageantry, are memorable instances. Don Giovanni's 'Champagne Aria', while as swiftly moving and as lightly hovering as any of the 'Supper Music', lights up a complete aspect of human existence with embracing clarity, and with a keen-edged insight which no emotional rapture, no awed pondering of the most sublime ambitions obsessing the spirit of mankind, could surpass.[1]

The timorous essays in musical jesting attempted by composers who specialized in the 'lighter' forms dwindle before this assured mastery. Neither Sullivan in his parodistic operettas, nor Tchaikovsky in his Dance Suites and Ballets, to cite extremes, ever attain a tithe of the scintillating wit of that rapidly unfolding Mozart aria. So much can be established before the touchstone of musical perfection is applied.

The ostentatiously humorous composer often appears the most solemn animal, and his music easily the most tiresome and dragging. Tchaikovsky happens to belong to the more gifted ones who manage now and then to be entertaining in a cheerful vein. But, as might be expected, he was rabidly eager to be regarded as genuinely at home only with the over-

[1] Busoni has in his *New Aesthetics* singled out this air to present a similar moral.

LAUGHTER UNHEARD

poweringly tragic sides of human experience. And Sullivan, who could display a light hand in his familiar cum-Gilbert part, became unbearably noble and soulful when the injunctions of his admirers betrayed him into the writing of what he considered really serious music. Where he was determined to appear dignified and elevated, he became as distinguishedly soporific as the most awesome models of Teutonic solemnity beloved of the academic nurseries.

It is significant that Mozart, who was witty above all others, and ready for a jest at his saddest moments, was also the one composer whom nobody can deny a talent that will stand any comparisons whatsoever. I have found that when I say how witty Donizetti or Offenbach could be, I am told they don't count, or otherwise that they were funny without knowing it. If one discounts the personal dislikes that beget such hostile judgements, one must still allow for a residue of ignorance. Repeatedly I have heard humorous intentions of composers denied by people who did not understand the language of the text employed. They knew works in translations that blunted every edge of wit, or they knew no more than the music alone, and purblindly passed by treasures of humour. It is a thankless task to argue with musicians who cannot see a musical joke unless it is fully annotated by the literary context. And it is disheartening to have to give explanations, only to be told that anyhow it proves nothing because the composer is not a great enough figure. Rossini may be witty—granted!—but he is no Beethoven. Offenbach may be without a rival in comic characterization—admitted if you like—but he moves in too low a region to call for 'the serious attention of a serious musician'. He may be entertaining. His unashamed venality, his cynical defiling of a minor talent make him all the more contemptible. What can one say against such maddeningly wrongheaded arguments? A composer may not make it his life's task to cultivate the traditionally ornate forms; that does not imply that his humorous utterances could not, by sheer perfection, rise to the highest heights of excellence. The most felicitous products in the sombrer vein do not, as such, command a greater respect, even if they are the work of the universally venerated masters. If a thing is admirable, it is admirable in all circumstances, as a beautiful woman is beautiful wherever she is. We may be shocked to find either the lighthearted music in staid surroundings, or the lovely maiden in a bawdy-house, but if the 'thing of beauty' is not always 'a joy', its 'loveliness' is not decreased, though it may be tarnished in some moralists' minds.

There is a Hindu saying that 'the cup loses not its grace whoever drinks from it'. I have in one of these essays set down my conviction that the occasional rape of Euterpe does her no great harm, that it is in fact a useful experience for a lady inclined to be a shade too serene, and encouraged in this by pompous admirers. A rare, blushing touch of impudicity within reason, would seem to keep her up to concert-pitch. For fear of losing our lofty adjustment we risk becoming as solemn as undertakers' mutes in our musical pursuits. We ought to be a little *canaille* at times; not quite so *nobilmente*. High kicks bring ventilation; too many *dessous* are heaped on the poor Muse.

But it should be understood that I am not referring to the futile affectations of modernist blatancy, the knowing leer of the painted jade, the hollow grin of Dada, the noisy buffoonery of the French and Russian fashion-plate idiots who are so anxious to tell us about this age of machines. The composer who, like a spookish, clinking ape, beats his empty tin-plate chest to let us hear how hollow he is, and whose foppish giggles proclaim the spruce delight he takes in his own rattling emptiness, is such a piteous figure that one does not grudge him his commercial triumphs as long as it is understood that as a musician he is miles beneath Grock.

Rossini or Offenbach in their most unguarded moments of mechanical witticism never sink to the depths that would be summits of inspired achievement for these nightmare brats of a gloomy couple of half-impotent parents, the one being over-satiety of undigested tradition, the other lecherous appetite for the quick successes of sensational novelty. I wrote of Hellas and Olympic laughter, of the sunny shine and the spring breezes of glorious mirth, of Bacchantic rapture, not of the squeals and stench of the litter in a hyena's tunnelled lair.

The men on the heights, with clean brains and full hearts, are worthy of our admiration whether they ask us to laugh with them, or meditate with them and share their melancholy. Erasmus and Rabelais are as great as Bacon and Montaigne. If masters of musical wit cannot be so readily quoted, it is partly because most composers fear to be caught unbending, and partly because most music-lovers dare not see their idols subject to what they think is a weakness.

The advocates of merciless sublimity in music above all arts, offer one superficially presentable excuse when they insist on a single standard for all. But on examination it proves a double standard for any single work. If one ridicules this inconsequent critical severity, it is objected that not all ways of expressing spiritual experience demand respectful consideration. The Comic Muse is denounced as a poor relation of the Tragic Muse. Lest it should be believed that her poverty is even respectable, it is hinted that she is also the Ugly Sister, incapable of collecting the wages of sin in spite of her willingness. Or, with the roles reversed, the plain but impeccably clean and severe Muse of the unfunny composer is, for our discomfiture, unfavourably contrasted with the abandoned sister and her too-pretty prettiness. The impermissibly seductive one is pictured as the inspirer of comic talent—her favours are held responsible for reciprocal defilement, and a reprehensibly profitable one.

It is true that Offenbach did make capital, and income, out of his gifts, but so after all did Max Reger, whose music owes nothing to flightiness, whatever renown he gained in other fields. The anomaly is fascinating. Offenbach exhausted his whole store of wit on his music, and was, outside it, a virtuously dull dog, as his *Reminiscences* prove. (How pitiful, when one remembers his reputed evil eye, which caused one critic to omit his name in all notices, the blanks to be filled in afterwards by his daughter!) Reger was famed as a wag and a raconteur whose numerous cronies repeated his titillating quips with infectious chuckles of boozy glee, but he kept all that out of his compositions. There, in fact, he preserves a colossal, simian, flat-footed high-mindedness which ensured the purring approbation of the Apollonian arbiters of German musical etiquette.

One might believe that sundry demolishing facts like these should have caused a wavering in the army of goose-quills with little men attached that fight for the rights of respectable dullness. But it takes more than truth to discourage these pests, as it takes more than light to make them see, more than wit to make them smile—however ready they are to scowl when others threaten to relax. These snickering crib-biters, antagonists of candid laughter, presumably are descendants of Rabelais's tiny men that were borne on a very ill wind which failed even in its proverbial redeeming quality. It fits them all the better for rushing about between the legs of the great, snorting aloud their disapproval. They are not heard by the great, perhaps, but all the more distinctly by the majority of reach-me-down semi-wits who lend a sympathetic ear. They are the bearers of banners on which they inscribe such truths as that whatever is generally assumed is necessarily right. Nothing could be more flattering to the innocently immodest public of these soured disapprovers, who would deny the unrighteous their part of sunshine. We are asked to take it from them that music built on tragic elements presumes greater penetration and higher gifts in its makers, and more persistent application than that in which wit, satire, irony, or any of the comic moods predominate. The absurdity of this superstition is not soon admitted unless one's demand is put as a pure abstraction. As soon as the personality of a composer enters, the picture changes. What seemed a simple, logical admission to ask, suddenly appears as a monstrous assault on the integrity of ardent

'... NON LICET BOVI'

partisans who feel that a holy cause stands or falls with their devout loyalty.

There have at all times been composers who in spirit felt inclined to humour, broad or narrow, but who by temperament were slow of motion, as others felt naturally impelled to dance but, restraining the urge, affected a solemn pace in deference to what they had been taught was an inexorable requirement of their art. When the gaieties of Beethoven appear crude it must be remembered that he was not remarkable for a light touch in any department of life. He was Olympian, but not Mercurial; Jovial, no doubt, but never a swift-footed thrower of feathered darts. If he, too, carried away Europe, it was once more in the guise of a bull. His is the thundering laughter that suits one whose lightning kills; there is no lightning wit about him.

It is all too evident on the occasions when Beethoven, in a work conceived in profound seriousness, wants us, for the duration of a few bars, to join in a rush of tremendous good-humour —his renowned unbuttoned jollity. Is there conviviality so enticing that it can wipe out the deep-grooved deprecating frown of a man who felt the weight of human suffering so heavily upon him? The essential gravity of his obsession with the grandiose survived all his youthful fooling; his tight-lipped, Dantonesque conviction of the towering responsibility in which his self-imposed task of moral redemption involved him proved unsettling when he gave way to a jocose mood.[1] He readily relaxes but not unnaturally finds an awed public shy of following this lead in his company. 'Gentlemen, you may laugh!' he seems to say first, and his own burst of laughter follows to emphasize the encouragement to unrestrained, simple joy. His hearers still tremble to the reverberations of the lion's angry roar heard a moment earlier, and while they anticipate its prob-

[1] Danton's injunction to the executioner, 'Show my head to the people, it is well worth seeing', is truly Beethovenian. Prose could come no nearer to the themes of his 'monumental' middle period. It is interesting to compare the heads of Danton and Beethoven with that of the aristocrat-demagogue Mirabeau. Physiognomists please copy.

able return, their enjoyment remains a little uneasy. Everything connected with Beethoven bears the imprint of the legendary leonine grip. We can read volumes in the sole enumeration of the contents of his library. Austere classicism is heavily stamped on all the labels of the books he left behind. Homer, Euripides, and Sophocles are there in force. His correspondence and his conversation-books provide numerous equally revealing documents. Whatever the primitive force of his mother wit, it was not strong enough to save him from committing to paper such things as the notorious 'Heiligenstätter Testament' with its schoolboy heroics. There is no attitudinizing: he felt like that. 'O ye people that would see in me a hater of mankind, how are ye deceived. . . .' &c. And this diffuse rhetorical rapture persisted as strongly as his childlike veneration of The Great Ancients. It was not just the symptom of the excessively tragic mood that overwhelms adolescents at the approach of puberty. He kept it up; one of his last works, in which is manifested his immense humanitarianism, characteristically turns to the grandeur-that-was-Schiller: 'Schöne Götterfunken' . . . 'Seid umschlungen, Millionen' . . . 'ahnest Du den Schöpfer' . . . 'Dieser Kuss der ganzen Welt!'

Beethoven felt a Moses with the stone tablets. And as ready to smash them, as we know from the trampled 'Eroica' score (restored, however, without any corresponding Mosaic acknowledgement!). The pathos of his use of the Schiller Ode is enhanced by that of the preceding recitatives, which serve as an orchestral annunciation. How well the fervent apostles have felt this is shown in the numerous proposed texts for them, invariably of the most exalted moral and philosophical tone. Beethoven himself cannot be acquitted, whatever shamefaced disclaimers other disciples have subsequently exhibited on his behalf.

In his unadulterated *scherzando* moods Beethoven has, without a shade of malice, distorted the playful Mozartian tradition, yet the fact alone that he did write such things as the Rondo mentioned, supports my thesis that unblushing fun in music is a thing no composer need disown. If Beethoven did not trip lightly it was only because he was physiologically incapable of it; he was a great man for all that.

His tempo was essentially the tempo of conventional musical structure. In his symphonies he had moments of inspiration where he succeeded in speeding it up. When he is occupied with the implications of a text, he neglects the brevity which a jest demands. However unambiguous the words, he no more trusts his hearers than himself for quick appreciation. He pokes them in the ribs, slaps their shoulders, and stamping on the floor shouts in so many notes, 'See the joke? Good, what?' until the little jest is all pounded flat. In his song, 'Ich war bei Chloen', a man kisses a girl who protested that she would scream, but waited until the deed was done. Beethoven developed this into a kind of instrumental scherzo which requires several repetitions in the text, culminating in a childish reiteration of the concluding words that contain 'the point'. He is not so desperately afraid that his hearers may entirely miss it. He dwells on the typically brief musical phrase until it is developed into the form his instinct prescribes as appropriate treatment. Nothing could be more instructive. The music tells us explicitly:

How she giggled and wriggled.
How she pretended; her chastity being all my eye. . . .
Not to forget Betty Martin.
How the man was nearly taken in, but her duplicity exposed.
So much for her bashful shrinking, and airs *and* graces.
And how the girl did scream—(Scream? Oh yes, she screamed! She screamed all right!
But you know when? Long, long—afterwards she screamed! Long, long . . . afterwards!)
And how the whole business was a joke, becoming funnier the more you think of it; how he feels tempted to tell it you once more.

By this time the musical form is satisfactorily rounded off. The procedure reveals where we must seek the germ of the

Beethoven scherzo when we are without the help of detailed references.

We must, however, remember that then Beethoven's indigenous wit functions on a much higher plane. His self-consciousness makes him slow when he has to provide room for as leisurely a setting of the text as he believes necessary. It is different when he considers nothing but his musical invention, and need not resign his sovereignty.[1] He evolves his scherzo on the same principle, but the pulse beats quicker.

His musical snippets have a germinal power which makes them shape like ice-flowers on a window-pane into naturally enlarging designs that obey an inherent logic. This proliferation is independent of the humiliating need to adjust the movement in subjection to the obstinacy of mean literary directions. Beethoven's powerful themes only submit to this drilling with reluctance. Where he forcibly subjects them to the snaffle one is reminded of the wretched spectacle of a thoroughbred ridden by a monkey to make a yokel's holiday entertainment. Where Beethoven alone directs, the development of his thought may run to equal length, but there is greater concentration. Nothing could better demonstrate the intrinsic difference between wit in words and wit in music. His methods were unsuited to literary treatment. Words attract him for their ethical implications; their own rhythmical laws and measure of speed embarrass him.

The Beethoven influence has been so lasting and overpowering that after him no composer, unless he would risk the shame of being called a musical buffoon, had the courage to display such wit as he was capable of in symphonic works or chamber music.

Wagner's occasional excursions are mainly remarkable for their monumentality. His musical developments in amusing

---

[1] It is a curious fact, deserving of protracted examination, that the Beethoven who disdainfully repulsed singers' pretentions and who would say 'Do you think I can bother about a miserable fiddle while the spirit is moving me?' would fawn upon the poet in his setting of words, his sin being one not of peremptory curtailment but of exaggerated annotation beyond the stage of musical repletion.

situations are habitually planned on the Brobdignagian scale. They are not numerous, and it would be hard to find an example in his earlier works. Vast stretches of the later ones are curiously devoid of humour in view of their intended universality.

We have to fall back on the 'Meistersinger', where his Saxon wit is unveiled in all its pot-bellied nakedness. Beckmesser is not just a cantankerous fool; he must be a fool as big as the Niederwald-Denkmal, that pyramidal memento of Imperial Teutonic grandiosity. Wagner does not only poke you in the ribs: after he has told his joke you feel as Beckmesser must have done when the whole population of Nüremberg had joined in a nocturnal orgy of bashing and smashing. The full-orchestra-and-chorus that has contributed to this prodigious hilarity is even enlarged in the last act for the childish caricaturing of a Rossini theme which, in Wagner's mind, was connected with tailors, whose occupation for centuries has appealed to cock-eyed German wit as something irresistibly comic. (Richard Strauss in his earliest Wagnerian mood made his début as a musical wit with a 'Schneiderpolka'; the fact of a man being both a Pole and a tailor is obviously almost too unbearably much for the Teuton sense of humour.) The more subtle fun Wagner managed to introduce between these two peaks is that of Beckmesser's serenade and his visit 'the morning after' to Hans Sachs' studio. The wretched Merker (in a first version he was named 'Hans Lick'!) is now pilloried in his envious impotence. Sachs-Liszt-Talent is going to have an easy prey in Beck-Messer-Hanslick-Pedullard. As earlier, in his numskull pedantry, he put his scansion consistently wrong, and exposed his bovine stupidity in the stodgy clumsiness of his bass parts, so now, properly 'beaten up' *à l'allemande*, he cannot move without stumbling and saying 'Ouch' and 'Aie' at every bar. In case the wit should lack transparency there comes a side-splitting extension, when, from the semi-purloined manuscript, he sings about 'liver' when it should be 'live', and 'bleich wie ein Kraut', for 'gleich einer Braut', and so on.

The wit in the 'Ring' is restricted to the earthly figures. Even then Wagner probably did not foresee that Fasolt and Fafner would appeal to us as somewhat painfully comical. He meant presumably no more than a sort of grim humour, and it says much for the exclusive seriousness with which he regarded his creations that he does not seem to have apprehended any incongruously burlesque effect from Fafner-as-Dragon lowing through a megaphone. The little there is of determined witticism has been lavished on the figure of Mime, and we are not permitted to miss it. With repeated he-he-he's and ha-ha-ha's, Mime ingratiatingly tells Siegfried that he proposes to cut off his head, the joke being that only Siegfried and the audience are aware that he believes he is saying something very different. Such choice morsels are served up over and over again, and as relentlessly exploited as the landlady's joint, which from shepherd's pie gradually becomes transformed into rissoles and broth—very much like the Wagnerian *leit-motiv* —until the guests become so desperately familiar with the stuff that they swallow it without investigation.

There is presumably some tepid good-humour connected with most of the stage-appearances of animals in the 'Ring', but we know how immensely seriously Wagner took his fauna, from dogs to Rhinemaidens. It is notorious that the less humorous the intention the more mirth-producing the result of the introduction of animals before the footlights. On such occasions as Siegfried's leading in a bear to frighten Mime, although the incident is conceived in a spirit of happy laughter, it does not carry one beyond a wanly tolerant smile. (History mentions one occasion when Brünnhilde's horse showed—as an unkind critic reported—what it cared for the whole performance; but such can happen to all horses . . . in the 'Muette', the 'Fanciulla', the danger is always there. A ribald historian has suggested that Auber chose a 'Cheval de Bronze' as the only safe one.)

Berlioz was too much of an iconoclast to respect the fetish of obligatory solemnity in composition, but it is in keeping with the tragedy of his life and the exuberance of his sardonic moods that his humorous passages are either wholly diabolical, or shattered with the convulsions of his Titan's laughter. I do not mean anything like the stale accusation that all he does is too cataclysmic for graceful measure, I mean no more than that his humour is too much coloured with the terrifying intensity of his passion to let it rank with the polished, allusive witticism that is one of Mozart's great charms, and which I have throughout kept in mind as a criterion. Berlioz's unsurpassed joke against his critics (the 'unearthing' of 'L'Enfance du Christ') was so to say extra-musical, although it shows the master hand sufficiently to be eternally resented. But his purely musical 'petards and rattlesnakes' provide a Mephistophelian illustration of the reckless mirth in which he exulted.

The French comic-opera composers approach the ideal of elegant pleasantry more nearly; many a passage of Auber or Hérold survives the application of the exacting standard I mentioned. Their music, however, lacks just that ecstasy of genius which makes occasional drolleries detach themselves naturally as delicious touches on the magistral breadth of the whole picture. In this respect Offenbach provides a more convincing example. He has revealed shuddering depths of tragic intensity in the 'Contes d'Hoffmann', and the sheer power of his dramatic grasp imparts to his witticisms an added perfection.

I am not referring to such threadbare stage-jocundities as the stammerer and the deaf man, although often enough he lends even to these a new brilliance by his consummate musical finish. I am thinking of the subtle turns of humour abounding in his dialogues, which serve as illuminating strokes to his accomplished character-pictures. In his most rollicking mood he can still fascinate our musical perceptions with jesting of a finesse and universality as exhilarating and engaging as that of Mozart's 'Impresario' or the 'Musikalischer Spass'. There is an excellent piece of fooling in 'La Belle Hélène', where the outraged husband asks of Paris 'Qu'avez-vous fait de mon honneur?', the catchword being taken up in true grand operatic fashion by the others on the stage, who repeat with slight variations, 'Yes—*what* have you done with that honour?' The musical ensemble, from an evanescent parody on the conventions, develops into an etching ironical comment, every part taking the form of a vocalise which delineates the character of the stage tenor, the stage bass, and of all the singers' '*singeries*'.

The composer who next to Mozart is distinguished for the grace and transparency of his wit is of course Rossini. Unfortunately, while most musicians are prepared to admit that the 'Barbiere' is a masterpiece, they have the irritating habit of always referring to it as a masterpiece *of* something or other. They show a peculiar hesitation to regard it as the flawless work of a master, pure and simple. It surely is not only distinguished for its wit. It has many admirable qualities besides, as worthy of study as any work whatsoever. It is a pity that the outrageous popularity of the 'Barbiere' has made the majority of people forget that there are other operas of Rossini which do not lose by comparison. Mr. Sacheverell Sitwell has drawn attention to some of these in his little monograph on Mozart, and he will deserve the gratitude of many music-lovers if his plea rouses opera impresarios from their pessimistic lethargy sufficiently to bring about a revival of at least 'L'Italiana in Algeri'.[1]

The composers who are most eminently representative of the nineteenth century were characteristically averse from the frivolity which habitual indulgence in humour implies. They submitted to the faith of the grim leaders of thought in that period. After the much-abused lack of seriousness of the eighteenth century there came the reaction of the half-worldly, half-mystical religion of human progress, which for its deepest

[1] Has this happened already? The management of Covent Garden has announced the revival of 'Cenerentola', a work which few living musicians can have heard in London. But one fears that it will be modernized *à la Respighi* before it is presentable with modern singers. (Since this was written 'Cenerentola' and 'L'Italiana' have realized my apprehensions.)

origin derived from the probings and hopes of Kant and of Rousseau. This was enough to exclude the undignified conception of a composer's ethical obligations which Wagner was shocked to discover in Mozart. The position of Kant was that he simply had no time for anything beyond his immediate investigations. His face alone shows that he was by no means incapable of humour, or likely to despise it. This, however, has not been understood by many of his followers. The artists who were at all occupied with a philosophy of life mostly took their Kantian ideas from Schopenhauer, whose grating churlishness is incompatible with any but the most lugubrious humour. As for Rousseau, whose occult influence on all nineteenth-century artists has been deeper and more comprehensive than is suspected, his case admits of only one interpretation. He was fundamentally and physiologically incapable of wit to an extent that borders on insanity. Anything less mercurial, anything less Pagan and Hellenistic, further from Nietszche's 'divine laughter' and 'le gai sçavoir', than 'ce misérable pisse-froid de Genève', as Anatole France (who on this account felt an almost personal grudge) dubbed him, it would be exceedingly hard to discover. What the pervading mood of the nineteenth century has done to Beethoven and Wagner and Brahms, I have attempted to show. Of the masters that are generally considered to be in the straight line of descent, Richard Strauss claims attention because he has acquired a considerable reputation as a musical humorist. One has seen him described as a musical Rabelais, a musical Molière or Dickens. And he himself has done what he could to foster this strange idea. His choice of subjects and his methods of treatment, alike, have powerfully assisted in the shaping of it, although he is really as owlishly solemn as any of his German models.[1]

He lacks the sympathetic humanity which is a first requisite.

---

[1] For reference one should consult Claudius's *Wandsbecker Bote*, a true compendium of all quintessential forms of the national wit at its most un-Hoffmannesque.

He may have something in common with the Dickens whose caricatures descend to very low comedy, just as he has something in common with the other weaker Dickens in the slimy oleographs of pure women. To the best of Dickens he is as little related as he is to the real Mozart, in spite of all his smug posturing as a Mozartian reincarnation. His comedy is rooted in the old German peasants' farce, made up of slapstick and knockabout. His 'Till Eulenspiegel' acutely marks his predilections. In his symphonic poems the fun invariably culminates in rowdiness, broken heads, and broken crockery, and people being knocked silly or kicked up and down. Sometimes there comes with it a rasping grin at the persistent nagging of fools, at the mulish obstinacy of old men or the disturbing hysterics of young women. He revels in every situation that deals with such motives. And he deliberately contrives them where the course of events, or the natural line of thought, would seem to be leading to almost anything except a resounding fracas. This has little to do with the *vis comica* of the antique authors on which the outstanding European humorists modelled themselves. Anything less humorous or less comic in the classic sense than Strauss's 'Sinfonia Domestica' would be difficult to cite. Here is not even the fun of some one slipping on a cake of soap, but only of the dratted infant howling in its bath when getting the suds in its eyes. With the uncles booming through the deep brass: 'Exactly like Ma', and the aunts squeaking through the high brass: 'The spit of Pa!' we have descended to the wit of the mummers' booth at the country fair. The 'musical clown' with his little fiddle, sliding his finger up and down the E-string while saying 'Ou-i Mossieu', is more picturesque and more amusing. Even so, he belongs to the 'variety' show and the circus, we do not expect him in the Queen's or her Consort's Hall.

If there are things in the 'Alpen' Symphony that fetch a laugh, Strauss did not so much plan it as that 'he asked for it'. In his later, unrelentingly jocose operas he is supposed to continue the *métier* of Mozart—the kind of thing the musical roué does to find a haven after a stormy life! He 'comes back' to Mozart. As if at one time he had outrun him. He comes back more like the drunken husband who tremulously sneaks up his own staircase in his socks. The situations of the Hoffmansthal 'books' may somehow belong to higher comedy, but Strauss's treatment of situations remains unchanged. His little operatic vignettes show an appalling likeness to the old symphoni-poetic ones that illustrated nothing so graceful. One sees a heavy character-actor in an unfamiliar role; Arlecchino with Pantaloon written all over him.

To find the incongruity particularly pointed we need only compare the apparatus of Strauss in his facetious vein with that of Mozart. The relative charm varies with the lightness and heaviness of the underlining. The allusion that is presented by the one with a subdued chuckle is heralded by the other with the bellow of heavy ordnance.

Mozart is so completely a man of the world that his most risky asides can pass muster anywhere. Strauss's coarse instrumental jokes, wanton orchestral puns, and polyphonic blasphemies are presented with a rosy smirk and a simpering air to the accompaniments of courtly and elegant gestures, that make them all the more suggestive of a fancy-dress ball in disreputable surroundings, to say the very least. The rococo exterior does not hide the familiar ribald jesting we remember from the symphonic poems. The uproarious hilarity still pivots round old tested laugh-raisers, the musical counterparts of pulling the chair away, crushing people's toes while gazing at the ceiling, soaping the stairs, slipping slugs or caterpillars down ladies' bodices (a 'try-it-on-your-friends' one!), and of course such delicious bagatelles as putting dry-flies in the soup, &c.; I need hardly mention them, one can buy them gummed to cardboard.

There is a fair amount of horseplay in Beethoven, but if it is crude it is not coarse, if his jocosity is profane it is not obscene. If he scandalizes the squeamish, his jollities never sound offensive; it is all very harmless if a little rustic. The smell of the earth and the stable are never revolting, as musk and patchouli can be. Beethoven develops the simple comic stroke with unexceptionable good humour. The pervasive impropriety of Strauss in his ormolu manner is an altogether different affair. There is a mixture of suspicious linen and grimy jewellery, of slippery, snivelling civility and smutty elegance which evokes a far more unpleasant atmosphere than of mere boorishness and gruff jocularity.

Beethoven, although he has a marked place in the musical hierarchy, is by force of character *sui generis*. He lends the colour of his personality to every facet of his existence, and to every bar of his works. Things that would be damning in others only give an attractive accentuation to some unexpected side of his character. The unquestionable purity and sincerity of his thought make us see his very weaknesses as welcome revelations of another corner in a curious mentality which never becomes repellent. One forgives what in others would, to put it mildly, make one feel uneasy. When, either unexplained, or in deference to the implications of the words to which his music is wedded, he discards the armour of ethical superiority, he becomes more lovable for his naivety, or at least for the entire absence of sophistication. For fastidious tastes he is too clumsily explicit in his somewhat ponderous jollity, too roysteringly matey in his honest outbursts of bucolic merry-making. Haydn, the peasant's son, never was so much of a bumpkin as the genteelly democratic scion of the middle-classy artistic Beethovens. Still, the important point is that, if the playfulness of so big a man makes one feel a little shy because it appears more primitive than it would otherwise, he never dreads frank laughter as the small men do.

When the academic Festival-heroes leave the aula, the organ-loft, and the rostrum to unbend for the delectation of mortals, we are offered nothing so fleshly as Beethovenian jollity to serve as a sop to our depraved tastes. Their orderly, well-behaved pleasantries, their seemly and controlled moments of diversion, the very measure they preserve in their

OWNER-COMPOSERS

occasional descents into extravaganza—even the maidenly oh-quite-mad pranks to which they will recklessly commit themselves—can bear any prurient censor's scrutiny. The most Savonarolian snuffling could not nose out anything objectionable in those works which bring so much wholesomely innocent mirth to the unspoilt audiences that find an hour's entertainment in the merry tone-pictures, the bright cantatas, and the sprightly tabloid operas of our musical Knights and Dames. But these ravishing charades, for all their unimpeachable cleanness, are never as funny as the most reprehensible funniness of Gounod or Puccini. There is more amusement in the mild pleasantries of Gounod's Dittersdorfian 'Médecin' (although the addition of an 'Apotheker' made the earlier work appropriately more spicy), or in 'Philémon et Baucis', notwithstanding the trills and glissandos and bassooneries, than in the most ladylike efforts to make music approach the Himalarious heights of best-selling biscuits given and taken by Messrs. Jerome and Jacobs. If one can get a laugh out of the 'Musikdrama' treatment of human foibles, it is sooner found in Puccini's orchestral poker-game between the top-hatted villainous Sheriff and the Angel-woman for the life of the Clean-limbed Boy, whose blood trickles through the ceiling on to the cards, as the drip-drip-drip of the orchestra tympanitically and pizzicatocally explains! This inspiration in the 'Fanciulla del West' must have grown from youthful recollections of the Puccini who used to betray his 'hand' to his partner at the card table by whistling B-flats and C-sharps for kings and aces. If the 'Fanciulla' did not catch her opponent's 'hand' from the orchestra, it may have been that the pitch in the U.S.A. is not the same, a fact that would upset the best-laid cheats.

The symphonic and dramatic humour of our own peculiar genus of English composers in this *genre* is unfailingly in impeccable good taste, clean, healthy, and proper; there is nothing for the Devil to gain by the closest attention to their most unguarded moments. But this does not lead us beyond the achievement already marked by Sullivan, for whose success these qualities are largely responsible, as according to Thackeray, they are for that of *Punch*. Stanford and others who shared his predilections have shown us what the next well-meaning composer can do on these lines.

The unassailable excuses for so much bourgeois decency do not hold good for the humorous attempts we find in German modern music. A Brahms or a Reger has little to gain from the qualities enclosed in the casket of perfect cleanliness. They fail on their own grounds.

The elaborate display of wit in some of the music of Hindemith or Křenek represents nothing so much as a strain in their honest-to-goodness wooden structures which makes them creak worse than they would do by the sole virtue of their ploddingly steadfast build. It makes them appear slipshod in spite of the reliable fabric these schooled craftsmen cannot help producing, however reckless they are determined to be. Their guild-instincts, and their lineage prove too much for them. No advertisements and no trimmings can hide the essential pulpitiful groundwork on which they mechanically start. When it comes to the unequivocal equivocalness they all take from Strauss, one can only wonder that so many connoisseurs listen to this music without furious blushes. The unbiased critic when he watches audiences at concerts and in the opera-house, if he keeps in mind the hearers' pretence to genuine understanding, can only wonder how they stand without quaking such numerous offences against modesty and morals as would make their sensitive souls squirm with repulsion if plain language were used instead of unplain music, although your very spade becomes an excavator here.

If Tchaikovsky or Scriabin's musically suggestive tribulations, Wagner's epileptic eroticism, and Strauss's own blustering musical indecencies were presented to the same public of dilettanti in simple terms of everyday speech, we should after the first minutes of pained embarrassment witness enough scandalized protests to make further performance impossible.

THE MAN OFF THE STREETS

But although we find 'Paterfamilias' and 'Pro Bono Publico' and 'Victorian' grappling the newspaper correspondence columns and brandishing the bludgeons of indignant protest as soon as a comedian introduces gags which daughters are supposed to understand too well, or when they find in their favourite showrooms mannequins showing off by showing nothing on (a spectacle which they rightly think should be kept for visits to Paris music-halls that cater for 'ces messieurs'), there is never a one, be he ever so Balliol plus Whitehall, who will not swallow the musical whale with Jonah inside and all. Straining indeed at a filter-passing virus when they will let a sea-serpent pass without blinking.

Nothing could show better how little the plain man—who is supposed to have the last word—and how little even the bulging woman who, according to Beardsley, makes the 'Musikdrama' audience, know what is happening before their ears. People graciously smile at symphonic jests that would make them feel degraded if they came from a red-nosed comedian. In the place where it does not belong they like 'drawing-room entertainment'. Perhaps that is why the in-betweens, with just an inkling of the dangers, prefer to have their composers undilutedly solemn, although they are among the first whom this episcopal pomposity sends to sleep.

Thirty years ago European student-centres were greatly stirred by what was then known as 'Sexuelle Aufklärung', which meant: 'No old-fashioned nonsense on *this* point.' The desperate liberality of the present generation looks like a repetition of that bravely indulgent movement. It is again mirrored in the contemporary composer's anxiety to be frantically indecorous as soon as he gets a chance. One of them, in search of a 'red-hot' libretto, disgustedly rejected a famous confrère's much talked-about manuscript as 'not nearly indecent enough'. Yet, being in possession of a copy of it, I can truthfully say that it was full of 'the stuff' which hopeful booksellers keep in their back rooms. Strauss's manner is at least superficially gentlemanly; only the nearest bystanders catch the leering winks and sniggers, the 'you-know's, the 'I-mean-what-you-mean's. It is noteworthy that in the humorously inclined compositions of older musicians we find none of the deliberate harmonic and instrumental shockers with which to-day we expect to be regaled. Composers seldom chose texts which gave the right opportunities.

Some of the songs of Loewe, 'Der alte Goethe', for instance, are really witty, but even when he works on this small scale he rarely selects words which allow his wit full play. Most of the old ballads are either full of blood and funeral tollings, curses and omens, or else are of the abstract poetic type which leaves scant opportunity for the somewhat esoteric humour to which he was temperamentally disposed.

Loewe's compatriot Weber, with a similar preference for a circumscribed folk-loristic style, could at times be as sardonic and as grimly humorous as the anonymous 'Wunderhorn' poets. Most of the instances in his work are, however, reminiscent of that grisly Swabian ballad, 'Grannie Cooksnake', where the woman asks her dying daughter about a 'little fish' she had eaten:

> Maria, my only child!
> Where did Grannie catch that little fish?
>
> In the herb-garden she had caught it!
> Oh, mother how my belly aches!
>
> My only child, with what did she catch
> That little fish in the herb-garden?
>
> With forked sticks and slings she caught it!
> Oh, mother how my belly aches!

Lest the English reader should still think it was a matter of eels, and not vipers, I quote the further information: 'What happened to what was left? Maria, my o. ch.; The little black-brown dog had that! Oh, Moth. how m. b. a.!; What happened to the black-brown doggie, M. m. o. ch.?; He burst into a thousand pieces, Oh, M. h. m. b. a.!'

Where Weber becomes sprightly in any other than this

eerie, medievally lugubrious tone, he invites us to laugh at such girlish fun as the ghost story in 'Freischütz' where Aennchen recounts the hair-raising, goosefleshy spookeries of growling and groaning and rattling of chains, with the infantile conclusion: 'And ... What ... Was ... It ... ? ...: Haha! ... Moritz, the watchdog!' Yet he was neither solemn nor childishly grotesque in his wit, as the spirited elegance of his chamber music shows. He was bursting with ideas to incorporate in his novel dramatic style; only he did not live to reach the windswept clarity of thought that permits the same mastery when dealing with laughter as with the austere, the tender, and the heroic passages. His style generally is anything but mirthless, but he failed to attain the stage where in the dramatic picture a smile is never far away. Mozart's phenomenal precocity endowed him with the indulgent irony of the old and wise, while he retained the youthful grasp of immense conflict in life, which is not so strong in a Cimarosa, who in many ways approaches him so nearly.

Most young composers, when attempting humour, failed to carry out what their ardent senses inspired, what rarely anything less than the matured powers of full years permits. Hugo Wolf tried, in his 'Corregidor'. Peter Cornelius came rather nearer to it in his 'Barbier von Baghdad'. All they aimed at was performed without effort by the aged Verdi. When the rough edges of Verdi's raging passion had been smoothed by the experience and refinements of ripe age, there remained undimmed the humorous sympathy embodied in his latest works. They conclusively show how increasing wisdom brings tolerant irony and generous laughter. The old Verdi was as little shy of them as the young Verdi had been of melodramatic violence.

Our twentieth-century, impish wits despise what their inhibited imaginings present as aesthetic hypocrisy. Thereby they automatically attract audiences determined to have the ancestral taboos ruthlessly derided on every occasion. Both appear to rejoice in the knowledge that they are lost to all sense of artistic good form. They have no relish for simple, natural attractions. But while they contemn the perfumes of the meadow and the haystack, they dare not candidly praise the odour of unholiness. The fashionable infatuation has no use for light and dark. It cherishes its own rank curiosity which, true to its pathological origins, keeps the fawning victims trembling on the border of the trench wherein crawl the pallid-and-dun-liveried question-marks of the vaguely abnormal.

With such things your up-to-date composer will oblige; if he could feel a leash he would be straining at it in his eagerness to please the neurotic fashion-devotees whose needs he divines with practised insight.

The reckless modernists jazz in their straight-jackets of inverted convention, gathering applause for their silly capers. Like Strasbourg geese dancing on a hot plate, they make their anxious yelps and croakings a fitting accompaniment to antics which ripen their 'big brothers, alas!' for the tureen, as they themselves ripen for the melting-pot of popular approbation. Thus, with crazy gawks and giggles, kindred consumer and consumed meet in the recognition of their advanced unhingedness.

Theirs is not the laughter that should 'purge the soul' as fully as do the 'horrors of tragedy'. Here are cathartics; no doubt, but the catharsis no longer denotes what it once did. 'When I read his work,' Heine remarked of a popular contemporary, 'I am never sure whether he ought to be described as cathartic or emetic.'

Among fashionable modernists we must choose between those that adhere to the solemnities of the solemn children of the age of sociological progress and humanitarian uplift, and the defiantly Bedlamite Dadaists rocking with hilarious screams at the sight of their own distorted nullity in the crooked glass of their time.

David danced before the Ark, and Schumann wrote a March of the Davidsbündler. (*Bund* means Covenant; from there we come back to the Ark; only Schumann did not mean all that, although he meant too much, anyhow.) His Davidian bondsmen were the musical Rotarians of his Tiecked imagination. They were defying all the doddering arrivistes and the proudest grocers that might stand in the way of modern advance. But let us not forget the scornful lady who watched David's *pas seul*, and considered that he made himself ridiculous. David's artistic weakness was that in his poems he remained unremittingly grave, while this display of exuberant frivolity (Levite-ation, Joyce might call it) was preserved for one of his rare public appearances as a mature and sovereign Duce. If he had been in his generation as wise as, reincarnated or Solomonized, he was in the next, he would have mixed the humorous element with his compositions and thereby have grown in artistic stature. As it was, the cruel censure of the critic at the window appeared justified.

Schumann's own wit was of the dismal, polysyllabic variety, however much he tried to stop its musical leaks by plastering Hoffmannesque titles over them. There is not sufficient power in literary references to raise the lame and paralytic musical jokes. Nor can any amount of open-eyed foolishness cure the dispirited incoherence of our Show-Mannin-ish moderns whose crimson scoffing and shrill bragging only draw attention to their infirmities.

There is no need to be ceremonious whenever the occasion is important. Important utterances can dispense with all pretence of hieratic stiffness. If David made no success of his gymnastics, Nietzsche's Zarathustra showed his divinity most convincingly by his triumphant conquest of the 'depressant law of gravity'.

Men of great genius have communicated weighty thoughts in playful terms. The universal appeal and the permanency of their productions justify the belief that deep thought leads to smiling statement, and often to what borders on flippancy. Pascal himself, although with his wretched physical condition he made much of the inevitability and dignity of bodily suffering (with self-inflicted Jansenist cruelty he kept it acute, so as to be mindful of human miseries!), did not suppress a certain sardonic humour in his most searching aphorisms. Every word reveals the incessant concentration of his lofty mind, yet there is always an unmistakable, subtle fragrance of irony.

The peerless exponents of lucid thought and fervid meditation, a Leonardo, Goethe, Cervantes, Balzac, all have conveyed that sense of the proximity of merriment and joyousness which proceeds from the divine itch keeping the sharpest intellect constantly at a point of tension where grave statement may instantly dissolve in disarming laughter.

All mythologies disclose how human intuition has invariably ascribed qualities of humour to the heroic figures and the divinities. The Gods themselves are invested with these attributes; and although the antique Hebrews are not generally conspicuous for their humorous propensities, they have none the less included in their most venerable legends occasional strokes of a fantastic levity entirely commensurate with the bigness of the theme.

The paralysing, clayey solemnity of more recent legends and traditions seems the outcome of a sulking, unproductive fanaticism which habitually confused the letter and the spirit of the great examples. As long as the spirit is alive among the makers of the new tales this danger does not occur. None other than Luther remarked that 'if God could not see a joke he had no desire to enter Heaven'.

If the great become greater by their faculty of candid laughter, the small can, by modest emulation, grow in stature. The Houyhnhnms listened to Gulliver with unfailing, courteous kindliness and gentlehorsely patience. The Lilliputians were full of intelligent understanding; the Yahoos alone proved dully incorrigible. Always the obstinately and impenitently mediocre exist in fear of diminishing themselves by deviation from the path of salvation-armoured propriety and reinforced-concrete righteousness, for they walk in the shade of tribulation lest their presumptive greatness should be called into question. Yet they only succeed in making themselves hatefully smaller by this unwilling display of their anxieties.

The frog who blew himself up until he burst, at least had the courage to undertake an experiment that must have filled him with enough misgivings to cause acute discomfort long before the final catastrophe. There is something pathetically heroic in this, if nothing but wind otherwise. How one wishes that all the toads who wallow exclusively in moderation could be seduced into so bold a trial by the secret ambition which they hide under the slime of reasonable modesty. But these disgusting amphibians possess a deprecatory safety-mechanism which protects them against anything so dramatic as self-immolation. When they inflate at one end they promptly deflate at the other, saved by their all-round, seasoned mediocrity. Curse as you will, nothing can hurt the slippery nonentity—but he can hurt you! Were it not so, one would not bother. And they derive a baneful power from their toadish solidarity. A number of them can always trip up a struggling giant and blister him with their loathsome exudations before he can rise. They themselves survive being trod on, and even the impact of the great body they bring down; in their own structure and behaviour are included all the elements that make for unobtrusive but noxious continuation. Their detestable instincts of unashamed self-preservation at once make them for a time feel comfortingly small when they are growing too noticeably big, but also make them avoid the bursting point, and by way of compensation again let them feel comfortingly big just when they visibly diminish before the eager observer's eye. Their levelling sense of seemliness infallibly warns them of approaching distinction before they need judge from which side it threatens, and to one's discomfiture, the thing your mediocrity-toad steadfastly and resolutely refuses to do is to burst like an honest frog when his ambitions and pretensions fill more space than his skin can contain.

In this way the middling flourish and outlast their actual

victims, as by what looks like a regrettable dispensation they outlive their potential victims, those men whom one wishes to live longest. Their 'ways and means' may have something to do with this longevity which appears in the species as well as in the individual. Toads and crabs, who, characteristically and significantly, share with fleas and lice the distinction of belonging to the oldest forms of creation, move in devious ways, whereas the unfortunates that are impelled by original talent do not feel constrained to be continually going 'back', or into odd corners. The attractive 'busy bee' has a frail existence, and moves in a 'bee-line'. The pleasant penguin, equally famed for its straight going, painfully struggles against a host of clever foes that exploit its honest weaknesses. The truly great are not crabbing '*back* to Mozart' or cribbing '*on* with the motley', any more than they are panting forward to the much advertised vanguard whence the light that leads is supposed to come.

By all means let us try to borrow some of the light that heads the column in which we all march. But let us not forget directive relativity. The luminous point appears to different eyes now at the rear, then at the van, of a movement in which no one consciously participates. If we seek the spiritual illumination that comes with freedom of mind, we ought to abjure the puny solemnity which marks the stride of the well-bred midgets, and smoothly leads to damnation.

Between clowning and pompousness there lies a road wide enough for the heroic gait. If all is not 'right with the world', God *is* laughing in Heaven, and we should not improve on the precept with the brass scowl of the conventional Dante just returned from Hell. After his subsequent Paradisiacal experiences he could smile as sweetly as any poet.

The spirit of the last century was dis-infectiously earnest. The Santa-Claus beards of Brahms and Marx and other popular idols make a dangerous mask. It must have influenced the wearers as much as the dickeys, Jaeger vests, and made-up butterfly-ties they constitutionally favoured. We should regard them as danger signs. The beard and the frock-coat replaced the ancestral perukes and swords, but not to our advantage. The artist's ambition ought to point to Apollo and Dionysus, not to the overtitled, overbemedalled Herr Professor Doktor Direktor Wirklicher Musikrat Remi Fasoldo, C.D.E.F., G.B.A., heavy with honours and symphony.

·❦ *Four* ❧·

MEYERBEER

Satan: That name I do not want to hear!
Witch: But why? What mischief hath it done?
                                GOETHE: *Faust.*

I. Small Pride and Great Prejudice

EVERY MUSICIAN KNOWS THAT THERE ARE NAMES WHICH goad readers to fury, names hardly to be mentioned in polite musical society. These are, apart of course from Liszt, mostly those of successful composers of grand opera, French or Italian. One may speak about Rossini, because genteel amateurs remember that after all he wrote the 'Barbiere'. Names like Thomas or Halévy can pass, because few people could say extempore what works they had written. But quite recently Donizetti was to be spoken of only in mild derision. The belated discovery of 'Don Pasquale' has restored some prudent forbearance to the critics of Italian opera. If Bellini is now tolerated as a subject for serious discussion, it is because his methods exemplify certain principles, and his works themselves are so rarely performed that, in this country at least, most musicians regard him as an antique from whom nothing is to be feared. If there is one composer who has not profited by these mitigating adjustments of critical opinion, it is Meyerbeer, whose name alone can still irritate contemporary opera-lovers beyond the point of gentlemanly patience. There is apparently something about him too bad for mention. In the period that has seen the triumph of Wagner and his principles, he is vividly remembered as the perpetrator of the worst vices against which pure dramatic aesthetics had to fight a battle that has left the temporary victors too exhausted to forgive.

No wonder that Meyerbeer seldom gets a hearing now, and is not treated dispassionately, in spite of the fact that he is described as so hopelessly outmoded, over and done with, as to deserve no further attention. Had he not been so phenomenally successful in his lifetime there would have been no need to single him out as a favourite target of operatic reformers. As matters stand, generations that do not know the works and cannot remember the antagonisms, evidently still sense the aversion he once roused.

Meyerbeer was an idol and he has paid heavily for the painful privilege. Frobenius describes a dynasty of Negro kings killed after a reign of ten years by the high-priest electors. During their reign they were considered divine, but their power could not surmount the principle from which it derived. There is no recorded instance of one having survived his term of office. If some of the European musical idols, as relentlessly killed by the high priests of aesthetics who first exalted them, meet in the valley of eminent shades, there must be prodigious winks exchanged. One can imagine kindly old Franz von Suppé passing Meyerbeer and sarcastically stroking his huge beard. And one can imagine how Meyerbeer would gulp. However carefully he guarded his copyrights, it must appear a barren effort in view of the relative sales of 'Robert le Diable' and the 'Poet and Peasant' overture.

All this seems very cruel to Meyerbeer, and yet it would be difficult to say whether it is any one's fault. The composer cannot very well be expected to defend himself against popularity, and an adoring public is not really guilty for losing its earlier enthusiasm. People are childishly sure that a discarded idol can have no right to a good word. They are relieved to see it found out and finally done with. With delight they snigger at the admiring pages of Goethe on Byron, wondering which bubble burst with the biggest bang and the smallest remains.

Perhaps this fulfils a purpose. We are reminded of the uncut copy of a first edition contemptuously preserved among the rubbish, for the delectation of a later, wisely sobered, and reconverted generation.

What makes the case of Meyerbeer hard is that he has been

reproached for a boundless adoration which he did not court. He was eager to please, but he had as much artistic conscience as any opera composer. His earlier successes were so fantastic that later he necessarily had to try and live up to the legend of his name. He did it with such determination that his work suffered in spontaneity for what it gained in craftsmanship. If he did his best to serve his public, it was with an irreproachable object.

His hesitations and uncertainties, his fears and self-questioning, were all caused by a desire not to disappoint. He hoped to justify the esteem and affection he had conquered. This is different from the commercial exploitation of popularity. There was no abject soliciting, such as one might expect of an ambitious young man in search of success. Meyerbeer was not crudely flattering a potential public; he toiled to show himself worthy of the admiration of a world-wide audience whose loyalty he had already secured.

It is curious that his most distinguished qualities should have been singled out for merciless criticism by his later detractors. His very modesty and conscientiousness have been denounced for meanness and commercialism. Yet how many artists would have remained equally unspoilt in the unparalleled position Meyerbeer held? Heine wrote, and with good reason, that the mother of Meyerbeer was the second woman in history to see her son accepted as divine. The description was scarcely exaggerated. Few people to-day know how complete the public's surrender had been. Everything was expected of Meyerbeer's genius. He was the unique personality who summed up everything that dramatic and symphonic music, through the individual efforts of its greatest exponents, had ever attained.

He may not have deserved such idolatry more than any man ever did. Nor did he deserve the almost universal contempt with which a fickle world avenged itself on him for its erstwhile infatuation. When his power and his influence (once so welcome to many a struggling composer) had gone, when his very nimbus had faded—how bravely the old lickspittles came hurrying to kick the dying lion! They never stopped to reflect that they attacked the taste of a public they had led. They found it profitable now to proclaim that Baal had fallen, and that they were the men who had hacked through the feet of clay.[1] At the same time they were ready to start a dance round a new brazen image, as convinced as ever that this time it was the right one. Yet, these Meyerbeer-haters had contrived to stay unheroically in the shade so long as his operas drew full houses.

When once audiences began deserting him, there appeared from dark corners an army of critics who had till then hidden their rancour with conspicuous success. Thus, during a revolution, appear from nowhere crowds of malcontents that have never evinced their vehement convictions before.

We have seen something like it happen, although in miniature, not long ago. Between 1915 and 1918 the London musical public, under professional guidance, developed an affectionate interest in the activities and products of the lesser natives. But they were rapidly forgotten in the relief afforded by the return of international figures. The guiding advocates not only abdicated their leadership, but became as sarcastic as before they had been generous.

Not so long ago Stravinsky was received in London very much as The B.P. is at a Scout Camp. Then he started trying to write like Czerny and betrayed a fantastic incompetence in his affectation of simplicity. He lost so much prestige that writers who hysterically lauded everything that came from him or his clownish imitators, unexpectedly re-

---

[1] One of the representative lexicographers, Reinecke (means 'the little fox'!), has told us that 'it was discovered that the colossus had feet of clay, but it still needed terrific efforts to overthrow him'.

It was 'der unbestreitbare Wert der einzelnen Gesangnummern' that made this such a hard job. He expatiates with blissful insouciance on the 'grim necessity' of getting him down 'at any cost', so that 'composers might breathe again' and have a chance for their own works. This was the authentic German tone. It is true that 'Grove' has an eminently reasonable article on Meyerbeer; but is 'Grove' ever positively unkind to any one?

vealed themselves as champions of the cause of musical purity. They became slashing now; their ruthless dissection cut right down to the diseased heart of the subject. But they had been hiding their fervour well and long. They had been reticent and self-denying when their services were badly required; when the abstract-ballet-cum-rational-heartlessness racketeers were having things all their own way. Most of them paid a heavy penalty, for, the fever once overcome, Fleet Street had no further use for their catchpenny-as-line-can sycophancy.

There is enough moral in this to last Aesop for an Olympiad. Artists and their advertisers when they specialize in popularity share the danger that immediate success may have to be paid for with the sacrifice of enduring fame. These ci-devant idols together experience the agony of watching their privileges dying within and out of them by inches. It is understandable that the painfully acquired knowledge of this ghastly process makes them antagonistic to any one suspected of original genius.

When we think of the torments artist and critic must undergo when their popularity wanes, we come automatically to the conclusion that the man of genius should bear the brunt. If he succumbs, there will be time enough to make up for it by the erection of monuments to his blessed memory. We console ourselves with the conviction that a great man can desire nothing better than posthumous homage, for in his quality of genius he ought to scorn 'the facile plaudits of the crowd'!

'As long as we do not commit the old mistake of calling a lame horse a certain winner', say the wise ones, acclaiming the newly discovered man. And the study of his work leaves them no time for others. The little artists who are neither particularly good nor bad, but just good enough, always profit. They are like the beauty chorus walking in a circle through the spotlights, when every girl gets her turn to display her attractions.

Occasionally the judges have a shock when they find that a man who deserved laurels has been first tortured and then judicially dispatched. They ease their consciences by indiscriminate generosity lavished on the next who comes up for judgement; if they think he deserves hanging they give him a spiritual pension instead, and sleep in the certainty of justice restored. Should it happen that history concludes they have let a guilty wretch go free, that, without praising him, they failed to see impartial justice done, they refurbish their magisterial severity and for a while distrust everybody's innocence.

When Meyerbeer's fame was at its height, there were found on all sides additional reasons to show why and how well it was deserved. Germany hailed him as one of her sons. Her academic critics proudly pointed out how he had stiffened the muscular structure of Grand Opera with the skeleton of Teutonic formalism. At the same time modernist German authors praised him for softening the contours of Latin precision with the fluorescent haze of Zauber-Romantik. Italian admirers were happy to see how the triumphant exponent of Opera Seria at its apotheotic summit—at its most Parisian—had adapted it to Italian traditional methods by his effective use of the unison chorus and Rossinian dramatic fioritura. France perceived a final justification of the triumphant artform and militant institution that had grown on her soil, when Meyerbeer came to the capital to pour into the mould that was its special creation the compound stream of his aggregate inspirations, at a time when none of these had yet resulted in a fully acceptable national form.

As, however, the time arrived when from sheer surfeit people had lost appetite, and Meyerbeer's works lost their hold on the public, a complete change occurred with astonishing rapidity. German critics now perceived that he had prostituted their country's chaste traditions; in Italy it was at last recognized that in order to give a spurious unity to a shameless jumble of styles he had abused the race's precious heritage, and by this time the French themselves recognized with disgust that a perfected shape on which they prided themselves had been exploited for personal ambition. Once it was too late, all were shocked to find how a charlatan had been burning borrowed plumes on the altar of success under their very noses, without by the warning stench waking them from their aesthetic torpor.

When there was no longer any risk, it was inquired on every side whether this purveyor of hybrid monstrosities should be allowed to parasitize further on the presumably undefiled body of operatic art. It was strenuously denied that only quietism and hedonism had made this scandal possible. Critics were anxious for their readers to understand they had not attempted any earlier revolt because it would have been premature. The time, they said, had not been ripe for scouring the sham blackamoor. How could one have called the bluff when vested interests were so alert that at the merest show of the critical sponge-bag they would have mobilized to keep the right tint?

But when the dangers of critical warfare had dwindled with the numbers of defenders, no words were bad enough for 'this banker-composer'. People who had made use of his exceptional position were the first to forget how they once expected moral and material support from him.

It is true that Wagner did not risk much when he aimed the arrows of his wit at the almost dethroned monarch.[1] He was comfortably drawn onwards with the anti-Semite current which he proposed to direct. We have seen too much of the complexity of motives that cause pogroms not to forgive Wagner for being 'Nordic' and 'Aryan', and 'Teutsch'.[2]

[1] It is painfully noticeable that in *Das Judenthum in der Musik* the name of Meyerbeer is never mentioned, an endless string of allusions making up for the omission. 'Mendelssohn-Bartholdy', and 'Heine', and 'Börne', but: 'a certain famous opera composer' or 'a fashionable writer of Grand Operas,' &c.! Did Wagner fear that the lion was not quite dead yet, and discretion indicated for even so valorous an onslaught?

[2] The Teuton of Teutons loves this legendary spelling. Nietzsche has explained how it derives from 'täuschen', i.e. to deceive. It reminds the German of his reputation of being very 'deep'.

'... THE WAY IT TALKS ...'

II. *Ineffectual Ghosts and Contemporary Caricatures*

'The People', according to the Encyclopaedists, were 'right, good, and just.' But Phocion did ask the crowd, 'What imbecility have I spoken that you should applaud me?' Meyerbeer was cultured and sensible enough to be aware of this, and more, to grasp the implied ethics. He honourably rejected the cynical precept to smile at the public's jeers and applause if only their gold flowed into his coffers. He knew all about the popular addiction to his music. Yet he had the artistic decency not to exploit it. He could confidently have written his dozens of operas. He could have palmed off on doting audiences *his* 'Legend of Joseph' and 'Ariadne auf Naxos'. But, whatever the belated insinuations of his enemies, he was too great an artist.

The timidity that has been accounted to him for weakness came from his conscientiousness. The doubts and apprehensions that in his later career impeded his production derived from his artistic responsibility. He understood well enough what were the tendencies that bred his popularity. If he took his public seriously he would not therefore be held in such subjection as to mistake its grounds. But he is no longer given credit for that, although it implies rare qualities of mind.

It has become the custom to treat his works with a supercilious smile. Midgets who at the height of his fame would have been tremblingly craving his favours, write him down as a musical *crétin*. They remember his unforgivable successes, and also the cringing of their ancestors. They now try to restore some of the tribal self-respect by an ostentatious contempt.

Meyerbeer was not, in the fullest sense of the term, a great man. Let us assume that he was one of the smaller of the nearly great. This still puts him far above the mediocrities that gladden the hearts of scribblers who thank their paper gods for minor artists to extol. It is revolting to observe the eagerness with which some of his critics are trying to repair the errors of their predecessors.¹ None of the tribe like to be reminded of the servility which erected a pedestal whose height in the end appalled them.

Newer leaders of public opinion are as lustily shouting: 'Great is Strauss of the Prussians', and 'Great is Stravinsky of the Choreographers', as their forebears roared the praises of the one and incomparable Meyerbeer!

I have often tried to find out whether people who were speaking of Meyerbeer's operas with confident disdain could have been acquainted with them. During the last twenty-five years there has not been much opportunity of hearing his operas. There were a few performances of 'Le Prophète' at Covent Garden, occasionally one of 'L'Africaine' at Berlin, and rare appearances of the same works on the stages of the Milan Opera House and the Metropolitan in New York. I have heard some of these, and I can say that the performances had so little to do with the actual music that unless a hearer had studied the scores with the greatest care, he could only have the haziest impression of what the music originally was. Some years ago Londoners might have had an opportunity of testing this for themselves, provided they had been acquainted with the score of the 'Huguenots'. Unfortunately, few people who heard the 1925 performances could have had many previous experiences by which to make comparisons. If any one had set out gratuitously to cause further harm to Meyerbeer's reputation, he could not have done better than present so offensive a caricature as was seen at Covent Garden on that occasion. But it could not have been deliberately perpetrated. The motives presumably were so mixed that they must remain obscure. Financial expectations were too unfavourable to make the possibility of bad faith admissible. But while the

¹ The author of a popular kind of tradesmen's catalogue of Orchestration refers contemptuously to a much-quoted passage for bassoons from 'Robert': 'The less said about Meyerbeer and his rubbishy thirds the better.' But it deserves mention that dealing with a passage from Berlioz which he admits he has never heard, the same author informs his readers that 'it probably sounds very nasty'. Presumably the world would be incomplete without such critics. (See C. Forsyth, 'Orchestration'.)

offence cannot have been committed with malice, music-lovers had no reasonable chance to form a judgement. If to settle an historical query we had recourse to exhumation, and found a coffin filled with stones, who would be bold enough to say that one of these must have been the tenant's heart? It would seem fairer to conclude that there was some mistake. Why pretend that the stones had any connexion with the monumental one bearing the name of the missing principal? But how many listeners could have an inkling of the situation when, at that lugubrious Covent Garden ceremony, we were invited to recognize in a fantastic abortion one of Meyerbeer's most vital works? The majority of the audience were defencelessly deluded into the belief that they looked on the ungalvanizable remains of a creation that had once been unaccountably glorified.

We shuddered at something that was not even the ghost of the opera. It was sheer nothingness. Apparently no one concerned in the production had any convictions about the work, or even the interest to simulate them. The mangiest stage properties had been considered good enough. The orchestra was evidently unprepared; there was nothing to break the intolerable tedium of the singers, and the polite audience could not have known that they heard an unforgivable pot-pourri of a score that for its effects depends chiefly on dramatic coherence and logical structure. Even then it proved impossible to destroy some of those vocal numbers that had preserved Meyerbeer's memory long after his position as an operatic composer second to none had been undermined.

The worst consequence of this outrageous affair was that it spoilt Meyerbeer's chances of a fair hearing in London for many years to come. Yet some one moved by genuine interest must have planned the revival. But apparently no one had understood the first causes that to-day militate against the acceptance of Meyerbeer's operas.

Almost every musician is so enormously cultured as to call Scribe's libretti execrable. It is generally conceded that good taste demands their rejection. But why the book of an opera should possess literary value is not so easy to see. The demand is irrelevant. As if one were to insist that a painter must only work on the finest material. When the painting is good, we do not feel unhappy because it is on canvas instead of silk or ivory. In fact, one feels that a simple panel or canvas is properly the material preferred by the best masters. Insistence on literary value in a libretto has paradoxically become most marked since Wagner's homespun libretti, in which no one today affects to discover exceptional structural or poetic qualities. See what a proud pretence can do! One would have to search long to find anything more preposterous than the 'hot-gospeller' treatise on disease and faith-healing dramatized in 'Parsifal', with its doyen of sufferers—an inoperable case—its authentic and its unorthodox practitioners, its chorus of trained nurses with Klingsorian instructions, and the dark lady spreading the troubles against which the most cunningly prepared remedies prove all but useless. All this conveyed in the true adepts' jargon, which makes one feel that only knowledge of the cabbalistic gestures admits to the privilege of the magic circle.[1] This allegory is treated with portentous solemnity, while the books of some of the greatest operas are spoken

---

[1] The subject deserves extended treatment. It ought to be shown how here we see the libertine's dread of consequences sublimated as religion. The surgeon's coat regains the ju-ju prestige of an ecclesiastical garment. The unfortunate victims fleeing from the familiar and unspeakable Kundry get metallic armour stuck over them in lieu of mercurial plaster. With this object-lesson before them, patients and experts together search for the perfect antiseptic, called the Grail.

The dove is the symbol of vivisection experiment at the clinic. The raw house-surgeon—the perfect fool—ignorantly 'shoots' his needle into a swan. After his hypodermic blunder he is told by the experienced physician-sufferer that this was an immunized animal and therefore 'one of them', experiments on whom are waste of serum and instruments. This would explain how one of the swans became a carrier and brought Lohengrin into human society and back without getting infected. Also, how Elsa 'got' the disease called 'Lohengrin', which did not affect her as long as she was not aware of it. Only when she asked for the name her chances went with swan and master back to the research centre, where the latter had to apologize for the risks run, and report another failure of a medico-religious missionary among the natives of the Darkest Netherlands. (Schweitzer was not the first to combine the two arts.)

of as abominations. Common sense alone ought to make us sceptical about this. To take a few proverbial examples: could the book of the 'Zauberflöte' be as bad as it is called? Would Goethe have been so impressed with it as to write a sequel? And 'Il Trovatore'? And 'Robert le Diable'? They must possess some exceptional qualities to have lasted in spite of plausible criticism. The fact that they enabled composers to write good music should be enough to make us pause.

Can one write a good opera to a bad book? Can one write good music to a really bad text? Does not the quality of the music speak for inherent merit in the text, although to any one but a creative musician it might remain hidden?

Probably there is a fine balance that represents the coefficient of useful failings and embarrassing beauties. The precise proportion of the factors is immaterial. What matters is that however much a libretto may now appear absurd, inadequate, offensively silly, it enabled a composer to write inspired music.[1] His inspiration was found in and between the librettist's lines. Whatever Wagner may have said about the texts of those Mozart operas which he liked least, they achieved something to earn our gratitude when they inspired Mozart to write music which he did not call forth from the chaos.

The appeal to a composer's imagination is a high distinction. When it provides a foundation on which the composer erects his edifice it fulfils its most ambitious purpose. The book for an opera should not be 'too good'. Composers who tried to use literary masterworks without adaptation, instead of a rough sketch like a woodcut over which to brush the colour of their music, invariably failed. When Boito the poet provided impeccable texts for his own operas, he failed, apart from his insufficiencies as a composer, to make them live

---

[1] Only when he mistrusts all poets to such an extent that he regards himself as the only one who counts, does he, like Wagner in the case quoted, provide a caricature of his own needs. As long as he treats situations provided for him and welcomes the lyrics, he avoids the solemn absurdities that become unforgivable in the critical composer who judges as if he had all the knowledge of a professor of literature and none of the innocence of a mere musician.

musically because he attempted to make one harness suffice for horse and mule. When he wrote a libretto for Verdi, he had to listen to the innumerable objections of a musician who could unhesitatingly tell when the words were too good for the purpose, or the exposition of the dramatic knot either too subtle or too precise for musical treatment. Verdi kept him to the practical point—to the merest poetic commonplaces, the best for the occasion. Whenever Boito became abstruse or original, he found himself pulled up by the composer who had learnt all the hard lessons of the theatre. Often against his will he was directed to produce something usefully neutral that could be made to live by the ardency of music.

Even gifted song-writers make the mistake which the experienced dramatic composer avoids, of obtruding music on perfect poetry. Seldom has a composer added anything to words like Goethe's 'Der du von dem Himmel bist', and then, significantly, in a setting which (like that of Loewe) avoids dramatic accentuation but gives the singer a simple symmetrical line that least interferes with the listener's familiar reaction to the poetry. Generally speaking, the best songs can be written only to words which by themselves are incomplete. These need music: not the others that by their loveliness move the musician to emulation.

Mozart found in Da Ponte's unpretentious lines all the suggestions he required for the ordering of dramatic conceptions which in embryo were crying out to be born.[1] Unerring instinct in all such matters makes Mozart what he is. He could not have written anything so true and profound if he had used Milton's or Klopstock's untouched lines. Neither could he have been so heroically comic or erotically witty if, instead of taking an adaptation of Beaumarchais, he had been ill-advised enough to set the original words of Rabelais or Boccaccio. Schikaneder was the man to write an opera libretto, not Keats. Metastasio produced better books for opera than Dante or Ronsard could have.

[1] Like the young lady inside the egg in Shaw's 'Back to Methuselah'.

RICHARD NARCISSUS

If Wagner believed that there was only one poet who could write books for his operas, and that poet's name was Wagner, it was because in his estimation there was one man who could do everything better than any one else—Wagner. Had he been able to overcome this megalomania, he might have found *his* Boito, and it would be easier to-day to admire Wagner without having to become a Wagnerian. It might have been better for him; certainly pleasanter for his audiences. Only he could not help taking his texts as paranoically seriously as he took himself. An occasional licence with the sacrosanct words might have been good for the music. But he dared not take liberties with his own literary products.

Wagner has been as fantastically successful as, at his hungriest, in his Paris days, he dared dream to make up for the depressing reality. So we are mostly inclined to take him at his own valuation and accept his own treatment of his own words by his own standard. Maybe this is justice. When, however, we apply that standard to the works of other composers we certainly commit an injustice. We appraise them by a measure never meant to be universally applicable. There may exist a natural equilibrium of text and music, but when the Wagnerians announced that only The Master achieved it, this was because they grew impatient when his highly personal methods were not admitted quickly enough. It has become the fashion to test operas for purity according to the Wagner standard, as if this were an unquestionable criterion, very much as, after a successful political revolution, all citizens' deeds and intentions are judged by their conformity to the victorious shibboleths.

III. *The Highfalutin Standard*

Meyerbeer has been ridiculed for his methodical use of reiteration. Reformed musicians laughed at his variations, which proceeded to their predestined symphonic end while the text introduced no new version of the idea expounded in the first few words. It is begging the question to criticize such repetitions for precisely that principle which brought them about.

Is it certain that the method is so contemptible? Is the protracted variation of a single literary phrase an aesthetically superior device? Meyerbeer makes his singers repeat a dozen times 'la vengeance et la foi'; true, but what is so very wrong with that? Only the musically uninformed, who listen to the performance of an opera as if it were drama with a bit of music going on, spiritually speaking, 'behind the scenes', could take exception. Since the music justly demands and must be given all the room it wants, verbal reiteration seems a perfectly legitimate procedure. The praises of Wagner's superior appreciation of literary responsibilities naturally make one ask whether his treatment is really much better, or even intrinsically different.

Meyerbeer, at least, sees to it that a repeated phrase is distributed over the choir, the various ensembles and soloists' parts. In the Wagnerian manner we get the protagonists endlessly addressing each other about such things as 'Liebe und Tod', 'Ew'ge Nacht, Welterlösung', without the relief that changing vocal colours might attain. While he works at his climax he unashamedly lets his singers go through a formidable number of permutations until he has developed the symphonic material. His justification here is no better than that which makes him call an opera a Musikdrama. His nomenclature frequently serves to affirm an originality which otherwise none but the initiated would discover.

> Unsre Liebe?
> Tristan's Liebe?
> Dein und mein,
> Isolde's Liebe.

or:

TRISTAN:
> Ewig einig
> Ohn' Erwachen,
> Ohne Bangen,
> Namenlos. . . .

and:
ISOLDE: Um ungetrennt—
TRISTAN: Ewig einig—
ISOLDE: Ohne End'—
TRISTAN: Ohn' Erwachen—
ISOLDE: Ohne Bangen
TRISTAN: Namenlos. . . .

Can this be poetry before which 'Tu l'as dit, tu m'aimes!' pales into insignificance or stands revealed as sheer rhetoric? Or can we say that 'Plus blanche que la blanche ermine' will not bear hearing next to such doubtful euphony as 'die bräutige Schwester befreite der Bruder, zertrümmert liegt was je sie getrennt'? Generally speaking, Scribe's unpretentiously mellifluous lines stand repetition better than Wagner's barbaric alliterations and grating consonants which stick like burrs.

Even if nothing could be said against the Wagnerian manner, and if three-fourths of all the criticism of that of Meyerbeer could be maintained, it still does not follow that the former is preferable. When we know that singers are only repeating words which at the beginning of the section fixed the mood, we can give our attention to the musical development instead of wasting it on pretentious depths of meaning in a mystical disquisition proceeding on the stage. Closer examination, moreover, reveals that these are not only as tiresomely redundant as mere repetition could possibly be, but mostly as bombastic as the worst lines of the worst libretti in the old style.

We can better assimilate the course of the music towards a dramatically conditioned point when our attention is not deceived by a pretence of poetic and ethical significance in a text that consists of sheer word-spinning without an honest admission of the fact. The display of symphonic apparatus, by which the Musikdrama evinces its superiority over mere Opera, mostly makes the hearer feel all the more embarrassingly that he is kept eternally rotating round one dramatic spot. He has to seek compensation in the seductive assurance that with a proper understanding of the text's literary beauties he ought to feel his 'soul is moved and purged'. Wagnerians may feel this is a consolation, but there are also intelligent opera-goers who prefer to remain unpurged, and hear the composer get on with the job. Get on, that is, with all of life, instead of a subtly prolonged preparation, slowly, slowly, with the maddening deliberation of Achilles' tortoise-partner, moving to one orgiastic climax in order to have one act of complete collapse, or perhaps one should say, have one complete act of collapse. And to think that there were people who complained of the 'Rossinian crescendo' where a composer lets us participate in a light-hearted vitality which renews itself continually by its own freshness. They didn't know when they were well off.

What has kept opera as a form alive, through all vicissitudes, is not 'the combined appeal of all the arts'.

People like dancing not for theories they may have about rhythm or melody, but simply because they like dancing. And they like operas not for the love of poetry and painting and movement, but simply for the music. They prefer to have music more or less explained to them as it goes on. This, opera does better than 'programme music' could possibly do, and so opera survives the perpetual offensive. If the critics who despise the attitude which sees in opera primarily a musical entertainment needed a test, it could easily be supplied. Present the miming and the choreography of an opera separately, have the drama acted without music; there is not an opera-enthusiast who would sit through it. But we know that in a concert-hall the music of an opera can be completely satisfactory. Wagnerians are the first to acknowledge that many fragments of The Master's works gain rather than lose when played in the concert-hall. But I have yet to hear of a Wagner fanatic who could stand a theatre performance of 'The Flying Dutchman' or 'The Mastersingers' without the music! The very thought makes cold shivers run down one's spine.

Meyerbeer is, more than is generally realized, reproached

THE CONVICTIONS OF IGNORANCE

for extra-musical aspects of his works. Few of his critics would hear all those hateful insincerities and trivialities in the music alone if they should hear it outside the opera-house. They would not in his 'Struensee' music or in his 'Fackeltänze' discover the fearsome sins imputed to him. Probably not even in the old popular favourites, like the Bridal March of 'Les Huguenots', or the Arias of Fides in 'Le Prophète'. When it comes to 'Le Pardon de Ploërmel' or 'L'Étoile du Nord', one can safely wager that of twenty who turn up genteel noses, less than one has ever heard or seen a note of the work.

Many operatic conventions called unforgivable in Meyerbeer occur in the work of composers not so diligently explored for weak spots, simply because they had not been so irritatingly idolized by the largest public. None of the critics that gibe at the book of the 'Zauberflöte' would risk being so sardonic about the music Mozart mysteriously managed to write to it. And although Gluck is often described as a forerunner of Wagner, few experts would care to deny that his 'numbers' lose nothing when taken out of their context. Most of Beethoven's 'Fidelio' can perfectly well stand on its symphonic legs, without thereby becoming weaker as a setting of the text. Berlioz, a most consistent composer of programme music, has given us in 'Les Troyens' symphonic movements whose appeal is quite independent of their dramatic meaning.

The structural intentions for which Meyerbeer is frequently pilloried are exactly those that give his music a coherence which holds good in and out of the theatre. It was never denied that his works were theatrically effective. But too often it has been assumed that therefore they must be insincere and trashy. This criticism is founded on the mistrust that inclines radical thinkers to the belief that every theologian is a Pharisee, every preacher a hypocrite. It may often be true, but ignorance and prejudice combined here tend to raise suspicion to an axiom.

Meyerbeer's method is to let his 'book' arrive at a situation that can be symphonically summed up. There was an originality in this which impressed his contemporaries. Before him, the procedure had been to lead to a lyrical summit where concentrated emotional intensity gave a poetic illustration. Meyerbeer selected the dramatic clashes as props of a swift musical development which cumulatively employed all the resources of his musical powers.

The 'tableau', alternating with the deliberately conventional aria, was a striking innovation of Meyerbeer's; one which legitimately gripped his audience.[1] These thrilled listeners were nowhere near so silly in their admiration of his originality and monumentality as his modern critics would have us believe. It may seem cavilling to censure the expert knowledge of his detractors, but how shall we overlook that they evidently disliked his capacity for extensive melodic structure, his easy-flowing line and luscious orchestral sound, all sustained at once without effort. Yet that very facility is what too serious musicians find difficult to forgive. They prefer a tenuous musical tissue unrolling while the action is tying its knots on the stage, the composer building up a theatrically sound, but symphonically neutral, body of tone. At the climax the protagonists are expected to hold the audience by their histrionic powers. That Meyerbeer should not only have been able to shoulder all these tasks, but also to obey strict academic precepts without neglecting the charm of sound—otherwise considered the prerogative of the technically incompetent—proved more than flesh could bear. It had been taken for granted that it could not be done. When it was done for once, respectable musicians concluded that apart from a slight smell of sulphur, there was the unquestionable stamp of charlatanism discernible. Others mistrusted Meyerbeer as they would an astronomer who discovers a new comet every week, or a physician who cures everybody by unexpected and yet rational

[1] Before him the alternative to the aria was the ensemble which, as the Lucia sextet, fulfils a similar function to the tableau. The aria gives a lyrical résumé of the preceding action, the ensemble was mostly a momentary freezing of the situation—the moving picture stands still—while the composer gives a comment (on this actual situation, not, as in the aria, on what has gone before). Meyerbeer anticipated Moussorgsky in bringing ensemble and chorus into the action and with their help making of each tableau a miniature symphonic poem.

methods. One knows somehow that it cannot be done, and while waiting to expose the trick one might warn a gullible public they are obviously being swindled, and that they need but a little patience before one can tell them how. Schumann gravely drew a funeral cross on the score of 'Les Huguenots' at a time when he would have been hard put to it to say why this was a dead work waiting for burial. Composer-critics, especially, behaved like exasperated heirs, on tiptoe in an ante-room for the sad tidings, ready to sit on the corpse if it should show signs of returning life. There was the feeling in the air that it was time to end this disgusting success of Meyerbeer. Every self-respecting young musician knew he could prove his artistic integrity by taking part in the movement to overthrow the unspeakable colossus that practically monopolized the market. It was an acceptable and expected feeling. What is not quite so straight is that later critics shared it, that, in the late nineteenth and in the twentieth century, writers adopted the intolerant tone to which their impatient and embittered predecessors felt constrained. It had become superfluous. Yet they made the old superstition so much their own that even now they fulminate against him with the antiquated fervour of a politician insisting on laws against witchcraft.

To some extent the cause of this lasting hostility is that Meyerbeer was at one time the chosen target of neo-classicists as well as of neo-romantics, and, what is perhaps equally important, of anti-Semites and militant Wagnerians. Later critics may not have realized that they identified themselves with German political schisms, French musical quarrels, and personal clique-antagonisms, persisting through generations of standard text-books.

Possibly there were some grounds for the stereotyped reproaches which Meyerbeer's critics monotonously preferred in their diatribes. He may have been even 'insincere'! What if he were? Are we always sure of the sincerity of great composers? One is inclined to question the sincerity of the most attractive figures. The indubitable sincerity of others does not become any more pleasant in consequence.

Savonarola, Luther, Calvin, Brahms, and Sir Hubert Parry were, of course, as sincere as any child born of woman. And, perhaps Leonardo da Vinci, Loyola, Napoleon, Offenbach, and Byron, were not. One cannot escape the impression that the good men are not always the right men.

Meyerbeer's enemies may have been honestly actuated by clean convictions when they attacked Meyerbeer for his alleged habit of offering impressive musical displays where a little less might have served better. Here, one should ask first whether, when musical climaxes were obviously indicated, he failed to give all that can be reasonably demanded. If, then, he gave as generously as one could expect with fresh recollections of the feast provided at less urgent moments, it would not be fair to find fault with his lavishness. On that score Meyerbeer has not been found wanting. His worst enemies had to admit that after the dramatic splendours of the 'Bénédiction des Poignards' in 'Les Huguenots', he contrived a further summit with the lyrical tenderness of the duet between Marcel and Valentine. Let us assume it was achieved by insincerity; we have heard how the whole thing was an afterthought, suggested by a tenor, if not by the legendary fireman. Who would not be insincere if it made him write such music, or the strangely moving last bars of the 'Ô, transports, ô douce extase' of 'L'Africaine', where the sheer emotional penetration succeeds in making us forget a frankly ludicrous situation.

If we judge Beethoven, Wagner, Strauss, or almost any composer by the standard of sincerity, can we be certain their work bears close scrutiny? Are the greatest men's purple patches always justified by the implications of previous symphonic development? Do not all composers welcome opportunities to let go? Is it not just this recurring chance which makes opera so irresistible to composers? It is this which makes it immeasurably more than the musical illustration of anecdote. How the erudite's logical respect for the text leads the conscientious composer to hell, Debussy demonstrates perhaps better than any one else. His emasculated mezzotints forcibly suggest what happens to a man's music if he thinks too much of the poet instead of thinking, as he ought, of music first, last, and all the time.

IV. Begone, Dull Care

If Meyerbeer had not been so excessively popular, there would have been no cause for the reaction against his success. Instead of admitting that the hatred of musicians in the last decades of the nineteenth century was largely the distaste that follows surfeit, Meyerbeer's critics searched for sound motives with which to justify their strictures. They found it easy to denounce his crime against literary good taste, but they took care to conceal that here he sinned in common with all composers.

It is undeniable that he often raised an impressive tree of music from apparently insignificant poetic seeds. But this is what composers generally do, although they do not generally reveal how they found inspiration in a line, a turn of phrase, or a thought which could have been stated in a couple of words. The composer's creative power roused by what seems slight provocation, appears too brutally primitive in its embracing directness for the faltering squeamishness of over-scrupulous aesthetes.[1]

The solemn writers who tell us in leading-article tones how far below contempt Meyerbeer's music is, never trouble to discuss particulars. They reject him without more ado. The wiseacres who write articles in books of reference will take fees to write about Handel or Schütz or Sullivan or Gounod, but they feel it rather beneath their dignity to deal with such stuff as Meyerbeer's in other than disparaging and contumelious terms. They make up for their uncles' failings by intensified severity; 'If the old man made himself ridiculous with his

[1] Peccavi! I have been a musical critic from the earliest time I remember. I have found myself in the situation of the man who is shown his childish scribblings by his old nurse. There is nothing I have not myself perpetrated. I feel at home in the barque of Don Juan and share its traditions of cannibalism.

enthusiasms', they seem to tell us, 'I will repair that now.' As if to preserve strength of conviction, they take the precaution of remaining as far as possible ignorant of the works they expose to odium. Otherwise they might find themselves in the humiliating position of the member of the anti-claque who had to ask his neighbour in the theatre to blow his key as he wanted to earn his money honestly, and just then couldn't, because of the sobs shaking his lips.

We have heard so much about Meyerbeer's impurity of style that less instructed musicians must form an undefined suspicion that there is something subtly indecent about his work. I have read a transatlantic critic who complained of the perfume of his works. Thirty years ago, when real ladies had no legs, the accusation might have been that there was in his music that swish-swish of... silk... dessous, which a woman who respects herself (a higher achievement than holding the respect of others) knows how to avoid.

Then there is, we are told, in all his work the cosmopolitan allure that inevitably suggests a suspicious character. A man who in an altogether too slick conversation continually falls from one language into the other, and occasionally mixes them, is as likely as not an international swindler. Here, once more, a social prejudice is by the gratuitous connexion of ideas raised to the level of an aesthetic principle.

But it is highly doubtful whether one can rightly apply to such a product as grand opera a test which presumes in the listeners an erudition very few can possess. Meyerbeer's detractors write phrases that could make a reader, unfamiliar with the habits of the former and the qualities of the latter, believe that his operas are comparable to novels written in several languages. He imagines something of a confusing and rather offensive mixture of irreconcilable idioms, in which ear and mind are plagued by the need for constant re-orientation and quick translations.

The picture is subtly deceptive; national styles of music are not, to that extent, mutually exclusive. On the contrary, they easily merge their identities in each other, very much as languages do in borderlands. This demonstrable miscibility actually is a desirable and valuable property of musical language.

It has to be admitted, however, that the fusion of such elements into one homogeneous substance is a process that demands considerable time. It may reasonably be questioned whether it can be achieved by one man in the course of a lifetime. These aspects of Meyerbeer's case are frequently overlooked. The failure of continuity and consistency of idiom on account of antagonistic ingredients is a weakness of only a small part of his work. Besides, a fusion of styles had been already largely accomplished by earlier composers.

Meyerbeer has written much music that is stylistically blameless, and composers whose musical morals are so completely above suspicion as Bach, Mozart, or Beethoven, have consistently and methodically tested the spiritual purity of the German muse by allowing her to have a child or two of French or Italian parentage. Not only has she come through triumphantly, with heart and soul unsullied, but she proved all the pleasanter to her later lovers. She had acquired a certain *savoir-faire* and *leggierezza* with which she could very well do. Yet it was to be expected that some of the little friends who craved her favours were by no means so much *hommes du monde*. Not only did they reject with horror anything that smacked of a triangular arrangement, but they incubated a sombre mistrust of her disposition, which made them savagely warn off any visitors whose homage seemed a shade too devoted.

They one and all felt in their bones what a danger in the house a fellow like Meyerbeer was. A wealthy German, quite at home in Paris, an elegant and instructed gentleman, a conqueror with the graces of a grand seigneur about him ... I ask you! As long as princes danced attendance on him, one could not very well show him the door, but when the welcome moment arrived at last when he was simply not received in the best salons any more! What could not be said about his vices then was only what was not even fit for whispers. And what made it all the more bitter was to have to admit that he must have known perfectly well what he was about; did he not start his career with cantatas that in Germany itself were considered rather too contrapuntally dry? Did not Weber himself look upon his fellow pupil as one of the hopes of the national romantic *Aufschwung*, afterwards, when he had grown a little more flexible? To think of his further career, in view of this early promise, freezes the blood in one's honest veins.

The German critical summing-up, which, by virtue of the immense prestige of German opinion at the end of the nineteenth century, became a direction for the whole of any international jury, was, as could have been foreseen, something like this: the tremendous success of Rossini, Auber, 'and others', drew to Paris a German Jew, avid of honours, who was determined to exploit on a grand scale the possibilities offered by the presentation of spectacular entertainment to a cynically 'blasé' cosmopolitan public, which had outgrown every feeling of artistic seemliness and aesthetic purity, and asked only to be excited and intoxicated by false gorgeousness and spurious raptures. Every word 'tells a story', and while I shall not bore my readers with bibliography, I can assure them that the picture is a true one, and that I have not introduced a word or a turn that has not been taken, true to its context, from some representative opinion on Meyerbeer.

The effect of this particular tone of condemnation has been to leave a general conviction that, while other composers may be nearer to, or farther away from, the heights of Olympus, Meyerbeer is one who has no honest rights in the neighbourhood at all. He is regarded as an intruder who only contrived to enter the company of musically creative spirits by an elaborate system of false pretences. No self-respecting teacher would refer his pupils to any music of Meyerbeer, although there is more to be learnt from him about construction and proportion and the expressive power of melodic line than from many of your true black-board composers who are continually being drawn on for improving and uplifting examples for the young.

Meyerbeer is, as a matter of fact, treated rather as if he were one of those artists whose works are not left lying about in the living-rooms of respectable families. His music is literally suspected of being harmful to tender souls, and assimilable only for the leathery organs of perception which their musical elders are supposed to have available for occasional indulgence. 'Les Huguenots' and 'Robert' are kept from the youthful musician somewhat as parents and tutors would spare the innocent from contact with drawings of Rops, or Louvet's 'Faublas', or the dubious Memoirs of Miss Fanny Hill and the twice-dubious ones of Mme Devrient.

Yet we have taught modern youth so well to beware of adult hypocrisy that to-day it would not be easy to find a daughter who could not tell her mother a thing or two if it were not for the fear of shocking her antiquated susceptibilities, or a son who could not warn his father against some of the dangers he might meet on the treacherous path of life. In spite of this laudable tendency towards Pagan frankness and methodical initiation, we have not progressed far yet in letting music share in the advantages of the abolition of embarrassing veils. A large number of musicians are still submissive enough when supposed by their artistic elders to be safer and better off altogether 'in purdah'.

Therefore Meyerbeer remains a painted and perfumed Jezebel amongst composers. To the careful mind of the pedagogue he is as one of the 'unfortunates' whose appearance on the highway makes a chaperon say: 'look at your toes for a moment: afterwards I'll tell you why!' The subsequent information assumes the form of a warning sermon dealing with the undesirability of knowing anything beyond the certainty that the subject ought to be avoided, in word and deed.

Many a time it has been my pleasure and my privilege to show to well-bred musical youngsters some of Meyerbeer's music, only to hear the amazed query: 'But what is there so terribly wrong with it?' I could only reply: 'If you can find out for yourself, it will be time enough to worry about that.'

Apart from its reprehensible ease, gracefulness, and theatrically effective manner, Meyerbeer's music has been reproached for its restless illustration. Now, to begin with, Meyerbeer sins far less in this respect than many operatic composers who can be discussed without bringing a flush to the cheeks of the oldest professor. But, admitting that any stick is good enough for an unpopular dog, we still have to face the very pertinent question whether dramatic music is any worse for 'meaning something' in every bar, and symphonic music better for being, or tactfully pretending to be, completely meaningless right through.

Let us look at such a characteristic instance as the Ballet of the Skaters in 'Le Prophète'. If the music were performed away from the stage, one might miss the illustrative significance of the basic figure, although the music would probably remain sufficiently attractive to invalidate bland inquiries about 'whatever does it mean?' A fully informed listener could conceivably judge the pictorial sweep of the musical theme to be somewhat naïve, but then it is only his 'knowingness' which spoils the pleasure for him. There sense surely is deserting censure, for it does not apply precisely to the circumstances under which the music was intended to be heard: in the theatre, while the movements of the ballet are being watched. Music that did not adapt itself to the tempo, the rhythm, and the meaning of the movements of the performers would be worse than inadequate; it would be aggressively ridiculous. An Australian composer once told me that to his socialistic feelings a king was a ridiculous figure, and that the pageant of a king's appearance on the stage should be accompanied by ridiculous music. But probably that was all he could write, and the argument is as poor as the talent must be of a man who is reduced to such specious reasonings.[1]

[1] Curiously enough this composer was for years the musical critic of an important weekly, until presumably the editor read one of his contributions.

SYMPHONIC INNOCENCE

If any one feels inclined to make fun of the operatic composer's candid illustration of happenings on the stage, he should pause to ask himself how often the most impressive phrases of symphonic music must have been shaped by visual conceptions. We need not descend so low as the comic picture of Beethoven's Fate wearing out its knuckles on the door in order to supply the unhappy composer with a happy thought to last him for a whole movement. It is bad enough to think of a composer who, like Brahms or Franck, is so afraid of revealing his particular childishness that he keeps away from opera altogether. He can then commit anonymous imbecilities by the dozen, and will probably be praised for them, while his operatic colleagues who cannot escape the necessity of finding parallels in sound for ideas which in words appear primitive, will be chastised for sins that are no worse for being honestly admitted. For being shy, the truant from opera is called distinguished; his very helplessness seems superiority to kindred souls who prefer him as long as he prefers violins and woodwind to brass and percussion for his statements.

If only we knew, how often should we smile at the Tweedledee-and-Tweedledum-mummeries of our old and feared friends the toy Brahmses and Schumanns, who hide in their 'absolute music' many an extra-musical impression which the operatic composer is compelled to reveal before the public gaze. The wise mean here, as mostly elsewhere, is not to laugh at either unless one is prepared to laugh at both. If we insist on making a distinction, we should first of all remember that the opera composer knows that he must exhibit the source of his inspiration, or at least acknowledge some suggestion received, whereas the symphonic composer comfortably hides behind the Noah's blanket of formalism, while enjoying the consolation that the farther-fetched the related ideas are, the sooner will he acquire a reputation for profundity. Where the one cannot help putting the tail in the bass and the head in the descant, the other, the abstractly lyrical writer, can afford to produce a symphonic movement that knows neither head nor tail, and his hearers will like him all the better because they are free to read into his music whatever their own mood suggests. The supposed meaning of his abstract tone-pictures of action in C sharp, or still-life in A minor, will be whatever the first acknowledged disciple commits to print. Once a tradition is thus founded, and consequently approved by the master himself or his spiritual executors, generations of listeners afterwards praise the composer for his adherence to a poetical programme. In this way, accidental spreading of the inversions mechanically brought about by recipe of construction, eventually acquires the value of a poetic symbol. It just shows what poetic symbols amount to, and how careful one should be before one exalts the strong, silent composer, and hurls contempt at the assumedly weak, voluble one, who at least must have the whole courage of his musical convictions.

Nothing is more difficult than to describe details of the actual music characteristic of a composer's style, without using an unlimited number of quotations. I hope, however, that my argument may bring some readers to revise unfavourable impressions derived from reading about Meyerbeer unsupported by personal experience. Unfortunately, there are not many opportunities of becoming acquainted at first hand with any of the works, except the few performances of 'L'Africaine' and 'Les Huguenots'. The very best one can hope is that revived interest might justify the venture of presenting anew some of the other works, so that a new generation of musicians shall have a chance of judging for themselves instead of being dependent on opinions shaped by musical politics and personal quarrels of fifty years ago.

Without attempting to deal with the very bars of the scores, one can contradict in detail some of the generally tolerated beliefs.

It is not true that Meyerbeer is fully absorbed by orchestral effect immediately when the tension of a situation justifies any outburst. He never releases the full resources of his choral and orchestral masses unless there is a dramatically justified climax. The old accusation that he indulges in the most pathetic symphonic rushes when the book offers no defensible pretext, is a monstrously unjust one, which no critic could, with the score in his hands, rationally maintain. Since this is one of the most popular strictures, one would like to challenge the experts who speak so sneeringly of Meyerbeer to produce the passages that establish his guilt. But they never condescend to particularize.

Another criticism of which much has been made is, that to suit his phrases, he pulls about the words of his lines in a criminal manner, and that neither scansion nor poetic accent, rhythm nor period, holds sufficient meaning for him to stay his hand once the musical frenzy is on him. I have several times discovered that the most indignant critics of Meyerbeer's alleged unspeakable propensities in this respect happened to be entirely unaware that his operas had originally been written to French texts; they roundly damned him for his sins in the setting of German lines which he never knew, and that were nothing but a poor hack's twopenny-halfpenny translation. Honest study of any of Meyerbeer's scores will, on the contrary, reveal all the faithful consideration of finesses and subtleties of diction a poet can demand from a composer.

It is hardly necessary to say that the one serious shortcoming of Meyerbeer is one that is rarely, if ever, noticed by his most censorious antagonists, and that is his dreadful lack of all sense of humour. Some authors indeed have affected to find humour in such lugubrious canonizing as he commits in 'Le Prophète', where the three frightening male figures that upset Berlioz so much are being denunciatingly witty about each other. Now it would not be easy to say whether he was not dramatically sound even there. It would reveal a refinement of psychological analysis in which one hesitates to believe. Still, composers do penetrate some of the soul's mysterious recesses. Meyerbeer did, perhaps, write these dismal passages deliberately. While they fail in theatrical attraction, they could certainly not be surpassed as the concerted mirth of

Anabaptists indulging in a bout of acrid humour. The worst —i.e. the best—criticism one could make would be that such a display of gloomy, morbid wit is too depressing to tickle any listener in the way he has a right to expect when a quasi-comic relief breaks in on the sustained dignity of the previous and subsequent proceedings.

These questions at least make one feel how dangerous it is to dogmatize about Meyerbeer's intentions, and how astonishingly superficial is the bulk of the adverse criticism that is usually offered as a considered estimate of the strengths and weaknesses of his music. That a certain rhythmic monotony can be discovered in his more extended structures is undoubtedly true, but why he should be so severely taken to task for a technical weakness that he has in common with unquestionably greater figures, one may legitimately inquire. Some of Bach's fugues—a good example would be the D minor of the second book of the 48—betray the identical weakness; and when we think of the final movement of Beethoven's last symphony: I should like to know where is the critic who, with his hand on his heart, would dare to deny Meyerbeer the right to a seat among the elect on account of that failing.[1]

When Berlioz, on hearing the first performance of 'Le Prophète' said that he 'could have bitten the hand of the author of "Les Huguenots" for being guilty' of some of the dark and depressing pages of his later opera, he paid a marked tribute to Meyerbeer's descriptive power at the same time as to his earlier ensembles. However purist we feel, we do not quarrel with Beethoven's admiration for Cherubini's dramatic writing, while we cheerfully admit that he is a terribly dry stick, taking his works as a whole. Meyerbeer has been viciously attacked by competent judges who were anxious to atone for youthful weaknesses, and who thus were able to shore up tottering consciences. But there is no such justification for

[1] Meyerbeer's notorious 'insincerity' was not enough to make him write 1/4; 2/4; 3/4; 4/4; 5/4; when five 3/4 bars could be made to serve the purpose, although they look not nearly as 'interesting' as they are made to appear in some modern scores which exploit such devices.

the furious hostility of far lesser men, whose inexorable condemnation has supplied the bulk of the foundations on which most of his present critics build when they would justify their rejection of all his work.

Whereas we do not now think, in spite of Beethoven's praises, that it is worth while bothering much about the exact position of Cherubini in the history of dramatic music, no one can feel sure that in the same way Meyerbeer may be regarded as beyond the uncertainties of sympathy and dislike. He can still provoke actual hostility instead of being impersonally taken for granted as a figure that once was acceptable for some good qualities, while failing to hold the stage when the public had forgotten his earlier prestige. The very fact that Meyerbeer perpetually irritates certain writers to the point of rudeness to his memory, shows better than anything that he has not passed into the neutral atmosphere of historical assessment. After all these years he is as an artistic figure still sufficiently alive to make us remember his human failings, which otherwise we should see only as peculiar aspects of a generally assimilated style.

The influence he has had on later composers has been, on the whole, a good one, whatever sweet-thinking and high-feeling souls may say. To repeat his occasional perversities, a composer needs as exceptional a talent. Call it unpleasant, call him a power for evil if you like, he was an extraordinarily gifted musician, none the less. And he has taught something to all the opera-writers who knew his work; it would be very difficult to find a single one who has not profited by his example, where variety of orchestral colour, the broad sweep of melodic line, and the dramatically convincing construction of large ensembles are concerned. This alone should suffice for gratitude and ought to temper the tone adopted by the majority of writers who trouble to discuss his music; but even so our debt would not be nearly paid.

He left opera a distinctly more perfected large-scale musical form than he found it. This is praise which can be given to very few of the dramatic composers that came after him. No one wishes to deny that Wagner impressed his mark on opera; whether it was one for which he deserves nothing but praise while Meyerbeer should have all the blame, is a question not so easily decided. Besides, many a work of Wagner, not to speak of Wagnerian works (a great deal of Richard Strauss's best operatic music is obviously indebted to Meyerbeer), derives some of its principal features from his practice.

And, apart from a host of smaller figures, Verdi has had to thank him for much of the most valuable methods exploited in his works. This may to-day seem a left-handed compliment to many musicians, but it will probably appear different in another fifty years, when dramatically cogent speech, not depending for its course and inflexions on *leitmotiv*, has resumed its position. The signs are already visible.

I do not want to indulge in individual prophecy; I am really only epitomizing, with the mention of names, generalized appreciations of certain qualities of dramatic music which I have observed in contemporary writings. Although Meyerbeer's name is not openly mentioned in this connexion, I dare maintain with some assurance that it cannot very much longer be avoided. When modern authors on opera come to perceive some of the implications of their own assertions, they will give Meyerbeer credit for much that so far is only hailed in derivations observed in recent compositions where it obtains approbation without acknowledgement.

·ᛰ *Five* ᛎ·
SINE NOMINE

I

In the last twenty or thirty years we have become familiar with constant criticism of modern concert-giving. Perennial denunciations have revealed a widespread dissatisfaction, but they have not, on the whole, been constructive. Effects more than causes have received attention, and the reforms occasionally advocated have held out little promise of improvement.

It has been seriously proposed to erect temples devoted to Mozart, Bach, or Beethoven, where their works would be reverently performed. It is questionable whether there exists enough enthusiasm for the cult of any single master, of whatever eminence, to make that practicable in the face of the antagonisms such a proselytizing fervour is bound to arouse.

We have also been advised to search for flawless principles on which to found the acoustic and decorative features of concert halls, to keep them dimly lighted or in complete darkness, or to hide the performers; but none of all this touches the roots of the troubles that admittedly exist. Besides, widespread as discontent with existing conditions may be, it is by no means general. Reformers may easily obtain theoretical support, but they cannot formulate any general appeal that would bring forth material assistance substantial enough to allow effectual demonstrations of these proposed improvements.

The very works that can inspire so exclusive an affection as to compel the desire to hear them under ideal conditions, are seldom those that would ever become widely popular.

It is unreasonable to expect from wealthy philanthropists disinterested aesthetic convictions that fire them with the ambition to finance idealist undertakings of this kind on trust. To seek popular support for so recondite a cause as the worthiest representation of music is only more futile. The interest that is often demanded for it is hardly expected for any of the other arts. Public picture-galleries do not depend on popular support. Collections are almost invariably started through private initiative; when eventually they come under the control of some public body, the funds required for their upkeep are usually obtained from such patient and dumb things as tax- or rate-payers; anyhow, from people whose opinions are not particularly considered and who are frankly indifferent. The actual supporters rarely voice any opinions they may happen to have, but if they show no concern about the housing or the state of the paintings, nobody accuses them of callousness or barbarity, or the betrayal of a sacred cause.

Curiously enough, many musicians presume a profound and intelligent public interest in music. It is not easy to see why they should so persistently disregard facts. An astounding instance is the interminable controversy about opera in this country. It seems as if hardly any one realizes that The Public, in whose name and for whose benefit it is ostensibly kept alive, are not greatly interested, if they want the thing at all.

Interest in serious music of any kind is, anyhow, so infinitesimal that it would be wiser if appeal for public support did not so frequently take its existence for granted. Better face realities and conduct these wordy contests on an altogether more modest scale.

One of the saddest and most ominous consequences of this misconceived relationship is, perhaps, that composers, deceived by the frequency with which such discussions appear in print, and by the amount of space editors will at certain seasons allot to them, forget that they are—*cum grano salis*—read by fewer people than they are written by. They have come to think so much of the 'musical world' that they lose more and more touch with 'the' world and its plain realities.

Catering for a postulated fastidious few, they inevitably become remote and artificial. Some critics understand this so well that when a composer fails to achieve popularity they presume that he does not want it.

When one speaks of practical reforms, one naturally permits that precious minority that stands proudly and silently aloof from the crude ambitions and enjoyments of the crowd to realize its own ideals, as long as it is understood that there can be no question of demanding public interest, let alone support, for them. Composers whose music appeals in any way to the multitude can usually establish some vital connexion with everyday existence. Their direct grip on the imagination of the masses evokes an active interest that brings with it all conceivable possibilities, as Bayreuth has shown. No measure of rhetoric praise, or recommendation, or even vilification, could achieve anything like it. In countries where the composer and his public still meet more or less on common ground, that reasonable give-and-take is always possible.

One of the first conditions of a healthy, if sometimes over-robust, musical activity is thereby at least fulfilled. It is demonstrably not accident, for instance, that every Italian town of some importance has its Opera House, that every German city of some wealth manages to support its Symphony Orchestra, whether on the patron system or through municipal contributions. There is, no doubt, room for reforms there as much as here or anywhere, but in all cases the first requirement, in whatever phase of cultural development, remains that available public interest in performances be founded on a healthy connexion between the world and life, and the composer's activities. Such a balance has, wherever it existed, shown itself in the evolution of a harmonious organization of all essential elements. The absence of such organization exasperates those impatient devotees of musical morality who possess sharper powers of observation than of reasoning.

Sometimes an individual musician's sensibility has led him to a quest for circumstances and surroundings that avoided hurt to his feelings. Tartini, in his later years, played in the grave semi-solitude of the cathedral during the evening hours. Chopin renounced a virtuoso's career for the chaste gratification of presenting intimate pieces to a small, select gathering. The ageing Liszt, although fully initiated in the delights of popular triumph, abandoned them for the occasional pleasure of a transcendent interpretation of a late Beethoven sonata to a favoured pupil or a few close friends. I have heard it objected that he 'could afford it', many people having an irresistible desire to be unkind to the memory of Liszt. It is true enough in a spiritual sense, only that is not how the criticism is meant. In the material sense it is footling; for it is directed at a man of the most modest personal needs, who left his heirs not much beyond a couple of handkerchiefs. No other successful virtuoso ever believed that the right moment for retiring with an assured future had arrived. (When Patti abandoned public performances she built a private theatre which she filled with the reluctant villagers on her estate.)

All such anomalous behaviour by the morally well-favoured forcibly illuminates the nondescript role in the modern social structure of the musician who is not proud enough to be just a craftsman, or humble enough to become a business magnate. Similar, mildly perverse, orientations were not indicated when music had its indubitable position in the accepted formations of society. In the Renaissance period the enthusiastic cult of music at some of the Italian courts brought audience, executants, and composers together on equal terms. There was not really a commercial side to the performance of music then, for, although players, singers, and composers might be indemnified for their time, neither side saw in this a commercial transaction. The erudite dilettanti who conducted experiments in dramatic construction, and first codified the elements of operatic form, proceeded in an earnest spirit of investigation. No one would have estimated their labours different from those of poets, architects, mathematicians, or painters; none was expected, or felt obliged, to display any particular pride or humility. The state and the community generally had as many uses for music as for all other occupations, yet the status of the artist himself was not measured by the greater or lesser utility.

Since we have begun to look upon utilitarianism as a perfectly respectable attitude, if not even a philosophy, contemporary writers habitually affect to discern in the recognition of these facts some of the preciosity of the pedant and the bluestocking. But this judgement lacks sense of historical perspective. If so critical a view might be justifiably applied to present conditions, the fault is in the conditions, not in the principle. Musical life in Italy, even in our time, supports that assumption, because it has to a great extent preserved its direct contact with the daily existence of the people. The very ardour of the audience's participation demonstrates and explains the continuity of Italian operatic conditions. The *maestro* is still a popular figure whose social importance admits no question.

Almost everywhere to-day the sensationally successful composer aspires to the distinction of being honoured not for his gifts but for the soundness of his exploitation of them. He wants to be looked upon as a shrewd business man. When M. Prokofiev informed his big brother Stravinsky that he had allowed somebody to retain a manuscript of his, he got a severe scolding, culminating in the admonition, 'Mon chèr-re, c'est de l'or-re en bar-r-res!' In self-defence some creative musicians of lesser good fortune have tentatively and apologetically transformed themselves into a species of university don; of two evils they certainly have selected the less repulsive. But curiously enough, although it could be foreseen, both are agreed that any attitude is better than the candid one of the born musician who has no desire to be anything else. The uninformed public has easily adopted the same belief, and it is generally assumed that the traditional Italian state of affairs reveals simply a primitive temperament and an incorrigible national taste for the banalities of convention. All this would not be so bad if the prestige of the figureheads who stand for these convictions did not determine the judgements of the specializing students of music. When the student does not receive his information from a master whom he personally esteems, he has to find it in the standard works that constitute the nearest available substitute. He is seldom so wise in the ways of the world as to suspect that these are written by the same people, governed by the same bias. We all have to go through a hard school before we discover that the text-books necessarily propagate the vulgarly accepted notions, just because they are, with the rarest exceptions, compiled by officially recognized mediocrities. One may feel generously disposed towards necessity, but it would be foolish to close one's eyes to the fact that since universal philosophers have disappeared from this earth, there cannot easily be found an editor of whom one may reasonably hope that he will do better than collect the commonplaces which the acknowledged academicians mechanically contribute. It would be hard to assess the harm done by the respect which, for these obvious reasons, the lexicon and the dictionary claim. The trouble is not so much that they are not fairly reliable as regards information, but that the editor of an encyclopaedia is as human as the editor of a newspaper, and labours under the same limitations. With the best will in the world he cannot escape some aesthetic tendency that is reflected in the contributions, simply because he must choose the writers with established names who usually reach their position of eminence not only by concrete knowledge, but also by their proved immunity from subversive opinions and unexpected attitudes. A further aspect of the same infirmity is seen in a specializing lexicon, such as the musical dictionary must be. There emanates from the whole work the impression that events and interests in the occupation with music show some unbroken line which allows us to recognize a few basic principles, proceeding from human nature and physiological impulses.

Anybody who wishes to educate himself by the available literature will be taught that although all people of good will are always ready to fight to preserve the great tradition of music-as-it-should-be, there are a small number of malcontents and born anarchists who do their best to upset the idyllic conditions, and who should be resisted with all available power. Sometimes these are the anti-doctrinaires in one's own country, but as often they are the nationals of some other geographical or racial entity, with totally different ideals, who would seem to encourage the disruptive forces in our midst exactly as, at some time or other in English history, any unpopular figure was inevitably suspected of being a Jesuit, or a Spanish agent, or a Jacobin, or a German spy.

Naturally, musicians in all countries do think that some of the rules are universal, but what really matters is that a tradition, whether more or less local, should be allowed to grow unhampered. If any national art is to be allowed to grow, and it need not be particularly occupied with geographical frontiers, one of the first and most important requisites is that both the composer and his public shall be equally bound by it.

Whatever innovations the individual composer may attempt are then only the outward signs of his personality, not reaction against an academically-evolved universal system any more than concession. It is simply inane for a German, let us say, to condemn an Italian composer for his ignorance or disregard of principles that are unquestioningly accepted in Germany. But in England again, where until very recently the most doubtful German theses were taken most seriously, the student would easily arrive at an unfavourable estimate of the Italians' musical preoccupations, which is really vastly more absurd. The Italian himself, if acquainted with German ideas, would regard them as remote academic speculations that had as much to do with the blood and bones of living music as the assumptions of Chaldean astrology. Italy has a large, passionately interested public that for generations has with full attention listened to every original application of accepted dramatic formulas. Composers there could, for that reason, risk the introduction of subtleties whose significance would completely escape the foreign observer who is not deeply versed in Italian ways, and judges the works by canons derived from totally different needs, desires, and ambitions. He would be baffled by the, to him, strange duality of an artistic tradition which asks obedience to numerous straight-laced formalities while at the same time insisting on an unexpected treatment of familiar themes.

In the Italian Opera Houses, where the audiences participate whole-heartedly in the happenings and situations, without losing their appreciation of any felicitous turn that gives a new appearance to an old phrase, one is pleased to note the absence of that fatuous superciliousness with which, elsewhere, jaded intellectuals tolerate traditional entertainment. And neither, God be praised, does one find there the bovine obtuseness of our unspeakable old friend 'the tired business man',[1] who by his demand to be lulled into an agreeable stupor or excited to the just permissible point of indecorousness, tends to have all theatres transformed into conventionally camouflaged antechambers of petty brothels.

But wherever we meet humanly respectable traditions as directly shaped by reasonable artistic desires and spiritual longing, in whatever country or period, they will invariably prove to be equally far removed from pedantic austerity and from commercial routine.

Germany, in the seventeenth and eighteenth centuries, saw a high development of musical culture resting on traditions that rivalled in continuity those of Italy. The ardent patronage of composers at the many small courts constituted a powerful stimulus to creative talent, and provided fertile soil for their labours by evolving steadily a more refined and receptive disposition. Evidently there could be no question here of any popular movement, and thus there was the less

[1] When the 'serious' occupations of the day are over there comes a sort of second, very late 'children's hour' for the overworked money-makers. The people that cater for them have well understood this, and appropriately purvey entertainments calculated for infantilism, innocent and otherwise.

CONVENTIONS AND CONVULSIONS

danger of commercial temptations intruding. Against that stood the pernicious chance that the patron's trivial preferences or fastidious conventionality established arbitrary rules.

The abrupt social and political upheavals of the last century were unavoidably accompanied by a break in artistic traditions which were rooted in discarded forms of political and dynastic organization. Subsequently, the commercial exploitation of music in Germany and Austria rose to a fabulous plane, of which few people who had not looked behind the scenes in the pre-War Empires could have any conception. It was the time of the Symphony-of-a-Thousand,[1] and opera orchestras with a conductor seated in the centre of an army-corps of first, second, and third fiddles, and first and second violas. In common with Time, Music was Money as much there as it has ever been in the U.S.A.—so cruelly lectured for similar sins.[2]

The influence of the aristocratic patron diminished with the practical value of his once eagerly solicited support. The fanatics of liberty and equality who set out to destroy aristocratic pretensions to the prerogatives of individuality, at the same time—as some germs create a disposition to secondary infections—obliterated the distinctive character of institutions that owed their existence to the artistic interests of the 'enlightened despot'. We have not so far been offered any satisfactory substitute.

The antique republics witnessed what is now generally described as popular interest in, and support of, art and science. But the word here has a very different sense. The leisure that allowed the citizens to devote their time to abstract thought and artistic occupation was made possible by the existence of a slave caste. The mention of art and science together, in this connexion, would seem at first sight to invali-

[1] i.e. Mahler's 'Faust' Symphony.
[2] This was written ten years ago. Since then Germany has gone through a chastened period of chamber music and democracy, to turn with the first slackening of international supervision to Gebrauchsmusik and Hitlerism. Foxes and leopards have not changed.

date the denunciation of present conditions, since in the modern state the scientist appears to hold an eminent position. But that is by virtue only of his magnificent promises to industrialism. Princes used to keep alchemists as a speculative investment. The tame wizard would one day solve all his master's state and private problems by the production of an inexhaustible source of wealth out of the void. Our contemporary merchant-princes invest capital in laboratories, in the hope that one of their chemists or physicists will invent a death-ray, or disrupt the atom by means of a new 'Philosopher's Stone', although we are assured that the entire universe will follow—and 'si fractus illabatur orbis', carry his patron, if perhaps in company of all the rest, anyhow beyond all dreams, including those of avarice. Whatever contemporary patrons there are left have mostly lost touch with the actual practice of music. They hardly get a chance to learn much about it, since to become wealthy enough for patronage one must do without spare time. And it takes time to master any instrument, and much more to acquire the skill necessary to read a score. So that our potential protectors, if they are capable of affection for unfamiliar music, are usually as much as all others reduced to acceptance of commercially organized performances. Even then, their needs are very scantily met. The Italian gets the opera he wants; the provincial German amateur has a fair number of passable orchestras within reach so that he can acquire a reasonable erudition: but there is not much of either the one or the other in this country. For the various tastes, some known, and a great number presumed, professional concert-givers provide programmes which must cater for all sections. They are made up of most divergent works in the most contradictory styles, promiscuously bundled together. No one, had he the appropriate Gargantuan appetite, could possibly command the speed and accuracy of shift and readjustment of his receptive faculties needed to enjoy these crazy feasts. If one is not to develop an invincible distaste for all music, one must pay for a several hours'

'AS IT WAS IN THE BEGINNING'

entertainment to hear one single piece. And even that is difficult, for no time-tables are provided. The occasion is too genteel for the rational methods that suit railways or music-halls.

All this is admittedly depressing, and we hear as many proposals for improvement as there are reasons for disgust. None seems calculated to satisfy any but those concert-goers who happen to share the reformer's special foibles. The man with the proper herd-mind tells us that official control or a gigantic corporation would solve all problems, put the whole affair on a sound basis. The clubbable fellow believes in a jolly quasi-improvised concert, something approaching the old-time sing-song. The solemn specialist, on the other hand, assures us that if the public were only given Bach and Handel, we should soon discover how essentially solid is their aggregate taste. What has satisfied generations must remain satisfactory. He pins his faith to works of the commendable popularity of 'Elijah', which now the B minor Mass threatens to achieve. The promoter of concerts with miscellaneous programmes of a not too irresponsible complexion tells us that variety and light fare are all that is required.

In this confusion we naturally search through space and time for instances of a happy balance, hopefully assuming that it somewhere exists or has existed. But although it is attractive to consider, even at the price of some envious longing, desirable historical instances, it is at best a poor consolation to discover how good the past was, or how pleasant the present might be if only it would revert to the good old times.

One institution has, through all vicissitudes, preserved a venerable musical tradition intact in every country. This is the Roman Church, whose services have incorporated music from a date preceding the earliest responsible references to European music as an organized art-form. Music there is performed under conditions which, as far as it is possible to judge, are precisely those which hearers always expected, and the composers contemplated. These, moreover, have preserved their identity from what are, aesthetically speaking,

RESPECTABLE AND DETESTABLE RITUALS

prehistoric times. Even the few unimportant variations have, we can conclude on fairly reliable evidence, been always sensibly regulated after conscientious technical research under wise control.

The task of the composer who writes for the settled ritual is thus definitely circumscribed, and his idiom is severely kept within the bounds of a closely watched vocabulary and syntax. In exactly the same way, the hearer is predisposed to accept that idiom in its initial sense. Also, the surroundings in which the music is listened to, their spiritual associations, and everything implied in this relationship, here for once form a harmonious whole, with a universally understood meaning which appeals similarly to composer, executant, and listener. Further there is this very important factor, that a predetermined ceremonial places within the unified and balanced organism all constituents which if left to chance could destroy the equilibrium.

It is not easy to think of an organization which in this respect bears comparison with the Roman Church. Its roots lie deep in the soil of humanity's urgent common needs, and this alone gives it a standing to which no other body dealing directly or indirectly with music can aspire. An incidental advantage is (although it might appear a negative quality to people who do not feel strongly about music) that the tenderest susceptibilities could not be hurt by renderings under conditions so gratifyingly remote from those generally encountered.

Think of the familiar preliminaries of our ordinary concerts. Is there anything more painful than to stand in a queue of insolvent hedonists, advertising one's musical hungriness? When this unpleasant ritual precedes the performance of a work for which one has a real affection, the exhibition of anticipated pleasure is as embarrassing as a public honeymoon. The churchgoer, on the contrary, however much he is moved by the musical part of the service, does not display his purpose, even if it is a conscious one; his experience is ostensibly incidental. His emotions are no more advertised than those of an artist who is moved by the architectural beauties of a building which he passes, or which he enters to keep an appointment. In both instances the thing is inevitably there in its right place as much as a landscape, and the presence of an appreciative spirit is inconspicuous: the man becomes part of the picture, like a solitary wanderer in a forest.

When we wish to hear music, however, we have usually to be reconciled to a public display of our intentions and, worse, to the concomitants of a commercial transaction, and if we resent it, we are accused of sentimentality. One buys the right-by-contract to an organized orgy of musical delights. Are there lovers of music completely free from any aversion to that particular aspect of their enjoyments? I forbear to go beyond the bare mention of the horrific literature which is forced upon us at concerts to make us think about the music instead of listening to it.

II

If the music heard as part of the religious ritual moves us qua music, so much the better. It approaches here a function of which many composers have dreamed. I refer to its place in what Wagner called the 'Gesamtwerk'. The theories may be sound, but practice has not so far achieved a convincing fusion. With regard to the theory, one would welcome more attention for Grètry, one of the most distinguished among musicians who evinced convictions similar to those of Wagner. His lucidity of thought and his incisive and balanced prose, his graceful eloquence and profound erudition, should have recommended his writings to students. Where Wagner's verbosity and confused polemics and his irritating obstinacy frequently antagonize the best disposed, Grètry's logical simplicity and scholarly modesty charm us into sympathetic consideration of his arguments. But the impatient, brilliant pedagogue has by sheer force of personality impressed himself so irresistibly on the popular imagination that he receives credit for numerous theories and speculations that were no more his own than a great many features of his musical style for which he is particularly esteemed. The fascination of the 'alte Zauberer', as Nietzsche called him, has blinded generations of uncritical admirers to the fact that much of what he proclaimed as his personal conception of a deeper and truer artistic manifestation had not only been proposed before, but in a considerable measure already fulfilled. The attention for the thing available is deflected by the excitement which prophetic announcements provoke. But when the first heat of passion abates, a cool-headed survey allows one to see that the form of perfection called for existed already if not thus described and not to the extent declared desirable.

The greater power lies naturally in the steadily evolved tradition, representing the accumulated wisdom of countless generations, which while eliminating superfluous elements has constantly added such as lead to growing perfection. The personal opinions of the most gifted individual may contribute to this end, but he can no more contest the tradition or replace the constituents than he could have constructed the complete system. The fetishism of 'unique personality' may reject this humiliating truth, but what is such a puny effort likely to achieve against the imperceptibly rising monument which represents the connected, concentrated labours of the most eminent individuals devoting their energies to one common, if dimly perceived, purpose?

A mincing aestheticism, considering the possibilities of a combination of all the arts, conveniently ignores to what an extent the Roman ritual already achieves this. There it has for centuries been a stabilized organic unity, while megalomaniac artists and what Goethe calls 'haemorrhoidal professors' all failed to get beyond theory. Of course, the nature of the existing organization was not so crude as the theoretically propounded one. That the materialization of a hurrying artist-philosopher's dream was bound to prove even clumsier has been distressingly revealed in 'Parsifal', 'dies Bimbambaumeln; dies falsch verzückte Himmel-Überhimmeln'!¹ A composite appeal to the mind, through a single conception conveyed by numerous different but converging means, implies a delicate complexity which lies outside the power of any single artist, be he a Leonardo or a Dürer, to take two acknowledged magicians.

But this is not always fully understood by the very people who are most interested. Comparison with an intricate polyphonic structure is an obvious means of elucidation. Few things demand more concentrated attention than accurate listening to a complex contrapuntal phrase. No one can follow several melodic lines simultaneously with anything like the completeness that ear and brain permit for a single melody. Yet musicians, not quite sure of physiological limitations, fear that the perfection of their hearing might be questioned, and make astonishing claims to super-acute powers. When we come to think of the mental qualities that would have to go with such ears, we simply find ourselves in dreamland. In any effort to listen contrapuntally, one has to expend most of one's energies in an admittedly exhausting process of rapid elimination and substitution. The total of one's impressions, in fact, depends on the alertness with which one can sustain this constantly changing accommodation and ceaseless readjustment of focus. To hear the whole at once is as impossible as to see the whole surface of a painting at any single moment. One must let the eye rove over the expanse of a canvas, mentally fixing every separate feature, thus constantly adding to the sum of previously retained impressions, while one is actually occupied with the rest. In a similar way we build the illusion of continuity in cinema films. But with painting we have the advantage that we can every moment return to any spot for rapid correlation. If a musical point has at the moment of its appearance escaped us, it is too late to repair the hiatus. For the actual performance it has already passed beyond recall.²

[1] Nietzsche.
[2] To avoid misunderstanding I may point out that we are dealing with polyphony, not with the sort of music that repeats everything so often that no one could possibly ever miss anything.

The next performance, if we get the chance to hear one, brings its own problems again. And even then we would have to assume that all performances will be more or less similar and correct.

So that unless musicians can read scores as easily as they read a book, and they really can do nothing of the sort, they find themselves in a predicament indeed, when they wish to become well acquainted with intricate and seldom-performed works.

The process becomes infinitely more complicated when, instead of music built of independent parts, a work depends on the combined appeal of several arts, demanding entrance into our consciousness through the many distinct channels of sensuous apprehension simultaneously, and yet with their separate insistencies. Unless one is satisfied to abandon oneself unquestioningly to whatever gratuitous impression happens to reach one, it becomes a matter of restlessly grasping at every moment the vital point, while relegating the rest to a relatively diffuse background. The best one hopes for is that the single impressions thus modified will roughly correspond to those planned by the composer, if it is possible for any artist to calculate so precise and subtle a balance that he can foresee his effects.

On the other hand, it may be rationally assumed that such a complex appeal in a perfectly equilibrated form, which assigns an appropriate part to all the contributing forces, might be achieved in course of time by an institution that has grown from the spiritual ambitions of many generations of talented men striving towards the fulfilment of one common aspiration. The intuition that enables us to receive, through all our senses at once, a harmonious impression from Nature, may be similarly evoked by a human product when it is the result of continuous, unflagging, concentrated efforts to render some reflection of what the greatest minds have read of universal, directive purpose. One must imagine for this an infinitely complex, yet perfectly united work which, while permitting persistent analysis at every point, never ceases to grip by its continuity. None of its contributing factors would act on our perceptions at all moments with equal force but for the imperceptibly conveyed certainty that they all, and always, are indispensable parts of one indivisible and closely-wrought whole. The momentary suppression of a seemingly insignificant detail should be as noticeable as the omission of an instrument in an orchestral phrase, where we could not perhaps with certainty state what was missing, but would at once be aware of the changed tone-values.

Such a perfect harmony of ethical and artistic qualities would constitute the 'complete work of art', indeed that of 'the future', as Wagner with perfect justification called it. Unless one assumes that he would in his last hours have called it 'of the past', one can even say that this is his sole instance of modesty.

No Churches, apart from the Catholic, have achieved an appeal of similar perfection. Possibly outside Europe or outside Christianity there may be something that would stand comparison, but we are dealing primarily with music, and of non-European music we certainly have only very confused notions. There are evident reasons for the exceptional position of the Catholic Church where art is concerned. It has always been the bearer of a great artistic tradition in face of the antagonism of anti-Catholic critics who persistently attack the 'mummery' and the 'puppet-show' of the Roman ceremonial. The Reformation, from its inception, betrayed as part of its general iconophobia a pronounced distrust of the intrusion of music in the services. I have heard it argued that this aversion from the display of products of human hands and minds, with their invincible imperfections, *coram Domino*, reveals an appropriate humility. The argument seems to strike a painfully false note when we consider it together with the partiality to *viva voce* supplications in which 'our dear brother', or 'our erring sister', is by name recommended to Providence for suggested reward, punishment, or special assistance. I am referring chiefly to the Continental Reformed Churches, and those in the British Isles that resemble them; the Anglican Church holds a position apart. The creeds formulated by post-Lutheran Protestant theologians are pervaded by a mercilessly uncompromising spirit from which the Anglican reformers were mostly exempt. Political and national considerations weighed admittedly far more here, and England has seen little of the ferocious aggressiveness of Swiss and Netherlands Protestants. If we except a brief phase of fierce Puritanism, English anti-Catholics were evidently far more occupied with Spanish plots, French plots, Jesuit and Papal intrigues, and seldom showed that obsessive hatred and fear of sensuous beauty in any form that so largely predominated in the denunciatory preaching of the Continental specialists of fanaticism.

Wherever the power reverted to Calvinism 'sans phrase' there formed a host of sombre, dour, embittered enemies of all that was graceful, pleasant, sweetly appealing, or emotional, and consequently believed to stand in the way of spiritual purification. When art was not looked on with horror and contempt as one of the evident wiles of the Evil One, it was simply regarded as unworthy of connexion with worship because worldly, that is, trivial, childish, and deceptive, if not blatantly theatrical and lascivious. In the Netherlands, significantly enough, art was practised and appreciated almost exclusively in the regions that remained preponderantly Catholic. If outside these it was tolerated, it was in a spirit of haughty liberalism. This applies as much to the Golden Period of the early Dutch school of painting (when, incidentally, painting became as much a localized industrial craze as the cultivation of tulips a little later). The genuine herds of Calvinism lie in the districts that have least contributed to artistic glories. This is equally true of Germany, and still to-day a French author can write of 'ces ennuyeux Huguenots dont la race, si mal arrachée par les jardiniers de Rome, a poussé jusqu'à nos jours ses hypocrites bourgeois et de tristes et sots pasteurs'. Nothing could be more characteristic of the resentment Calvinism has roused in the mind of artists by its nagging crusade against art.[1]

Some of the less rigid Protestants tolerate music of a kind in the service, but on the understanding that it is divested of its pernicious charms, and parades its austerities. Music modelled with this submissive acceptance has been, for some centuries, the nightmare of most sensitive musicians. No one who has not suffered from it can have any conception of the utter depth of musical misery to which the last shamefaced remains of liturgy have sunk in Continental Reformed Churches. If similar terrors are to be met in the Anglican Church, it is through artistic neglect, not the consequence of an analogous moral obsession. Only parsimony or insensibility could have caused 'the howling wilderness of the psalmody in most parish churches of the land' of which De Quincey complained.

A fundamental distinction, which assures the unassailable musical superiority of the Catholic Church, is that it resolutely upholds the cult of beauty as an indispensable concomitant of communal worship. Adoration of the Supreme Being should be invested with every suitable attribute of dignity, and since creative genius is the unmistakable reflection of the Divine, the presumption to bestow that adoration ought to be justified by tributes of an artistic magnificence that bespeak a worthy application of the talents for which the Divine Distributor should, in this manner, be thanked. The pupil shows his master how he profited by understanding; the Scriptures extol the merits of the labourer who made the best use of the 'talents' with which he had been trusted.

A dyspeptic conception of Godhead denounces this as a flippant manifestation of faith, and presumes celestial rejoicing at the spectacle of cotton gloves and black coats, starch, pinewood, and whitewash. It implies that the only

[1] Unless it were the contradiction of Calvinist logic itself, which exaggerates the Platonic absurdities on artistic occupation by viewing it one moment as trivial and important, the next as unimportant but objectionable. The artist must give himself to his art to become ethically tolerable—but art in itself deserves no distinction in the ethical compound.

music which finds grace before the heavenly Throne is the dismal wailing of solemn elders and their cowed children, moaning, with pious contempt for pitch, the dreary tunes that the Reformation substituted for the wickedly florid melodies some of the greatest—but Popish—composers produced for the Roman ritual. Could there be a more perverse interpretation of the parable of the 'widow's mite'? No doubt the meanest contribution may, on occasion, be most valuable, but this cannot mean that the offering which would be valuable should begin by being contemptible, and that consummate craftsmanship reveals a frivolous application of genius. True inspiration made the Church a monument of ability as well as of faith. Such men as Brunelleschi were guides and masters of a fraternity which was known as 'Les Logeurs du Bon Dieu', because they built the churches and ornamented their portals, windows, transoms, and abscisses. They lavished their talent on the Good Lord's Hostel, asking nothing beyond their daily bread in exchange. This was the pure and ardent devotion of artists' lay orders. How 'many mansions' they visualized in the 'Father's House' one may gather from the allusions in the series of gargoyles of the big cathedrals. In the building and its enrichment, sculptors, weavers, and smiths proclaimed in stone and metal, wood and cloth, the unity of spiritual truths, within the enveloping conceptions of Catholic theology.

The most varied features, down to the smallest details of the priest's ceremonial robes, have been devised in accordance with Scriptural indications, and the interpretation of sacred texts by the Church's most enlightened adherents. An artist counts as one of these when his genius reveals the divine source of his inspirations. Ecclesiastical authority has allowed a comparatively wide licence to artistic ambition. Although the Church may not distinguish with immediate clarity of judgement in new and tentative speculations of philosophers and scientists, it has usually shown sensible discernment in its patronage of original artists.

OLD ADAM AT IT

The Church does not deliberately exploit art for its own purposes. It is understandably impatient of an exclusively aesthetic interpretation of its ceremonial institutions. I am extracting an aesthetic element from an established spiritual conglomeration. If I say: nature is beautiful, I do not mean that nature wishes to show off any more than that if I say: nature is cruel, I think she 'does it on purpose'. Every creative artist should, apart from his faith, gratefully recognize the rare milieu that offers to art a dignified and logically established position. None the less, most composers fail to appreciate the attractiveness of this exceptional situation. Some entertain so megalomaniacal an opinion of their significance in the universe that they would consider the dedication of their work to religious service as a humiliating subjection, although they see nothing incongruous in the foundation of centres of worship dedicated to Their Own Creation! But then, asylums are full of people with sincere religious instincts who have come to the conclusion that they are God, or the Messiah.

The Great Adventure of Bayreuth recalls an incident of the French Revolution. When the ci-devant Supreme Being of the Christian Faith had been disestablished by official decree, the 'Citoyens' changed the old forms of swearing. Instead of saying on appropriate occasions '. . .!', they positively cried 'by the Olympos!', or 'O, Juno!'. A few ardent young men resolved to enthrone Reason as the object of national veneration. A famous Parisian lady was, amid scenes of intimate fervour, conducted to the High Altar of Notre-Dame. An appropriately magnificent and concupiscent escort of pre-apotheotic worshippers carried this attractive and popular 'Goddess of Reason' along the Republican highways, singing:

Antoine Momoro

    Vive la Déesse Raison,
    Flamme pure, douce lumière!

'Pure' could not be bettered! And how can we help thinking

of this Mademoiselle Artémise[1] when we hear that some equally admirable baggage of music, by its virtues, elevates the surroundings in which it is performed? If it is true that Wanamaker's Stores were transformed into a Temple of Art when Strauss conducted his Sinfonia Domestica there, the Albert Hall would become a spittoon if one committed there what in a railway carriage costs forty shillings.

When we hear Bach's B minor Mass performed as an 'item' of a concert programme, it is unsatisfactory to ourselves and an injustice to the work. When such music is presented as an integral part of the religious ritual it acquires the dignity inherent in its conception. The works suited to the services are limited in number and character, but the principle of selection does not set up a barrier of aesthetic presumption. Most emphatically, I am not referring to any and every performance that takes place within the precincts of a church; the last thing I would wish to recommend is that abomination, the 'church-concert', where semi-amateur scholars, with little voice, and much gloomy reticence, execute fragments of those devotional works which every musician knows from the back covers of popular editions of the classics.

Ordinary concert performances are free from ecclesiastical restrictions, but instead, innumerable frivolous causes exclude even more works. The taboos of the concert hall hamper the freedom of the composer more than ritual exigencies ever did. The settled repertory of concerts could not be smaller than it has become under the narrow conditions of commercial necessity. People who know the ins and outs of professional procedure taunt the hopeful artist with his pathetic ignorance of 'hard facts'; indeed, few things make the lame duck of an idealist look more like Oscar Wilde in the witness-box, facing the inexorable Carson. He may be sure of his ideals, but he knows too well how reference to them will be received.

He knows how eagerly applauded is every appeal to

---

[1] History has preserved this *nom de guerre* of the 'battle-scarred, irresistible wench', as an eyewitness described her.

'common sense'. If he speaks lightly of 'commercialism' he will soon be told that reasonable compliance with its demands implies no inferiority, how eminently respectable it really is, and how the pride-swollen artist had better pocket his presumptions and admit the virtuousness of deference to commercial principles. How can the poor believer in his artistic mission hope to dispose of the irrelevancies on which he is usually tripped up, when he knows that a frank declaration of his ideals is bound to provoke derisive laughter. The artist who has preserved his early hopes, comes to conceal his affections, for fear of being grinned at, but he knows that artistic respectability demands more than the qualities that guarantee material success.

The weaknesses of the artistic temperament are easily condemned, but if an intelligent man sacrifices the comforts of existence to an unprofitable occupation it does not follow that he is mistaken in his devotion. Let us assume that the believers in art as an industry share at heart the ambitions of the less practical-minded. Both will pay their tribute to claims for music to be reverently presented. But artists cannot only play and sing to each other. There is a public to be reckoned with as well. Can that public have good taste, or any taste at all? Some people have such an awed confidence in the ultimate sanity of this taste that they are content to let public demand dictate the artistic supply. Supply and demand are supposed to be mathematically related; economists, in fact, speak of natural laws. Really it is largely a matter of anticipated sales according to the effects of advertisement. Only, when we touch the subject of economic laws we find ourselves caught in a vicious circle. Invariably we encounter *a posteriori* argument derived from *a priori* assumptions. When public taste is supposed to be on a low level, the type and quality of articles offered at once reflect it. We are invited to admit that the people who organize concerts may be trusted to know their business. But there does not seem much reason to believe in the disinterestedness and the spiritual chastity of dealers in music. When a man has something to sell, we naturally feel uncomfortable when he starts talking about artistic motives. If I try art plus business I am told it won't do because there is too much art in it, but when the other fellow does it I must respect him because there is so much art in it. And vice versa. It makes one blink. Yet, with unexpected indignation, the world boggled at the sale of indulgences even when they helped to build nothing less than St. Peter's of Rome, instead of a Thames valley residence for a concert agent.

One of the striking consequences of the situation is that out of a vast literature, we get to hear only an infinitesimal fraction. The rest remains unknown. If a performer speculatively announces an unfamiliar composition, he will interest, apart from his personal supporters, a few adventurous spirits, and perhaps a couple of musicians who are curious to hear at last some work they have long known by name. Before the promoter can expect an audience of any size, he must convert hesitating patrons with favourable reports of an earlier performance. But the authors of such reports are, without any particular fault of their own, probably as ignorant of the work as every one else. The effect of reports written after a single hearing of an unfamiliar work is as questionable as the reports themselves are bound to be, and anyhow, few concert-givers can afford to repeat the experiment. Probably it would only confirm the opinion that there is no drawing-power in neglected works. The exploitation of established favourites, on the other hand, may be considered perpetually profitable. This is simply another manifestation of the historical superstitions which the guileless believer in musical appearances unwittingly upholds. It does look as if public favour, as measured by frequency of performance, is a criterion of merit—the aesthetic sieve which separates the wheat from the chaff. The public are given to understand that they dispense ultimate justice, and the assertion is too flattering to be rejected. Who would not feel pleased to be invested with the semi-divine attributes of Posterity? But when contemporary individual opinion refers works to this terrible tribunal, it has to be very unsophisticated, or otherwise mighty sure of itself, since it appeals to a judge who has beforehand been declared infallible. Hardly any one would be naturally fatuous enough to accept such an enormity, but the personal responsibility is continually shifted to 'the others' so that one may feel the collective satisfaction without immediate misgivings. One intelligent man will admittedly achieve more than a hundred ignorant ones, although old-wives' wisdom informs us that there is safety in numbers. A century will do what a year cannot; five men together can lift a weight that is too heavy for every one of them. Cannot, then, five hundred men know what not one singly learnt, and cannot the next generation be trusted to understand things that have baffled an earlier one? The belief is silly enough to last.

III

We speak of the ravages to the works of human hands by time, and extend the conception to spiritual products, as if the wind and the rain, who are Time's chief condottieri, had power over these also. Time has not dealt kindly with Blank's symphony, we say, as if the stuff were crumbling here and there, and the water coming through the second theme. Having been taught that disrespect will call retribution on our heads, we rarely dare demur when the consensus of opinion of Time and Public Taste have refused to pass a work. We are told that innumerable works are reduced to a paper existence for their own sins. Had they only been better, they would have received the reward of posthumous popularity. If they are never performed it serves them right! The frightening imbecility of this doctrine is kept evergreen, but the truth at the bottom of the well that waters it is that no one knows the unperformed works, not even those that everybody talks and writes about. Music differs from the other arts in so far as the unperformed work remains unknown, while unknown works are not performed.

A student of literature who knows nothing of Diderot or Bacon would be considered an astounding animal, but a musician who knows not a note of Leonardo Leo or Donizetti is an everyday apparition. He is not entirely blameworthy, he is pathetically impotent, for he can know works outside the current repertoire only from study of the scores. He may say, for all one knows he may even believe, that he can read music as he reads books, but very few, even thoroughly trained musicians, really know a work that they have not heard. Beethoven could say that he knew Schubert's songs, although he only gave them a glance on his deathbed (when he said 'Ja, in diesem Schubert steckt die göttliche Funke'). We might even bring ourselves to believe that Wagner had good grounds for his strictures on Berlioz's 'Faust', although it is strange that after his study of the score he was not sure whether it was a symphony or an opera. At the time when Wagner wrote about the work, it had not been published; it had not even been written. That Wagner was a liar is neither here nor there; his technical proficiency is not in doubt. But one must not judge the average musician's capacity by that standard. Very few musicians know a single note of many 'historically significant' works on which they are ready to give opinions. They are not even aware that they are parrotting standardized pronouncements from text-books, whose authors are frequently as helpless as the readers who trust the accuracy of their information. Students consult works of reference with the simple faith of a tourist in his Baedeker. The tourist is inclined to accept its aesthetic statements, because he has experienced the reliability of the architectural and topographical facts. He automatically takes in some thesis on rococo together with the list of hotel charges, railway fares, time-tables, and opening and closing hours. Most newspaper readers are in the same predicament. They read the news as an unbiassed statement of fact, and when they come to the notice on last night's play or concert, they swallow it as more news. They see 'Gale in Channel' on page 1, and 'Unsatisfactory Play' and 'Superb Violinist' on page 5, and 'Basutos 3¼', and 'Barleycorn first, Oddsfish second' on the last page, and forget that two of the items were just personal opinions.

In the same way the reader of a text-book does not always realize how many of its authoritative assertions are based on nothing more solid than another writer's authoritative assertions—that he sees the last flea, dismounted from the bigger flea which relied on as big a bug as Fétis or Hanslick. The first wiseacre lays down the law on a subject in his Standard Work, and his opinions are repeated in the later compilations with ever diminishing acknowledgement. Works which are no longer performed pass from one book to another until what was simply the description of a work by some contemporary is accepted on trust, like the designations of an atlas. People look up their book and learn that Offenbach is contemptible, that Berlioz had no sense of harmony, or that Moussorgsky was an incompetent amateur.[1] As long as they have a chance of hearing the works for themselves, the harm is not irreparable, but the impression sticks fast when they read similar things about works they never hear. For all the average musician can know they might not exist, and the reference might be a hoax. What then is one to think of learned dissertations on music of which about as much is known as of the bread-and-butter-fly?

It seems reasonable to assume that somewhere in the living chain of historians and antiquarians there must be one musically educated critic who formed his opinions of unperformed works on conscientious study of the scores. But often even these are not obtainable. The reading of scores is

[1] Does not Donald Tovey himself write of the 'good fortune' (*the good fortune*) of Moussorgsky in having a Rimsky-Korsakov to revise and emend his operas? One of our foremost composers has even discovered that Berlioz has been given undue credit for his orchestration, which, according to this undaunted, eminent master of ponderosity, leaves much to be desired.

SEEING IS DOUBTING

not a simple matter. One should accept musicians' assertions concerning their facility in score-reading with extreme caution. The relation between sound and the printed symbol is an exceedingly complex one, and only remotely comparable to that between the printed and the spoken word.

One would not easily find a man of letters ready to claim as much for his understanding of a drama he had not seen as some musicians do for their reading powers. Schumann, who was a better technician than most, tells us (in his rather inane 'What is "being musical" ?') that the Really Musical, on hearing a work, ought to see the complete full score before their 'mental eye', with bar-lines, clefs, key-signatures, transpositions, in short, the whole ghastly paraphernalia one would so gladly forget.

It is impossible to enjoy music if one listens with this ambition. It is equally impossible to read music as one reads a book, the eye rushing down the lines while the mind takes in the meaning. After years of training under rigorous intellectual discipline, the reading of an orchestral score remains a perplexing feat. Students of drama know how difficult it is to visualize a stage production when reading. The mental reconstruction of sound and its effect from the score is even harder. The co-ordination of imaginative and reasoning faculties required would defeat many a mathematician and poet. 'But that is just what we manage', musicians say, and all one can do is to bend one's head in admiration, while making mental reservations. It may be rude to contradict a man when he makes such positive statements, but one retains the right to feel sceptical. What we know of the staggering difficulties, and of the average musician's intellectual powers, makes us suspect that he overstates his accomplishments. The greatest composer has to struggle with the problems of adequate notation; the elements of personal equation and vagaries of performers' interpretations always stand in the way of final precision. If three-fifths of his thought gets as far as the listener's ear it may be con-

THE GIFT OF THE GAB

sidered a miracle of exact communication. Even then he would not dare claim that he could reverse the process. If the eye-to-ear relation could be made reliable beyond ambiguity, he should be able to write down, without hesitation, sound-combinations not yet employed. This is a test by which the most highly gifted fail; they are liable to make gross miscalculations when they try to fix symbols for sounds that have not been heard before.

A man conscious of his genius can, without deliberate modesty, afford to admit his limitations. The less talented one does not know where he touches ultimate boundaries. He pathetically overrates the capacity of creative brains, and makes fabulous claims to technical proficiency. We find that the less endowed the musician, the more fantastic his pretensions. The conductor of an amateur choral society boasts of powers which would astonish Bach. The village teacher confesses with regret his inability to listen to more than four independent parts simultaneously. These people, of course, model themselves on such romantic legends as the one of Mozart writing down the 'Miserere' after a single hearing. They feel they ought to do as much. What really happened seems to be that Mozart's father put him through a special training, took him to several performances, after which, by concentrated application, Mozart produced a not entirely accurate score. (The reported excuse that the singers gave a traditional rendering, and that Mozart's notation was *much nearer the original*, is the real mystery about the affair.)

If students can read scores, they still have to find them. Printing or even reprinting a score is not a thing a publisher lightly undertakes. Music is not so much published for the expected sale of printed copies as to produce material for performances at a reasonable price.[1] The photographic

---

[1] In Mozart's time the copyist was the man who could amass a little fortune, and he did not forget it. This explains a thing which has puzzled some people, i.e. that with the advent of copyright laws the successful publishers proved to be erstwhile copyists! They were simply the men who knew, and kept the ends of the strings and the ropes in their hands!

process has greatly increased the number of miniature scores. Still, they are mostly used for the study of details and for critical quotation, not for the sheer pleasure of reading. If there were a considerable reading public music publishers would work on the same lines as book publishers.

If this does not happen it is because there is no market to speak of. How many musical bibliophiles does one meet? The most abominable type and the vilest paper appear acceptable to most musicians. Professional players use the most repulsive rags. No respectable book-collector would tolerate on his shelves anything like the stuff turned out by some of the greatest firms of music publishers. Several editions have, for instance, letterpress in three languages, in parallel columns, and other barbaric economical devices that in books would be abhorrent to the meanest pedlar. Crowded pages, margins the width of a nit's toe-nail, lunatic spacing, the vilest and ugliest abbreviations—all the blackest of typographical sins are virtually the rule. If there were an important body of readers of music we should see library sets on good paper, in clear, simple type, and composer's-text reprints undefiled by editors' itching fingers—in short, the good things which the bookman expects as a matter of fact. At present, music that conforms to these requirements exists only as a curiosity.

The public of reading musicians is microscopic, although they talk a great deal about it.

One does not deny that they look at the scores with honest application. A conductor has to do that, but he need not therefore pretend that he mentally hears the music. He is content with the fair degree of orientation which careful study of the design and the indications ensures. Afterwards, when his orchestra plays the music, he will be able to give the necessary guidance. He does not know the score as if he had heard it. For the popularly admired feat of conducting without a score, little more is required than the memory and the penetration which suffice for a performance at the pianola.

THE MASTER'S EYE

A capable musician should be able to improvise some sort of piano version of an orchestral score. This gives no final proof of the reliability of his inner ear, but it shows his grasp of the notes. Few musicians can do it satisfactorily, and one knows pretty well what to think of the non-executant who says he could do it better.

In the changing phases of our contemplation of the tree of experience, we see its branches alternatively as cause and as effect. Every one can interpret the relations with so many dialectic twists that an old question may be discussed for centuries with the perpetual illusion that new light is thrown on it. When we call a whale big, the sun a long way off, and a thousand years a long time, it is understood that this is measuring by our earthly standard. Only in this way can we agree on contestable matters without perpetually chasing the elusive 'bottom' which debaters invariably challenge each other to 'get at'.

When we touch the imponderables, we hide simple thoughts behind mouth-organ terms. Abstract, concrete, organic, inorganic, positive, negative. But so far from being warned by the sterility of the arguments that call for them, we apply them to facts of existence which we might approach with reasonable sense. We speak of an old rat, an old empire, and an old theme, of a white ant, a white race, and a white conscience, without blushing as often as we ought to. The habit leads to crooked analogies. We have become so inured to this allusive terminology that to our shame we understand the monstrous consistency of, for instance, Professor Pfitzner. He tells us how and where music was born, speaks of its toothless and clumsy infancy, of its finding its legs, childish stammering, school years, manhood, acquisition of coherent speech, and so on, through many pompously silly pages. With persistence, an author can hypnotize people into the acceptance of his similes. We forget to watch for the moment when he gets off the rails of exact parallelism. We have been told so authoritatively that music attained maturity about a hundred years ago that we have only begun to question it.

Goethe has put the case against metaphorical reading of history succinctly when to the Famulus':

> Zu schauen wie vor uns ein weiser Mann gedacht,
> Und wie wir's dann zuletzt so herrlich weit gebracht.

Faust replies,

> Mein Freund, die Zeiten der Vergangenheit
> Sind wie ein Buch mit sieben Siegeln.
> Was Ihr den Geist der Zeiten heisst,
> Das ist im Grund der Herren eigner Geist,
> In dem die Zeiten sich bespiegeln.

Where the history of man and of nations errs, that of the arts becomes positively ludicrous. The anthropomorphic attitude is remarkable for the ingenuousness of its distinctions. What to one generation appears clumsy and inaccurate, is as likely to be aesthetically right as what another generation substitutes in its new conviction that an unassailable norm has been obtained at last.

In historical criticism of music, we come across imbecilities before which the worst of histories of plastic art pales into reasonableness. We are told of a time when great composers were helplessly groping along paths that any little fiddler to-day is supposed to tread blindfold with assurance, and that modern musicians have developed a sense of harmony which eminent composers of past ages lacked. But can one believe that composers wrote consecutive fourths and fifths because their ears were not ripe for thirds and sixths? It seems more rational to assume that they wrote what they considered right for what they had to say, exactly as a competent composer would now. We have discovered in the abodes of cavemen paintings which no R.A. would presume to surpass.

When musicians sigh, with resigned patience, 'If only Monteverdi had had Wagner's technique', or, 'If only Beethoven had had chromatic brass . . . Mozart an adequate librettist', it is as if one were invited to deplore that Queen Elizabeth could not shop at Woolworth's. What these regretters of past disabilities forget is that if Leonidas had had machine-guns, the other side would have had them too.

IV

When we survey the picture drawn by the Pfitzners, we gather that Music, emerging unaccountably from the mist of the Middle Ages, went through a brief process of refinement in Italy, to be further entrusted to German hands, when Bach, Haydn, Mozart, and Beethoven moulded it into a medium good enough for Wagner's unprecedented genius. A rapid decadence since that glorious reign justifies the fear that, after a few more perversities of the purulent Ultra-Moderns, we may see music perish by spontaneous combustion, unless the last latest-composer snuffs it out before. Such ideas naturally incite to ribaldry; only that is not enough. They want serious watching, lest they should be thoughtlessly accepted on the strength of constant repetition. We have little in the way of reasonable marshalling of facts to oppose. While we know that music does not develop *in vacuo*, about all we can honestly say is that we may observe that it develops as one composer succeeds another, and that this development varies with the personality and the individual talent of every successive one. It is not subject to natural forces; it has no ebb and flow. It has no being apart from the thought of which it is the expression; its changing forms reflect the adventures of the human spirit.

None the less, we are often informed that the particular merit of a composition is that it was written fifty years ago. From this one would have to conclude that music, unaided, marches forward, while some composers lag behind, and others go so fast as to overtake it. When we say that Berlioz anticipated the development of music by half a century it really means that he had so original and logical a mind that it took musicians these many years to appreciate his music and

CHOOSING THE WRONG MOMENT

learn its lessons. In other words, they are only beginning to imitate him now. When the epigoni start polishing and smoothing, filing away rough edges and decorating surfaces, they are not 'perfecting the form'. All they do is to repeat in a finicking manner what has already been finally done. The form of a Beethoven movement is not an 'improvement' of that of Mozart. Symphony composers after Beethoven, from Mendelssohn to Mahler, are not the harbingers of final perfection, growing flowers on the plot Beethoven had laid out. Every original mind is a cosmos in itself. The new beauty it produces remains dissolved in the whole of humanity's spiritual experience when an individual name has been forgotten. But the inspiration which one man, by the radiation of his own incandescence, kindles in humbler souls, persists as the source of the modest works which build general tradition.

An Adam de la Hale, Dufay, or Orlando Lassus wrote, with perfect craftsmanship, music which surpassed Music as it was conceived by his contemporaries. The phenomenon repeats itself in every generation. Compassionate aesthetics have even supplied a euphemism for this irregularity: such composers are said to have been born before their time. We must conclude that all their contemporaries were behind it. But creative artists, even composers, do not really commit the mistake of the scowling foetuses suspended in rectified spirits because they entered the world before it was ready for them. For every composer, however disturbing his originality, there is a potential public. The essential difficulty is for them to meet. No gifted composer has been wholly bound by temporary convention. He writes as he must, style or no style. This may turn out to be his misfortune or otherwise. The public, although without precise notions on the subject *per se*, love or hate personality wholeheartedly, and the devil of it is that there is no telling which they will do next.

If Haydn was accepted it was not because he lacked originality; he had quite enough. It was just his good luck. He might also have been rejected during his lifetime, as he is

WHAT ANCESTORS DON'T KNOW

by many people now. He often writes like older composers. There are passages in his work which might come from Arcadelt or Dunstable. There are others which now sound to us much bolder than anything Beethoven ever risked. The whole point is that his particular thought, in the search for an appropriate idiom, accepted suitable elements of musical speech, and added to them when they did not suffice. The differences between his music and that of earlier composers are irrelevant; the ones that might be interesting are those between his earlier and later manner.

Arnold Schönberg, with his faith in coherent progress, evidently feels generous when he tells us, in his *Harmonielehre*, that 'we are not the first who think!' But he does not seem to believe that the earlier thinkers, whom he approves somewhat patronizingly, thought quite as much as we do. He is obviously of the opinion that Lassus or Martini could not have known what Schönberg knows. They had not heard 'Tristan' and 'Parsifal'. That the older composers had a different goal does not apparently occur to him. He believes they could not find a path which Wagner was to hew through the rocks. This thought rests on a false analogy. Leonardo da Vinci would have constructed a practical aeroplane if he had known the petrol motor, and one could hardly expect of even him that he should have gone through the whole sequence of discoveries that led to its invention. Similar limitations, however, do not apply to artistic invention; there is no reason why a painter of Leonardo's time should not have painted like Cézanne. Very probably some one did. Pisanello and El Greco were only some of the artists left for us to rediscover. After centuries of supercilious scoffing we take alchemists and astrologers seriously once more. I am not referring to fashionable faddism, but to the thoughtful interest of competent scientists.

When Bernard Shaw, following in Butler's footsteps, became flippant about germs and their clinical habits, he was not the pioneer which the intelligentsia saw in him. In scientific circles his unorthodox views had long been a commonplace.

Since Ste Beuve and Taine, serious critics of the Fine Arts aspire to the dignity of scientific workers. They think in terms of Evolution and Positivism, and such portentous orientations as remove their writings farthest from those of the mere Janins. They despise the methods which via medieval scholasticism were derived from a classical philosophy that rejected empiricism for cosmic speculation.

Many an author reacts to the slavery of his concert-reporting by improving on Aristoteles and Plato. He reviles the addle-pated ignorants who, disregarding the imposing march of events, would rely on artistic instinct. According to current belief such fellows must be egotists who, in their solitarian conceit, cannot leave our methodical cooks undisturbed at their system-broth.

Scientific investigation has not succeeded in bringing us any nearer to the unambiguous understanding of a work of art. The man with the greatest talent will produce the best works in spite of all theories, including his own. This holds good for the critic as for the composer and the composer-critic. No one has devised a touchstone by which we can do more than distinguish with a nominal margin of error between genius and mediocrity.

When we examine the parallel threads of the tissue of historical observation in cross-section, we find more or less the same pattern with slight variations of scale. It is when we look along the bundles of threads that they seem to converge, just as the surface design looks simpler from a distance. One consequence of this delusion is the belief in a patriarchal golden age. If we had a time-microscope we should probably find the distant picture very similar to the one that surrounds us in our day. In the same way, a section at any spot of 'horizontal polyphony' reveals harmonic relationships, and here also we find a persistent regularity. Superficial variations of fashion disappear under the levelling majesty of a few universal elements. What at first seemed an infinite variety consists of a few transpositions of unchanging types. Musical theorists become embarrassed when dealing with such simple facts. They seek escape in sententious complexity to hide their despair. Teachers of harmony speak of an immense number of chords with the same bigoted awe and futile exactitude that physicians apply to the classified forms of disease. In both cases we find a pitiful conscientiousness in the ordering of things that have no ascertainable existence; but the case of harmony is demonstrably the worst. The harmony text-book classifications read like a village-idiot zoology which distinguishes fishes that eat and fishes that are eaten, or short-horn cattle and such as are kept in temples. 'The beaver beats the water with its tail', but, on the other hand, 'the salmon tastes excellent with cucumber'. Such are the labels put on a number of coloristic units that grows as editions follow each other. The theoretical root of a chord is inalterable, therefore we are expected to recognize its identity in every inversion, independent of instrumental colour.

Few scientific systems would survive such latitude. We know little about the physical phenomenon called sound. Where the authentic scientist in his laboratory appears handicapped by the absence of acceptable postulates, we can understand what is to be expected of the technically untrained who undertake similar investigations. Especially when they wish to combine them with aesthetics. Most of them are incapacitated from the word go. Yet they are sufficiently ambitious to be constantly wavering between what they consider scientific respectability and what they feel to be their duties as musicians. The science of the musical research worker has a Looking-Glass complexion. Romantic musings and fabulous mathematics inspire it in turn, and we meet mechanical section of spiritual aspects as often as sentimental interpretation of figures. If we grant that a D major chord can elate our spirits, and a D minor chord depress them, can we further believe that this effect varies with pitch? One major and one minor third, superimposed, are, we learn, 'majestic', or 'heroic', in the key of C; but transpose them a tone up, and they become 'gay, if somewhat common'. The corresponding minor chords are 'dark and gritty', or 'tragic and slightly ascetic'. When we rise another step to E, we find the major 'brilliant and noble', but with the lowered third it is 'decidedly vulgar and ranting'. Readers of textbooks know what a diverting variety of these descriptions there is to choose from. The more extravagant the nomenclature, the higher will be found the author's prestige.

When examining historical disquisitions we find frequent evidence of similarly preposterous assumptions. The difference of pitch is replaced by the difference of period, and something done in 1500 sends an author into ecstasies, whereas the same perpetrated in 1900 fills him with disgust. This is again largely the consequence of the study of the printed note as opposed to the hearing of the sounding one. As for the sharp observer the columns of to-day's newspapers carry a more significant message than the specialists' legends on past happenings, so contemporary music that we know from frequent performance leads us nearer the core than the fallacious erudition which constitutes the science handed down to us.

Nearly all the writers that for short we call sources[1] have been seduced by their passion for regular shapes to arrange recorded facts. On the other hand, if one rejects the official accounts, one cannot hope to retain the respect of the cultured public, with its veneration for scientific standing.

Students, unfortunately, are taught from the tenderest age to honour the pronouncements of so many accepted authors that their opinions become prejudiced before they have had a chance to acquire individuality. The insistent authority with which orthodox critical procedures are impressed on them

---

[1] Documents an author is supposed to know at first hand; but in nine cases out of ten the successive writers take their consultation by the preceding one for granted, without 'looking them up'.

shields them against early discovery of personal bias in their exponents.

However much we may detest iconoclasm in early youth or advanced age, we must pass through a stage when we begin to distrust the reliability of venerable sources. We have a hard time after we discover their fallibility, and before we recognize that we come to no greater harm when, in doubt, we rely on our own judgement, even if we have to trust to intuition. Once we have started daring, we find that we walk pleasantly in our new freedom. It is true that we must acquire a measure of hypocrisy if we wish to preserve the dignity of ornate bibliography for our writings. An author with the requisite sense of academic exigencies feels he must produce himself cloaked in a mantle of references, very much as a Councillor appears at Court spangled with orders and decorations. But he is a more desirable companion when he is not so fully dressed.

Year in, year out, there appear new writings on music of which we have no reliable record. There is a peculiar prestige attached to occupation with Art's early manifestations. Yet our instinct and our experience tell us that the one thing we really know is that the oldest music conveyed human emotion in the same way that familiar modern works do. Contemporary references leave no doubt on this point. When we read these, we cannot tell whether we should be disappointed if we heard the works that inspired the old authors' dithyrambs, but even though their taste might have been at fault, the feelings they describe are immediately recognizable. It is a very different matter, however, when we come to ecstatic appraisements of the chaste beauties of Greek music, by a Bellerman and his followers, none of whom, for obvious reasons, could ever have heard a note of it.

Where manuscripts of antique music are procurable, we are by no means sure what they signify. The interpretation of obsolete notations varies. Many plausible decipherings are offered, and one unavoidably suspects that our antiquarians have never successfully resuscitated the actual products that roused enthusiasm in the balsamed bodies preserved side by side with them in our museums. There is a separate danger in this department of science which is often overlooked. The expert faced with a baffling document or inscription, is fascinated by the hope that it may prove related to his particular interest, whereas he fails to attribute as much to material already appropriated by other specialists. When Courbet received an illegible letter from a patron, he asked his chemist to decipher it, for chemists have to be experts at reading the unreadable. The answer was a bottle, to be shaken, etc., after meals.

A similar *quid pro quo* must occur often with palimpsests. The specialist is from all sides driven to one-sidedness. If only he would keep to the comic monstrosities, like Greek or Chinese music! Scholars who take up music almost invariably sink to a level of childishness that would seem unbelievable in any other form of scientific investigation.[1] One of their characteristic assumptions is that old music is as clumsy as its appearance on paper in the original notation. Where so few musicians read between the lines of contemporary music, it is to be expected that the musical theorist (who, usually, is a theoretical musician) will be more helpless than ever when he is confronted with the unfamiliar notation of little-known works.

One wonders what old composers would think of their scores after they have been through the hands of modern editors. We seldom know how much was implied in earlier graphic systems, and probably the alleged angularity and clumsiness of much old music is the reflection of editorial pedantry. This, in turn, accounts for the self-conscious solemnity with which players approach such music. We get thus a distorted picture altogether. There is as much reason to believe that all the

---

[1] Readers may be referred to easily accessible examples of the almost incredible silliness of which musical authors are capable. For a start they should look up the entry 'Rosalia' in *Grove's Dictionary*, or the article on 'Leitmotiv' in the *Encyclopaedia Britannica*.

composers of a certain period were awkward and stiff-jointed as that all Greeks were red-haired, old Egyptians had two left or two right big toes, and that Assyrian squires went a-lion-hunting in their night-shirts.

When we read yellowed records of the emotions roused by music which we only know as somewhat stilted and solemnly sad tunes, we marvel how any sensitive spirit could have been so moved. The sensible conclusion is that what is presented to us is a libel, resulting from the editors' systematized ignorance.[1]

An American professor of physics, recently, while extolling the enlightenment music receives from scientific collaboration, innocently exposed one of the processes of historical music-tasting. Dealing with the black-legged fact that the cunningly wrought polyphony of 'Sumer is i-cumen in' had 'i-cumen in' at a time when, according to theory, it simply couldn't have, he tells us what on similar occasions other professors had established, viz. that it was only 'an accident'. One is forced to the diagnosis that occupation with musical research exercises a baleful influence on the intelligence.[2] Could one imagine a professor of physics telling us that if light rays were found to pass around an intervening object,[3] it must be an accident? If the fact could not be denied any more than the winsome old canon, he would be expected to modify his first hypothesis accordingly.

In the field of music research authors, with almost disarming insouciance, dismiss unsettling facts as irrelevant, or otherwise they disregard them. If the expert thus abuses a prestige that may have been, on the whole, earned by earnest labour, what hope can there be for the majority of his readers to free themselves from the time-honoured prejudices? If one con-

[1] Gevaert quotes the Flemish 'Kapteyntjen der Grillen' (Il Capitano Grillo), a roaringly jolly tune which, read by the light of our own notation, seems a most dismal dirge.

[2] Cf. footnote on p. 214; I withhold the name only for fear of securing him perhaps another reader. There are more than enough fatuous productions for any student's entertainment.

[3] Einstein; subsequently confirmed by experiment.

sults a text-book on algebra or geology, one does not apprehend deliberate misdirection. Should an author say (to borrow from Fowler's pungent illustration): 'My dear fellow, it stands to reason that if A plus B equals C, then A squared plus B squared must equal C squared', one would know what to think of him. But when the musical historian says 'It stands to reason', there seems to be a general conspiracy to listen to him with trusting respect. And this although the sources we have to consult are tainted to an extent that would not be tolerated in any other subject. But while one may approach them only with strict precaution, one cannot discard them. The process of investigation is too complicated, as every one knows who has attempted independent research. The *ex cathedra* tone which, in spite of this, most works of reference adopt, convinces the majority of readers. Consequently, musicians, not to mention 'general readers', come to believe that they hardly lose if they never hear a note of ninety composers out of every hundred, and that time and tide have already determined the relative value of the rest. How is one to discover, then, if unperformed composers are greater than the popular men, or if the latters' unperformed works are greater than their popular ones?

Books and teachers tell the student that he need not worry about the music that has not 'lasted'. While 'antique' music is absorbingly interesting, Dufay and Binchois are deservedly shelved museum pieces, and while middle Beethoven is great Beethoven, in his last years he suffered too much from his abdomen to use with the old discernment the little hearing he had left, and his odd-numbered symphonies are his best. On the other hand, composers after him no longer soared to the sublime moral heights that were the natural abode of Beethoven's spirit. Brahms is the anointed heir of the great tradition, and, in spite of denigration, Wagner's star is steadily climbing, as is that of Bach (be it only at the London Promenade Concerts).

Now, where in any field of human activity are things as

simple as all that, so conveniently generalized and summarized? Can we possibly believe that with music it is always such plain sailing? Unfortunately, few people happen to ask themselves whether by any chance all this could be incorrect. One is reminded of King James and the Royal Society. He desired an explanation of the curious circumstance that when a fish is dropped into a pail of water it does not increase the weight. Various thinkers advanced ingenious theories, but it transpired that no one had made a preliminary test. In their zeal to please the august questioner the professors fulfilled his cynical hopes, and for once rose to the heights on which musical theorists habitually move.

Still, it is easy enough to procure a pail of water and a fish, but a correct score, a capable orchestra, and an intelligent conductor are not so soon collected. For every masterpiece more or less regularly performed, there are numerous ones which we never hear, and the scores of which few musicians have seen. All the same, they will talk about them and write about them, and thus spread false conceptions.

The Catholic Church, despite the inevitable circumscription of its interest, escapes most of the prejudices which hamper other institutions. Its traditions are too old and too continuous to permit lasting neglect of the masters of liturgical composition. But private patrons of music, however generous, are commonly subject to the caprices of individual tastes. They can only know one corner of that subdivision of the literature for which their resources are adequate, and even in this little circle they are restricted by a hundred circumstances of place and time and information. One occasionally hears the Church criticized for its restrained support of contemporary production. It may seem to proceed with undue caution in its acceptance of modern works. Ecclesiastical authorities must, somehow, be convinced of a composer's absolute artistic integrity before they dare admit his idiom if it noticeably differs from that of the acknowledged masters. One could, judging on purely aesthetic grounds, easily be unjust towards this diffidence. It should be remembered how slowly the tradition moves when the number of writers is so relatively small as it has become since the Reformation banned all music, or tolerated only that remotely connected with composition as a form of emotional communication.

Of this diminishing number, only a few again have preserved the faith that moulded conception to the style of undoubted models. This does not mean that, before, it was sufficient to copy externalities; most of us have met the slightly cracked enthusiasts who play 'with the bow of Tartini', or the lame idealist who writes exactly like Palestrina, and yet again, not quite. Without talent, no amount of conviction and faith will achieve much. But where the talent is sufficient it still needs the faith if a composer is to write music which moves us with him in the direction of mystical fervour and surrender that provides for its existence.

V

The Church has prescribed for its musical advisers definite principles to guide them in the selection of modern work, which in practice amount to a test of faith. No pretension to musical criticism contributes to their formulation. The better perhaps do they constitute a fairly reliable criterion, certainly one by which the manufacturers of sham-religious stuff can be detected. Human fallibility enters into the application, or rather, its possible omission, but this hardly touches the principle.

It is only rational if the Church insists on adherence to the tradition of the masters. One could not hope to encounter better founded precepts than there where aesthetic and spiritual motives have become completely identified. If the Church treads warily in its adoption of modern liturgical compositions, it is not because it holds, as do some disgruntled secular critics, that musically speaking the world is going to the augmented fourth. It does not entertain the shifting fears of hoary-head-shaking people who have long seen artistic dissolution coming on, one day in the guise of a forbidden interval or progression, next disguised as the organ-tuner's 'wolf', and then again as a composer. Whether in this most dangerous of incarnations he threatens us with whole tones or five tones or twelve, it is always Luther's 'alt bös' Feint'. The Diabolus in Musica gives no peace to virtuous musicians.

The Church's fears are founded on different grounds. It does not aspire to the ludicrous authority of the aesthetic policeman who stands in the middle of artistic traffic making exasperated gestures that no one notices, and who writes denunciatory reports to an imaginary executive, like a child posting letters to Santa Claus.

The Church simply insists that certain formal usages shall be maintained. This does not endanger the composer's prerogatives, or the free expression of original ideas. If anything, this unequivocal insistence on formal decencies is a help to him. For once he finds himself guided by venerable conventions that assist him in his search for dependable rules which our theories of musical composition notoriously fail to provide.

Only mediocrities, whose obstinate striving after originality seeks to hide weakness of native talent, need fear the influence of a tradition moulded by triumphant achievement. A composer of pronounced individuality feels no embarrassment at restrictions evolved by a process of selection which preserves the most impressive features of the rare masterpieces as examples.

Some artists conduct a continual warfare against material conditions that limit their medium, as well as the narrowness of our receptive faculties. They seem to resent the vulgar necessity of legs being fixed at the bottom and the poll at the other end—always the dull sameness to which emperor and crossing-sweeper, Helen of Troy and the old charwoman, submit with contemptible bourgeois resignation. Unlike the averagely sane artist, who is thankful for the common elements which constitute his instrument, and allow him to render his meaning with a minimum of wasted effort, the dissatisfied composer's ambition usually makes him yearn for a grammar, a vocabulary, and a syntax exclusively his own. His apparent ideal is that, at the risk of being obscure (this, of course, places him in the company of the Great Misunderstood —though misunderstood, perhaps, for other reasons), he should never be obliged to make use of motives, melismas, or chords that can be found in other composers' works. In fairness it ought to be remembered that almost the entire musical public shares responsibility for this crazy ambition. If they condemn a composer for this slavery to greed they denounce one of their own cherished foibles. The composer's spirit demands originality of form as well as of ideas for its realization, but he finds by bitter experience that if these are not actually resented by his public they are regarded with alert suspicion. But, illogically, originality of idiom to the meanest detail is inexorably required of him. The hunting of reminiscences and alleged plagiarisms is a favourite sport of people who pretend to knowledge of music. In this miserable game every unavoidable commonplace is examined for a wrinkle or a pimple that has been seen on some other face. No poet or prose-writer hesitates to say: 'On a dark night', because Dante has already done it, or, 'Ah! this was ale!' because Borrow said so, but should a composer write six consecutive notes of the D major scale, from the third upwards, he is sure to be told that he has robbed Beethoven's Violin Concerto.

Bacon's 'It would be self-contradictory and unsound fancy to believe that things that have never been done could be done except by means which have never yet been tried', does not apply to the bricks of the structure, but to disposition. It does not require a new language to express new thoughts. Originality of ideas lends individual character to common terms. If they appear incomprehensible it is because the idea is not grasped; unless sheer poverty has dictated its own terms for every occasion. This is the predicament of the word-starved scientist who has learned from Humpty-Dumpty that a word should mean what it is meant to mean by him, and no argument, please.

Exact thinkers and clear-headed philosophers have, almost without exception, managed to communicate their ideas in simple and generally accepted language.[1] Unfortunately, clotted verbosity suggests profundity to the unsophisticated mind. When the clear reasoning of deep thought is considered obscure it is because nature hides her secrets from the unworthy, and provides the spiritual plebs with an armour of obtuseness. Without this precaution even more saints and prophets would be burned and crucified than those which the envy and malice of the murderous man-in-the-street singles out as propitiatory victims.

The noisome urge of musicians for ferreting out similarities reappears in the popular notions of style, with their confusion of man and method. Instead of style being understood simply as the best balanced relation between aim and execution, it is looked for in the external likenesses of different composers' works. If they belong to the same century, the average listener imagines that he is coming into contact with the whole of one period, instead of with part of one man. But a composer represents a period only in so far as he resembles the preceding composer who influenced the initial phases of his thought. People who talk about 'Bach and Handel' do so for more reasons than the amenities presented by mnemotechnic coupling of names. Think of Racine and Corneille, Chesterton and Belloc, Goethe and Schiller. This Sally-in-our-alley weakness reveals an elemental craving of the human spirit. Many a musician welcomes the aid to knowledge which such 'amphibiguous' hyphenations provide. He is perpetually struck by the differences between familiar recent works, and the apparent sameness of much old music. If that seems all alike to him,

---

[1] The contrast I find in such technical obscurity and mazed involutions as Schleiermacher's. But all the same, how I wish, myself, I need not say 'Pity my complexity'!

MODE À LA MARIAGE

it must be, he reasons, that the old works stand for their age. Their individualities disappear before the contrast they collectively present with the idiom of his own day. People speak of Wagner and Meyerbeer[1] as opposite poles, but will lump together the work of twenty highly individual masters as 'sixteenth-century music'. Possibly, in another hundred years Wagner and Meyerbeer will be similarly hyphenated as composers of 'nineteenth-century music'. Later historians may in turn find it hard to explain what precisely was the unfathomable cleft between the two, and why it should have been so passionately discussed.

Some authors have already observed that Debussy does not derive from Liszt, that Elgar is not the spiritual child of Brahms; yet many of them complacently speak of 'the' sixteenth-century Italian polyphonists[2] as merely 'the' Southern representatives of the Netherlands School. Possibly the Netherlanders influenced composers in other countries in the same way that German classics influenced minor composers everywhere, but no Italian of genius was indebted to the Netherlanders for more than a few formal principles.

Their contrapuntal technique summed up conventional methods of workmanship that had proved eminently suited to the handling of intricate polyphonic structures. The acquisition of such craftsmanship was part of a complete technical equipment; its neglect denoted, not independence, but a lack of understanding and imagination.

On the other hand, the very manner in which a Palestrina applied their methods marked his originality.

[1] Gevaert still has the courage, at the cross-roads, to describe them as the two great figures of modern dramatic music.

[2] Counterpoint and polyphony are terms used indifferently by musicians with, evidently, the vaguest notions of what either means. The Italian composers of clock-work music were without a doubt imitators of the Netherlanders, but such have existed at all times (including our own with its Neo-Gothics of Chicago, as Busoni called Bernhard Ziehn and Wilhelm Middelschulte). All had this in common, that they could build staggeringly complex musical edifices—on paper. As the notorious canon in 124 parts, or some of the worst Reger, these compositions usually *sound* like one prolonged common chord, or like all the world's five-finger-exercises played together.

THE MATHEMATICS OF EMOTION

The music of classical contrapuntists is frequently as barren and lifeless as the most crabbed and shrivelled stuff of the Netherlanders at their poorest. But the melodies of the early madrigalists, and of Palestrina and Vittoria, are not only entrancingly lovely, they are always full of nervous force, yet supple, and drawn both delicately and firmly. At the same time, while as full-blooded and vibrant with energy as any operatic melody, they combine in threes and fours with perfect naturalness and enhanced effect.

This living polyphony is one of the miracles of human achievement. The schoolman dissects the organic structure, laying bare technical similarities, but there is danger in these anatomical demonstrations. The unformed mind of the pupil acquires a habit of regarding the most sublime emotional utterances as blackboard examples of scholastic counterpoint. This is usually no more than a puzzle, mastery of which enables the dullest mechanical brain to simulate the gestation of creative activity.

The 'strict' contrapuntist, with his double row of figures and his arithmetical juggling with intervals, represents an unchangeable type, whether in the sixteenth or the twentieth century. In the Italian motets and madrigals, however, appears the Latin genius for clean design and lucidity coupled with sensual charm, as unmistakably as in a Raphael painting or in Manzoni's prose. They reveal an art technically and spiritually as accomplished as that of Verdi in 'Falstaff'. It has little in common with the sterile pomposities of the Netherlanders, which display Gothic decadence in all its starched gorgeousness, like the chronicle script of a medieval cleric with its load of fantastic curls and frills.

The old Italians do not represent an isolated apotheosis of polyphony. English Tudor composers, whose style is based on identical principles, achieved a characteristic independence.

The revival of Tudor music provides an instance of the good influence the Church can exercise. It has also drawn attention to the existence of neglected treasures hidden in our libraries.

RENAISSANCE OF THE RENAISSANCE

Generations of writers have perfunctorily dealt with the early English composers. A German critic's work on keyboard music contains the significant chapter-heading: 'Alt-England, Ein Märchen'. The author thinks it is so strange, in view of the notorious nothingness of English composers, that there was once a time when their music counted, that he calls it a fairy-tale. His whimsical allusion tells its own tale better than the fairies could.

When the fairy-tale became tangible fact once more, it was at once evident how many respected critics had been as ignorant of the actual music as the public that had been constrained to turn to them for information. Here were works which for years had been 'of historical interest' only, and which proved astonishingly alive. Far more alive than many of the popular works of celebrated moderns on which musical authors had been doting.

The rediscovery and production of old English masterpieces of religious music were a more important event than the appearance of Richard Strauss's operas, or Stravinsky's ballets, which about that time kept the musical world in a state of hysterical ferment. While the majority of musicians were staring themselves blind on the eccentricities of nihilist composers and the Russian Punch-and-Judy show, Sir Richard Terry, by his discerning initiative and his indefatigable labours with the Westminster Cathedral Choir, contributed more to the musical renaissance in England than all the folklore-cum-ancient-modes composers and the French-cum-Russian fanatics together.

Our prayers are for those scholars who claim the faculty of translating the dead note into the quick sound. We hope they will let us benefit by the unbounded knowledge that must be at their command. They have Terry's example.

Remains the question whether they are likely to find a helpful instrument to realize their intentions. Without adequate performances knowledge is confined to those few that conquer knowledge whatever the obstacles. If they work without such effective help there is all the more reason for them to insist on the importance of works which the general public can at best know by name.

The people who want to know still more about Wagner, Strauss, and Stravinsky need no encouragement. There is a sufficiently voluminous literature available.

Our adolescent tone-poets have few such opportunities of hearing music performed for a worthy purpose in ideal surroundings as the Church offers. Yet they need nothing so much as its example of creative discipline. The masters who wrote for the liturgy kept a coherent view of spiritual values while having constantly to reckon with material demands of texture, dimensions, and exact duration of the constituent sections. The elasticity their idiom preserved under the incessant imposition of these several necessities constitutes a very valuable lesson.

We have become inured, by the immature pretensions of ever more youthful artists, to the preposterousness of their dictum that a man of talent needs no law beyond his sovereign right to do as he likes. We therefore forget sometimes to examine the changing prerogatives claimed on this account. One of the consequences of such cheaply-bought freedom has been the monstrous growth of every element of the musical organism in turn, as new claimants advertise the aversions and predilections of the latest fashion.

If for the majority of nineteenth-century innovators this amounted to an obsession with harmony, it was because the rules governing its use were so absurd. No rebellious excesses could be reasonably denounced (even when Insanity was inscribed on the banners), after the exasperating commandments of orthodox practice.

When the harmonic revolution was accomplished, twentieth-century bloods proceeded to the emancipation of rhythm. Here the opportunities for barefaced swindle proved even greater, and were even more relentlessly pursued. But instead of a new variety came a new monotony. The insistent exploitation was carried to a point where the hearer was mesmerized into forgetfulness. From there to conviction was only one step. A subtlety which long ago had been achieved was forgotten for the four-squareness of otherwise good music that intervened. In the intoxication of all-conquering anarchy there arose a strange faith. Every one seemed to overlook that only perfunctory rendering had obscured a much greater refinement which once existed. A more appalling rhythmical imbecility than that of Stravinsky can only be that of Jazz. The principal discovery of these young Rips Van (Louisiana) Winkle appears to be the exciting difference between 2, 3, 4, 5 and 3, 4, 5, 2.

At present level-headed composers are industriously seeking a way out of an impasse into which we were forced by the fiery revolutionaries who caught us on the rebound of our despair at the misgovernment of hopelessly muddled systems. For a time most of us had lost our bearings and we almost believed that negation of the self-evidently nonsensical is bound to produce some sort of sense. Experience demonstrated that, while there may be different kinds of sense, the varieties of nonsense are legion. We now explore old paths and fields with a new interest.

One escape from the chaotic confusion is an orientation which finds fixed points in polyphonic discipline. With this we renounce the chord-block conception of harmony that has been the cause of much musical distortion, and misery, and aesthetic squalor.

The alleged problems of euphony that obsessed theorists solve themselves in well-balanced polyphony.

We must remember, however, to what extent most modern composers are slaves of the keyboard, and the shuffling of timbres necessary before the chord sounded on the piano can be rendered in another medium. The orchestration of most music requires redistribution of the harmonic ingredients. This demands a special skill, and the dexterity of the pianist on one side and the orchestral virtuoso on the other have between them made music what it never ought to have been.

Few ears can distinguish in the welter of colours with enough certainty to detach them from harmonic contrasts. To people who study orchestral works in piano arrangements this is a matter of overwhelming importance. Incidentally, it adds to the atrocious cruelty of the 'black-and-white' test.

On the other hand, no clever instrumentation is quite clever enough to make poor part-writing presentable.

When separate parts have melodic meaning, the individual player makes his strand of sound vibrant with life, and the whole will glow with internal energy and, as the saying is, sound well. Where every chord is an orchestral miniature, the majority of players are most of the time counting bars. Then only lightning reaction to the wrigglings of the conductor induces some musical emotion in the performers. If the conductor is sufficiently voodoo this semi-epileptic trance may even reach the audience, and conceal from them the rottenness of the music, or what is politely described as occasional structural defects and shortcomings.

For a long time musical brains were so filled with the almightiness of harmony that they began hearing it everywhere, as spiritualists see manifestations in everything, and drinkers see alcohol assume bodily shapes that look like Wagnerian or Straussian motives. Some ears are sensitized into a state of susceptibility where they hear implied harmonies in plainsong.

The pioneers of this systematized perversity proposed to demand aesthetic citizenship for the harmony that escapes notation. The silent 'grounds' on which all tunes move were to be made preserves.

All this sounds aggressively trite, but that does not alter the fact that few musicians sense the expressive power of 'unsupported' melodic line. To the layman this might seem strange, but probably every unvarnished statement of the realities of the music world would astonish him. Even Wagner held that melody derives its significance from its inherent harmonies, a belief well founded in his practice (and the other way round). He appears incapable of conceiving a melody not definitely composed of 'broken chords'.[1] The associations created by memories of long assimilated tunes are evidently stronger than the reasoning power of musical intelligence, even of one so keen as Wagner's. Rameau stated pontifically: 'La mélodie naît de l'harmonie.' He admitted that it looks at first as if the opposite happened, but he found on reflection that harmony had first to provide the paths for the wanderings of melody.

Many critics who elsewhere display astute judgement question Berlioz's musical sensitivity because he was largely dependent on melodic speech, and in their opinion neglected the extra chances offered by harmonic colouring. But consider the instances where composers tried to emend what they regarded as incomplete utterances of earlier works. Think of the appalling mess some of them have made of the attempted harmonizing of plainsong or of the completion and correction of old music that was supposed to be too bare, too skinny and bony, as to the nineteenth-century mind most music written before the eighteenth century appeared. The barbaric horror of Schumann's piano part to Bach's sonatas for solo violin is characteristic. Schumann presumably was as talented as most editors, but not the most incompetent pedant among them could have committed anything more gruesome.

This strange incapacity to hear melody alone is a significant hiatus in some composers; it is not merely accident when a Schumann or a Brahms, and nearly all those composers that one critic calls neo-classic, another late classic, a third late

---

[1] As his harmonic conceptions deepened, this aspect became diffused by refinement in the increased frequency of seconds that are not 'gliding notes' only. To perceive in this a proof of my argument one need only examine the various ways in which chords of the ninth and eleventh can be 'broken' as compared to triads, and compare the melodies of 'Tristan' with those of 'Tannhäuser' in the light of that revelation. It will incidentally show how a closely related principle yielded characteristically different results at Brahms's hands.

romantic, share this weakness. The music of the self-conscious romantic, as well as of the would-be classic, frequently reveals his contempt for the sensuous charm of sound. It is full of opaque, greasy concord. This is inextricably intertwined with the predilection for 'abstract music', music which makes its best effect on paper. On the paper battlefield it gains its most glorious victories, but in the ear of the hopeful listener it cannot even put a flea, the one thing in which some of the very wild moderns usually succeed.

A pertinent illustration of the relative value of harmonic factors appears in the forms to which polyphony tends. The combination on which they are founded reminds us everywhere of the fact that tonality or key signifies, as in the old modes, not much more than difference of pitch.[1]

The ear trained to refer every note of a melody to the chord that could contain it within the limits of tonality, hears parts moving organum-wise in fourths or fifths as a statement presented twice, in separate keys. The unprejudiced ear, hearing a canon in the fifth at short distance, cannot easily escape a similar impression.

That is how the demands of tonality led to those alterations of melodic design which we know as the 'dux' and the 'comes' of a fugue, prescribing the substitution of fifths and fourths. Once the principle is admitted, this is a perfectly legitimate concession, which, by emphasizing the interdependence of the parts, promotes structural unity. But at the same time, it is one of those dazzling conventions that have so far blinded theorists to the melodic origin of part-writing as to make them taboo parallel fifths on the pretext that these destroyed the independence of parts. In reality it was their extravagant independence within the key system that caused them to be abandoned, except on the few occasions when they were 'unavoidable'. There, academic hypocrisy demands only that, as a concession to etiquette and decorum, they shall be skilfully concealed from the profane. By a refined abuse of

---

[1] Cf. note on page 214 *re* 'Rosalia'.

prestige, German teachers and their emulators all over the world proceeded to sanctify mere expediency by offering simple working methods under the imposing name of Theory and Law, even where originally seemliness alone was involved. The convention of the fig-leaf was transformed into an ethical commandment.

Their dictates were meekly accepted because they originated in a country which had produced composers of genius. But those very composers frequently cared less than a fig for the leaves on which the rules were written. Still, the alleged laws were, demonstrably, to some extent distilled from their practice, and the secret of their academic impropriety was anxiously kept.

When students accepted these rules as universal foundations of musical construction, they mostly overlooked to what extent the idiom from which they were derived was a national one, with all its peculiar limitations. This seems all the more curious when one considers the preoccupation of musicians with racial and national features, and it glaringly exposes the hollowness of their ideas about picturesque 'local colour'. They obviously do not rise above dress-designer's vision of Spanish, Russian, or Scandinavian 'touches'.

The German language was first made into an independent instrument by Luther. The physical and spiritual lineaments of that most estimable, voluble, hearty, voluminous, and bluff Swabian cannot leave us wondering that he should have laid the foundations of an edifice in which a monotonously steady formality became wedded to a certain childish exuberance.

The exasperated anti-fatherlandic outbursts of Goethe, Lessing, Heine, and Nietzsche, to mention but a few, about the semi-barbaric state of mentality manifested in German poetry and prose were anything but gratuitous. The same mentality persisted long in German music. This is only a natural concomitant, for music is the language of choice for the rapturous expression of uncomplicated passions. The Germans' familiarity with their national poetry attuned their ears to the simple metres and close rhymes of its least sophisticated and most popular exponents. Obvious correlatives can be discovered everywhere in typical formulas of German musical idiom. The bulk of German music never reached a stage beyond the rhetorical furies of primitive poetic speech. Its briefly articulated phrases demand a corresponding harmonic substructure, and thus were evolved the pedestrian cadences of academic, 'correct' harmony. Afterwards practitioners desperately strove to find justification in physical phenomena of sound, however slender our knowledge of these. This determination proceeds from a conviction that reference to science lends dignity to theories which otherwise would be too clearly reminiscent of the instructions and prescriptions of Mrs. Beeton. We are asked to see musical perfection in such models on account of the insistently emphasized, irrelevant eminence of a few composers of unsurpassed talent. But while the great name of Mozart is perpetually appealed to, it must have struck most students that standard text-books are distinguished for the paucity of quotation from his works. Beethoven, and afterwards Brahms, have been largely drawn on for the simple reason that in their works it is so much easier to show 'how it is done'. With Mozart this is difficult; he manages to say something completely original by the unaccountable use of commonplaces. The wonder of other German classics, as well, is that they often achieve such freedom and flexibility of line in spite of the severe restrictions imposed by the harmonic scaffolding. It illuminates the German saying that 'in der Beschränkung zeigt sich der Meister'. Only, we must remember that this does not, as vulgar interpretation assumes, mean that restriction is, as such, a praiseworthy manifestation of mastery. The point is that only a master can overcome the implied difficulties. Nothing could be more unreasonable than to flourish such deceptive maxims before youthful eyes, demanding of the immature artist that he should repeat a culminating *tour de force* by which consummate genius crowned its attainments. Yet that is what the propagators of

Leipzig methods would seem to expect. What they really do is to teach tricks that enable the tyro to ape the stylistic mannerisms of a few widely admired composers.

The result has been a continuous stream of dismal epigonic products, for more than a century poured out by mediocrities standardized in the conservatoires.

The few Germans who rejected their methods have been obstinately neglected by theorists. To find favour in their eyes, composers must build on the narrowest symmetry. The popularity of a Hindemith shows once more how people are deceived by a slight modification of old tricks when the juggler appears in a new costume or before a new drop-curtain. Practically all professors of musical Halma are completely stumped when it comes to carrying analysis of a fugue beyond the exposition of theme and companion. One would wish to see an analyst laying bare the inner workings of a song of Schubert, or of large-scale compositions of Liszt or Wagner. Although with Wagner it remains a debatable point whether he proceeds from his musical theme or dances attendance on the text, note by word, there are many fragments whose symphonic construction deserves study. But these compositorial longshoremen let pass, with their telescopes under their arms.

Where original genius evolved a musical structure that is equally convincing whether it employs academic devices or methods which were never systematically taught, one feels humiliated to see fellow humans reject it altogether rather than admit their helplessness. It happens with Mozart, to some extent with Wagner, and most strikingly in the case of Berlioz. If there is a treatise on composition that tackles the structural devices of Berlioz, I have missed it. As far as I know, all writers repeat his observations on orchestral technique. They do not always acknowledge the author; on the contrary, they often make a point of abusing him.

But when it comes to Berlioz's melody, they are at a loss for a word of good sense. One does not expect that any one should reveal the secret of its unique power, but it is remarkable that no one has even attempted to convey some notion of what makes his melodic draughtsmanship different from everything else. It will not do to say that his music is not good enough to call for professorial attention. This condemnation would carry more weight if his critics would anatomically demonstrate his alleged weaknesses or faults of construction, to make them serve as a warning example. How apotheotically our gowned and capped pundits would justify their occupation if they could point an admonitory finger at the weak spot! Instead, we find the distinguished author of the Berlioz article in the *Encyclopaedia Britannica* making a contemptuous reference to Berlioz's wild volubility, explained by the foibles of his race —Berlioz being 'a typical Gascon', which might seem a shrewd blow unless we remember that Berlioz was no Gascon and did not come from Gascogne.[1]

Berlioz's subtlety of construction is beyond the cerebral powers of authors of pedagogic treatises.

Our professors appear as much embarrassed by the methods of a composer to whom musicians with good-natured insolence refer as *Papa* or *old* Haydn. They forget that if Mozart did so occasionally it is no good reason why every one who can scrape a gut, blow on a pipe, or win a few letters behind his name should arrogate to himself the same privilege. Mozart knew more about Haydn than they can ever do. Haydn's methods are too elusive for the academy to unravel. He is usually looked upon as a decent old bird, and quite a pleasant composer. But there are few that so nearly approach the faultless rhythm, the 'Horatian junctura' whose simple perfection precludes discussion. For a parallel to the haunting simplicity, the compelling sweetness of his themes, the superb sweep of his periods, we must go to the work of Vittoria or Bellini, or some of Rossini's best. (Has any one found them mentioned in the usual books of instruction?) Haydn, for all his strength and brilliance and his limpid profundity, is not only practically ignored by teachers; he is one of those masters of whom we read

[1] Cf. 'Busoni'.

and hear constantly, but whose works are not really well known to the majority of musicians. When I speak of his power in long sustained melodic lines I am thinking of some of his totally neglected operas, a few piano sonatas, and other chamber music, not of the oratorios of his last period when his manner appreciably changed.

VI

There was a time when Germans themselves revolted against the tradition that had been their pride. Here again, they were slavishly followed by indefatigable admirers who would sooner take the second-rate from them second-hand than the best coming from other countries. When they deliberately abandoned traditional forms they found it impossible to replace them by others.

Instead came the anguishing dream forms that derive from structural suggestions conveyed by the sausage and the centipede, the jellyfish and the bandworm. Richard Strauss, representative of the last word in specifically German technique, looks a dolt and a clodhopper beside Haydn. His organized harmonic ruthlessness and the obtrusive vitality of his metre cannot make up for his deadly inability to attain balance between melodic periods and polyphonic accents. His so-called counterpoint is so much finery and no woman to wear it. That is because his melodic invention is like most people's musical memory. It is all beginning and no end. He sets out with tremendous assurance, to become rapidly diffuse and wind up in a state of mollusc indecision. He seems to be striving to repair a flaccidity of which the critical artist in him is aware, by storing up the progressively weakening extensions of his melody with all the props he finds in his vast harmonic arsenal. He is like a father who requisitions the whole family goods for the feeblest of his offspring.

In spite of his affectionate efforts he cannot hide that, almost without exception, his melodies lead to the lamest conclusions.

They are, as Peladan said of the lion, 'Only lion in front'; by comparison pathetic at the other end.

The German style itself leads to a similar clash between academic prescript and spiritual ambition, as soon as composers attempt originality within its boundaries. German critics are very patient with this failing when it 'remains in the family', they have a special, sensitive faculty in reserve for its appearance in works of sycophantic composers who seek the honour of being considered worthy of comparison with the native product. Leipzig's approbation used to be regarded as the label which distinguishes the 'genuine article'; César Birotteau's 'None genuine but those that bear the original maker's signature'. (Foreign bottlers are permitted to deal in high class French wines if they buy them together with *étiquettes, capsules, et bouchons*; the Château supplies these only to merchants of proved commercial position and integrity.) A composer once passed by the German Mandarins became almost as good as 'one of us'. It is true that Beethoven may have been a Fleming, Haydn a Croat, Mozart Tyrolese, Wagner a 'Speckjude'[1] (not to mention the numerous Jews that contributed to Germany's musical reputation), but to the German all acceptable musicians are naturalized Germans. So, we have been told, are Dante and Shakespeare.

Much German music of the classical period displays that bumptious self-consciousness we find in the pentameters and hexameters of poets who affect the antique style. Music, as well as prose, can dispense with rhyme and metre, although they are desired for the feeling of security they induce. To a considerable extent music depends on poetic analogy, and on the associations created by familiar settings of simple lines,

[1] It appears that recent research demolishes some of the old grounds on which pro- and anti-Semites built hopes that he might be proved a Jew. If it should remain uncontradicted, the chief remaining evidence in favour of a non-'Aryan' descent would be his own anti-Semitism. No doubt he found it politically helpful, and partly it was dictated by honest spite, but his diatribes make an impression of sincerity that is rare enough in Wagner's prose to engrave itself on one's mind. It suggests that the roots of his feeling on this subject burrowed deep.

which invest stereotyped phrases with a significance above their intrinsic value.

Musical forms are for the most part derived from extraneous principles. Apart from those borrowed from literature, the principal form-giving elements lay in the planning of dances. Very few have as directly grown from the essential nature of music as the exigencies of ordered polyphony. The insistent beats of the dancing-master and the shouted numbers of the drill-sergeant have in time become transformed into sacred rules of construction. Hardly a modern musician can find his way through an old madrigal without first imprinting some such drill on the free-moving limbs; he distrusts the early liberties. On the whole, musicians perceive in an impersonal way this usurpation by an alien power, but they submit because they have failed to organize internal government.

An attractive solution presents itself in the formal suggestions of programme music. Their drawback is that music is, before everything, the language of spiritual generalizations. The more it attempts to communicate concrete facts, the more it sacrifices of its innermost character.

Music conveys ideas where words fail. It degenerates if it attempts at its own length something that could be accurately stated in a few words. Generations of composers have worked at the perfection of a system which from first crude efforts should arrive at the verbal stage. They hoped to coin musical tokens that could obtain universal currency.

It is by now well known how Strauss voiced a conviction[1] that our ideal should be to make music describe anything, down to a teaspoon, in precise notes. The aspiration has been made egregiously ridiculous by its most earnest propagators; Mr. Frederick Corder, the grim-visaged but gentle-minded professor of rational composition,[2] has made all wags

[1] In the course of an impassioned speech on 'How far . . . we must bring music', delivered to Busoni and a few intimates.

[2] But then, he also advised pupils not to be impressed by the seeming intricacy of Italian operatic choruses, to reduce them on two lines for the piano, when they would see that the polyphony dissolved into a few chords, and simple

BESPOKE IDIOMS

his debtors by the compilation of a dictionary of musical terms instructing composers how to say in music 'After you', or 'Blast it!' It contains the latest information for any listener who, at a first hearing, should fail to grasp the plain English for

and no mistake.

This, beyond a peradventure, is music's passport to hell. It is possible that, as many other professors have told us, it is going there anyhow, but it does not seem necessary that composers should be shown how to go out of their way to smooth the pavement, or how to hurry the progress.

It cannot use symbols which, like the *x* of algebra, have to be taken for granted, i.e. for a spoon, or even one particular spoon, unless the composer appends a glossary to his score. (I have seen such a score of an American composer which to some thirty pages of music offered a good hundred of 'letterpress'.) Music is bound to produce every time a musical term which stands for all spoons, past, present, and future, the spoon-idea, the absolute and categorical spoon—the 'spoon-an-sich'. We could adopt the *-ino, -ello, -one* of Italian grammar, when what was a teaspoon on the fiddles would become a dessertspoon on the violas, and a tablespoon on the basses.

Composers who condemn such pea-and-thimble and performing-flea tricks can always make expressive use of the fact that music gives us the universal generation of each object instead of the special reference. The postillion's trumpet flourish becomes the rousing call to humanity of the 'Eroica'. A children's dance, passing through the mind of Haydn or Mozart, becomes the vehicle of sublimated mediation. The rocking of the cradle, the stamp of martial feet, the pulling of

ones at that—which is certainly as true of many an 'Andiam, andiam', as of the 'Improperia'. But he cannot help thinking that one Cord in the pianist's hand is better than four tunes in the Bouche.

oars, shape in music terms that convey an all-comprising sensation reached through the narrow gate of the original meaning. How abstract suggestion grows while direct associations are lost may be observed in the change of meaning 'titled' music undergoes. Generations that remembered how the antics of galliard-dancers were considered shocking and scandalous, rabidly licentious, may still have heard something wicked in galliards. But as satanic visions grew dim and old indignation was forgotten, later generations found nothing but a spirited tune. In music more than anywhere the style is the man, because its subject-matter is too undefined for intellectual appeal; only the wisdom of intuition can see here with precision. If by the coining of stock phrases we attempt to repair this disability, we turn the speech which could be almost free from material shackles into the most petrified medium. Wagner defiantly turned material objects into abstract symbols, methodically confusing ideal and technical aspects. He applied this method to a number of warlike implements not much better than forks and spoons, and produced clichés which already appear more fossilized than the old-maidenish conventionalisms of Mendelssohn or Brahms.

The products of polyphonic structure, fugal, canonic, and other contrapuntal devices, are—of the older forms in general use that have been at all satisfactorily described—those which have grown out of the very being of music. They are perhaps the only organic forms that are inherent in its nature; distinct from those that depend on literary associations. One would not advocate their universal adoption but, of available models, only these seem capable of lasting fecundity.

That they are largely evolved along with, and as the expression of, a dogmatically regulated faith may be accident, but it is not wise to credit coincidence whenever our credulity appears to be tried. After such totally diverse minds as Plato, Bossuet, and Morris, so rational a thinker and sceptical a critic as Mr. Bernard Shaw has observed anew that 'Art has never been great when it was not providing an iconography for a live religion'. Several thinkers of the present century have come, after Jeans and Eddington, to admit that possibly some spiritual entity may be at the foundation of the universe. Older self-styled freethinkers represented the conventional reaction that impatiently condemns an undesired discipline.

The first composers who discarded this discipline together with the conviction which made it, need not have been conscious rebels. Many of them had probably no spiritual interests whatsoever. With such emptiness inside him, an artist cannot fire others as he might with the glow of his personal faith.

Programme music supplies an instance of composers and hearers at cross-purposes, and the futility of historic and aesthetic justification in the absence of a direct faith and an unequivocal tradition. The recurrent controversies on the programmatic meaning of classical works, with their equally weighty arguments pro and contra, are signally diverting. A pleasing sound of innocence is the frequent view-hallo of investigators who have found yet another piece of incontestable programme music written in the fifteenth century: 'Hundreds of years before Liszt or Berlioz!' They overlook how much work, meanwhile, was, explicitly or not, intended to describe extra-musical events. Every generation has its cranks whose ambition is to turn music into a glorified Bradshaw or Who's Who. But the ascription of a similar tendency to other music is seldom permissible. Much confusion, however, is caused by the deficiency of rational criticism and the ease with which musical frenzy can be simulated. Any irresponsible composer can jump to ultimate conclusions, and write 'music of the future' with a vengeance. He need only exaggerate recently fashionable ways. A barely adequate use of technical resource will, if coupled with enough impertinence and obtuseness, achieve straight away what takes Time and Genius half a century.

STEEPLECHASE

With one man it is a matter of determination, with another of dissatisfaction—probably with his own talents, although he may not realize it—with others it is just unadulterated shamelessness. But crude challenges to artistic decency lead no nearer to the evolution of new, logical forms.

Schönberg, after years of hard work and hard thinking, risks the statement that he intends to eliminate the common chord. But while so redoubtable a virtuoso struggles on through his career with considerable trepidation, some implacable logician from Mowbray Stoke or Woonsocket (S. Dakota) has already, while no one was looking, jumped over the last obstacle, and made further progress an occupation unfit for serious workers.

It is true that a Schönberg will write better music than most composers, even with common chords. Almost any one can make a revolution; not every one can govern. When Weber demanded of orchestral players what then seemed impossible, it was for the new tone-colour and for the sensational effect consequent on the strain of its production. These were ingenious calculations of an experienced composer, with ordered imagination. He achieved an original orchestral style from which a new departure in tone-painting took its beginning. Since then, instruments have been improved until his dramatic effects were perfected away.

The only people who still become excited over effects that made our fathers feel delighted or disgruntled, are antiquarian students who read about them in out-of-date treatises. For the enthusiastic reader, imagination replaces a lost reality, but he may as well believe that conductors still beat with a violin-bow as that he hears, now, the music as its composer originally intended. Only, how is one to know?

If in ignorance there is bliss, there is also much possible bliss lost. Unfortunately, few people clamour for reproduction of music as it was meant by the composer. Their votes are not likely to count with organizers of concerts who, from experience, know very well that they can get on perfectly

AD MAJOREM DEI GLORIAM

without taking notice of discriminating but numerically ineffectual demands.

Most composers avoid the application of an effect that was familiar to previous generations. Later, when again it has become sufficiently unfamiliar, it regains for a time impressionistic value. Then the process starts all over again.

Among the few forms that cannot be in this way exhausted, an overwhelmingly important place belongs to those of polyphony; the fullest practice has yet failed to show a limit to their number. And they contain life in a very practical sense, because independent parts keep the executants interested. On a more intricate groundwork they support the same vitality that inhabits such diverse forces as plainsong and the unison chorus of Italian opera. These naturally obtain a glow and a pulse which a few incontestable masterpieces of concerted music may reach, but only after endless practice and by sheer brilliance of performance. I am alluding to such pieces as 'Non si fidar' from 'Don Juan', the quartet in 'Rigoletto', and the sextet from Donizetti's 'Lucia', a scandalously under-estimated work of a scandalously under-estimated composer.

Many of the greatest productions of the most skilful polyphonists were intended for the Catholic service. Conception, performance, and reception being all conditioned by its demands, a considerable measure of harmonious give-and-take is beforehand assured. The audience is also a religious congregation which does not manifest approval or disapproval. This need not be under all circumstances an unquestionable advantage, but it does remove the executant's temptation to attract attention to himself. He has no incentive to be noticed at any cost, were it even by a display of eccentricity, justified in his estimation by his personal merits. He rarely finds here a chance for the acquisition of profitable fame. But if his role is relatively modest, it is, more than anywhere, a duty to be reverently carried out. As far as concerns singers—and the music of the liturgy is chiefly vocal—the difference of result is striking. No other instrument responds more delicately to mental disposition than the voice. Composers of profane choral music who are not bound by ethical propriety, are, with very few exceptions, eager to provide occasions for the display of such vocal atrocities as are considered characteristic. (This is the musician's euphemism for what others would call outrageously picturesque.)

Some writers of religious music may offend similarly, but these coarse ambitions find a far more gratifying and profitable field in the unutterable oratorio. The concert hall is the favourite abode of this abominable form of music. Its suitability lies herein that it does not demand chastity and reticence. These qualities mark choral singing in churches whose musical directors are not infected with the bacillus bombasticus of the Handel-culture, for centuries methodically administered to music-students. There was as little choice for them as for the babies who must submit to inoculation with the scrapings from sick calves' bellies. The State-supported witch-doctors follow a Macfarren's instructions as docilely as they follow the lead of Jenner and his guileless notions of pathology. The law-abiding musician who wishes to keep his record unsullied must accept official beliefs with the hopeful submission of the father of a family who is informed that a statutory guarantee will keep his children's faces smooth.

The hopelessness of any festival-choir-tenor struggle for personal distinction is only one of the pleasing features of adequate rendering of music for the liturgy. Another that counts is the incomparable relief to harassed ears in the substitution of the clean, steady sound of boys' voices for the impassioned female vibrato that imparts a tinge of sultriness to the most austerely serene phrases.

If this applies to executants, it applies in a higher degree to composers. The composer of religious music, with convictions rooted in a defined faith, approaches his work with devout sincerity. However much quality may vary with individual talents, this attitude eliminates the vanity that covets before everything perpetuation of a name and record.

It is this vanity which most easily leads the secular composer astray. Each in his own way, however, has to become reconciled to the knowledge that, perhaps during his lifetime, but almost certainly afterwards (when for most men of genius the fun really grows fast, and fame starts rolling into the account), the one who believed in what he said and kept his tongue in the right place becomes more and more anonymous for the overwhelming majority of his listeners.

There are musicians who feel both proud and sad when they reflect that, to-day, there persist doubts regarding the authorship of a considerable part of the sublimest music. Works of Allegri, Vittoria, or Palestrina were habitually performed from unsigned parts. Full scores were not usually made. Composers were content with that anonymity which has been the lot of many of the greatest creative minds who dedicated their production to the Church, whose humble servants they considered themselves to be. Poets who wrote some of the loveliest prayers, liturgists who designed inspiring ceremonies habitually performed, are known by name to few worshippers. Most of the architects, sculptors, composers, painters, theologians, who built up the complex beauty that moves the unbeliever himself who witnesses the Services, remain legendary figures even for highly educated people.

The most eminent contributors to this venerable edifice seldom troubled to ensure preservation of their names. There is much meaning in the contrast with those moderns who never lose sight of the desirability of personal advertisement, who are even prepared to risk damage to the artistic integrity of their work for it.

They left their products unsigned, or used such enigmatic marks that it seems they only employed some form of signature to escape the charge of spiritual pride that makes an artist believe his work can never be mistaken. Unless in sheer humility they wished to avoid the danger that their faults or weaknesses might be ascribed to worthier masters. Their practice, whatever the motives, provides another instructive foil to the conduct of the sordid go-getter who manages to 'make a name' first, by cultivating social, journalistic, and other publicity-producing gardens, in the conviction that it will be time to start serious work afterwards, when the public is properly prepared to hail him. There have been superlative masters who never arrived at the stage which, by the grace of the Queen of the Earth, is nowadays no more than a preliminary to the composer's career. There is so much 'we have heard' about some nonentity or other 'in musical circles', 'from Paris', or 'from New York', that by the time he appears before us, we must feel the importance of the occasion if we are not to admit that like the American's 'sardine minus tin can' we are 'simply out of it'.

All this may have nothing to do with music, but unfortunately a great many musicians think otherwise.

The ambition of liturgical composers was to appear worthy of the service; music was their means of communion with the Divine. They had to renounce beforehand the adulation of the crowd. In so far as this is more or less true of every artist, he need not conceive his attitude as a specifically religious one; his respect for his own work may be his religion. One regretfully notes, however, that the smaller the artist, the greater usually his faith in the special sanctity of his personality. A steadying spiritual orientation raises men of modest talents to a high plane of aspiration by unswerving and sincere exertion. The works of lesser liturgical writers (not little composers who occasionally turn out 'sacred music') are invariably purer in spirit than the corresponding products of the ambiguously profane.

The music of Anerio or Lotti is vastly more attractive and cleaner in sentiment than that of composers who, like Grieg or Reger, have occasionally tried the 'genre' without achieving a similar unity of idea and execution.

Compositions destined for the service require a certain temperamental bent, a spiritual predisposition which does not thrive under different conditions. Bach was technically a

Protestant, but his instincts made him write music that possesses the intrinsic qualities of the more florid productions suited to the liturgy of the older church. In works where this is not immediately recognizable there is yet not a moment's doubt of their fitness.

According to Schweitzer, Bach expounds the dogma of the Trinity more convincingly than theologians do. The Catholic Gounod, on the other hand, demonstrates the impossibility of hiding garish sentimentality behind religious smirks. His 'religious stuff' is diagnostically typical of the gaudy shallowness which sees in the Church an angelic theatre. If it sounds there like unintentional blasphemy, it is not even that of the braying ass who appeared in the old mysterium at Christmas time. It brays as irresponsibly as any ass, but while the innocence is congenital, it is no longer touching.

Pergolesi, Rossini, or Verdi may sometimes seem to lack the spacious solemnity that Northerners expect in their churches, but this is a different matter altogether. Only people who feel at home in the house of God, and at other times than on Sundays, dare look at a woman there, or speak to her, without feeling sinful. They may attain the unaffected simplicity of Saint Francis meeting Brother Beast.

The unceremonious music of Verdi, by its clean truthfulness, by its candid honesty, approaches everywhere more nearly to the organic chastity of the old liturgical masters than that of composers who, like Mendelssohn,[1] copy externalities so glibly as to seem faithful to hallowed traditions. Verdi's critics could not stomach his 'Requiem'. Like the yokel who was shown a giraffe, they preferred to say: I don't believe it.

The case of Verdi, of course, chiefly shows what talent will do. But such versatile genius is too uncommon to justify generalizations, however careful. No one believes that a

---

[1] I refer to the odious Lutheran Mendelssohn of the oratorios, not to the erudite, polished composer of fairy music, of the 'Violin Concerto', the 'Italian Symphony', and similar compositions. None of these made German professors attempt to pass him off as a second Bach, as they did try for his 'Reformation Symphony' and his other loathsome heir-to-the-classics abortions.

devout musician is potentially a good composer, any more than that in every Catholic church he is sure to hear perfect performances. Only, the chances are distinctly favourable. The Church evidently realizes that it cannot expect all its musical directors to be enlightened musicians. One need not refer anew to the legend of the threatened expulsion of music which gave Palestrina his chance of dramatically converting the Cardinals. There is recent, unimpeachable evidence in the famous *Motu Proprio* of Pius X. The paramount fact remains that the Church can and will exercise an unmatched power to ensure the right hearing of the right work in the right place, at the right time, in the right mood. If there are exceptions it is regrettable, but, after all, irrelevant.

VII

The classics of religious music offer convincing models. They exhibit all those features whose absence is painfully obvious in most contemporary production.

Few teachers of the last century knew anything of the technique of the old masters. If we except specialists at seminaries who were educating musical directors or priest-librarians —but not deliberately forming composers—we seldom find any who knew more than the snippets quoted in books of the Richter and Riemann type, and those of their French and English adaptors and imitators. These sparse directions, moreover, rarely mention the origin of commended devices. The pupil does not know that his teacher reads from a book of the white-whiskered Emeritus who appears on prize-giving days, who himself relies on Cherubini, who never came out of his own little corner. The pitiable little scraps served up to him retain nothing to lead him to some superb sweeping phrase of Vittoria or some passage of Lassus, as emotionally profound as it is ingenious. Certain mannerisms of technique only have been preserved, and if these worn remnants prove inadequate, it is for no other reason than that they are imperfectly understood, because poorly taught.

MASTERS AND SCHOOLMASTERS

There are traditions of craft, not recognized as such, in the very music against which well-meaning preceptors warn serious youngsters. At one of our great public schools the boys had been given a lecture by one of our most distinguished academicians. 'He spoke about melody!' 'Indeed! What *did* he say?' 'He told us that if we wanted to know whether a melody was good, we must first notice whether it goes on for long on one note . . .' &c. This referred to bad melody; the definition of the other variety was omitted. Obviously the lecturer was aiming at Puccini, whose popularity at that time put thorns in many sides. But what must the pupil think when afterwards he looks at the best-known classics of choral and symphonic music? He understands that their greatness remains uncontested, but also that, measured by the criterion he has been taught, they must be wrong.

Much the same happens when a student who at the conservatoire has been taken through the whole of harmony *and* modulation arrives at real music.

All the worst things happen in the best works, and the worst music appears to be streaked all through with the most luscious bits. Can a young musician fail to make comparisons with the exasperating nursery and dinner-table lessons which invariably teach that all attractive things are bad for one, and that everything which for sight, smell, and taste one would not offer to a pet ostrich is bound to be wholesome, strength-giving, and a delicacy to one's elders?

A balance between the customary juggling with harmony-blocks and the earlier technique of writing melodic parts is found in the hieratic interjections of Italian operatic homophony. Here melodic elements rule; the harmonic formula is allowed only a subordinate place, and for sound practical reasons must avoid ostentatious originality. The German classics have allowed it to divert a certain amount of the attention which belonged to the singer. The exigencies of melodic construction curb the tendency to harmonic display, while tolerance of it rapidly leads composers to trust to harmonic resourcefulness in any emergency. Soon, they do not even wait for that, but on the slightest provocation fire off the harmony pistol straight through the pocket of the melodic coat. Not only does this procedure harm the texture, but it spoils all grace of *savoir faire* and puts a premium on impetuous brutality.

The prevalent obsession of the musical rabble is with the attainment of complete freedom, first in harmony and then in everything else. It commonly ends in the wily anarchy of the perverse doctrinaire, and music has seen more Marats and Robespierres than would suffice to break up continents full of kingdoms and empires. From chromaticism we have, by way of bitonality, atonality, poly- and peri-tonality, proceeded to the exemplary nonsensicality of harmonic inconsequence of Stravinskyttens and their premature, monstrous progeny.

Reaction, indeed, has so far overstepped the mark that we are again experiencing something like the confusion which once saved its face by the application of an imposing name. Esoteric humbug in this disguise was known as 'Generalbass'. Originally meant as a shorthand (Corporal Bass, as the Rococo joke has it) method, it soon became a symbol of regulations that attempted to make melodic structure obey the commands of harmonic order. Thus part-writing itself was reduced to the role of a helpmeet to keep the chordal household going. In this pedantic muddle-headedness the very essentials of music came to be regarded as mere factors of its all-important notation. When the printer, for economy, and ostensibly to assist score-readers, began to crowd parts together on the smallest number of staves, he started a pervading mischief. Making the eye his accomplice, he suggested that 'outer' parts held a position which deserved special attention. Nothing in the nature of music justifies the belief; they possess no merits to lend them particular importance. The highest part is no more in danger of toppling over than the lowest of breaking under the weight of harmony it supports. Similes like these are employed in all arts, but in music they are taken seriously. They have done so much harm that one must deal with them for all their preposterousness.

When parts are written on separate staves, the eye habitually expects the appearance of melodic sense. When they are pressed on two, or even one, the desire is cunningly deceived by a typographic swindle of graceful slurs and ties, which conveniently suggest melodic coherence where none exists. The eye cuts a dash on the inexhaustible capital of optical illusions. It makes us share this luxury until we believe literally anything. When we look at the printed music we accept as four melodic lines chords strung together on a single stave, and give the composer credit beyond his due.

For actual sound, middle parts may have no greater importance than others. But emphatically not less; sound is not merely a considerable factor in music, it is music itself, just as much as music is sound. In dealing with so intangible a thing as music, however, it is hard to resist metaphor. The simile-fed mind accepts with relief the repose provided by notions that exempt it from abstract thought. The 'bass' being the lowest part on the page, we are seduced into looking upon it as the firm 'base' that carries the edifice—an idea as alluring as it is false. What we call 'lowest' notes are no nearer the centre of the earth than the others.[1] No musical structure was ever in danger of collapsing or sinking into the soil. We know of the leaning tower of Pisa, but of no symphony that, in the course of building, fell out of the perpendicular. Many a composer, when he becomes aware of defects, is consoled by this certainty; he knows too well that neglect causes none of the dangers that elsewhere would necessitate revision of plans. Risk to life and limb would make composers more conscientious. If only a few had landed in gaol for manslaughter, or had been killed by their own towering tone-poems, much released energy of their critics could be given to neglected works of greater import.

[1] It would be more rational to speak of left and right instead of low and high, as Berlioz has remarked.

BUSTS—

When Wagner, in 'Tristan', showed off his middle parts, he was hailed as an innovator of unprecedented technical ability. They really suggest more formal coherence than there is in the music. Their harmonic relevancy does not rise above unavoidable implications of the chromatic scale. The perfunctoriness which Wagner here disdained was no older than the Rameau system of tonality with its array of standardized chords. They constituted the essence of the 'Harmonielehre', which neatly tabulates them for immediate use, like the little cubes of water-colours that are the birthday delight of juvenile artists.

The hosts of Mendelssonnies and Schumannikins, by reducing music to a marketable commodity with standardized spare parts, were responsible for many pernicious notions from which we now find it difficult to escape. Be it a charge to their souls; the little masters from whose practice they distilled their dreadful doctrines were not themselves such Philistines; they must not be made responsible for what their misguided worshippers perpetrated.

The older polyphony knew no such elements of minor importance as inner parts became when musical draughtsmanship was replaced by the childish skill of solving the jig-saw puzzles of figured bass and key-haunted harmony. These acquired popularity together with the ubiquitous keyboard instruments that facilitated their study, and made chunk chords seem as natural as the striking of them. Few things are better calculated to prolong the existence of the musically unfit. The practice of the polyphonists, on the contrary, frightens off fumbling composers.

At the conservatoire music is treated on the same lines as literature in secondary schools. Young musicians learn to hate Bach and Beethoven as profoundly as aspiring authors in their tender years learn to hate Milton and Wordsworth. Naturally, both develop a deep interest and an instinctive sympathy for any work that spells revolt against those things which seemingly hold unfailing delight for the pundits. Now, composers usually remain unaware of hidden deformities and sores as long as their garments are presentable. Rubinstein, von Bülow, and Liszt have in turn been accused of shocking young ladies by inquiring about the state of their underwear. The point of the inquiry was always that no neglect of personal cleanliness could be worse than indifference about such fundamental things as scale passages. An artist certainly ought never to allow himself any laxity. He must submit to standards that take no indulgent account of human weaknesses, even if they are slight enough to be otherwise tolerable. There is nothing against which an artist should guard more carefully than the temptation to hide a grimy technical singlet (one might say slip) under a cloak of aesthetic distraction or distracting allegory. It is one of those things that are not done unconsciously, and unsuccessful dishonesty and unsuccessfully concealed impropriety are unforgivable sins. The cantankerous insistence on a mechanical use of 'Leitmotiv', as employed by Richard Strauss, has done a great deal of harm here. The first composer who exclusively applied it knew he spoke a language understood by the initiated. But most of his followers felt that as long as one could present a list of numbered motives and text references to them, hearers ought to be sure that all the demands of structural precision had been rigidly obeyed. There may be unity in the organization of Wagner's thoughts, but as he had the constant choice between two ways of being understood, the adepts of his school can reproach a critic for his obtuseness if he does not choose the one that the adepts know to be right.

The confusion of these two necessities is responsible for as much clumsiness as lifelessness in music of modern composers who have lost touch with a definite tradition, and lack the genius to evolve methods of their own.

I referred to the despicable tricks that hide this tribulation from the profane eye. Composers exploit their successes to establish personal symbols of notation which enlarge appearances of technical proficiency. In this way they often succeed in passing as polyphonic independence counterfeit produced by the burnishing of clumsy outlines. They do not trouble about the material but all the more about surface designs. To superficial readers the lines seem to fit the grooves of key-system clichés that root in this very neglect. One finds it exemplified in its crudest form in the chromatically skidding parallels of alto and tenor in most modern choral writing. Pretentious manufacturers of intellectual jazz have applied the same methods to the lachrymose ditherings of their saxophonic laments. A composer who had grasped the methods of the old polyphonists, even if he did not attempt to emulate their spirit, would feel ashamed to employ such pestilent make-believes. No intricate chromaticism, or cunning anastomosis of unconnected tonalities, ever achieves the variety of half-tints resulting from melodic structure with rationally disposed separate lines. But we must, in extenuation, remember that talent and time are short, that a composer can seldom afford to sit still and think while his rivals go their rounds, capturing markets, and that to write four or six melodies that fit each other is eight times more time-consuming and twelve times more talent-consuming than to write a proper score once. Many, indeed, give it up in despair, 'go back' somewhere, and to show that they are not un-modern for that, draw attention to strangely modern passages in old music. They love indulging in allusions and adaptations which remind one of the poem of Richepin, that unexpectedly closes with: 'Now is this good stuff, without pompousness and beating about the bush? Well, then! Do you know it is number so-and-so by that old fogy Theocritus?' The surprise depends on people's ignorance of the details of the classics. In this respect, musicians are even worse than amateurs of literature. Their poor erudition can be illuminated by any one who will trouble to spend a few weeks in a library collecting prophetic fragments from familiar compositions.

The sullen monotony of text-book form and harmony,

however, is of a relatively late date. Popular consumption of its cut-and-dried rules became possible only when every house held a piano. Fux, in his *Gradus ad Parassnum*, still instructed readers to approach their studies with an 'In the Name of the Father, of the Son, and of the Holy Ghost', the ornamental capitals fittingly printed in red. Military drill methods appeared about the time that Handel's oratorios first fascinated the musical public. Poverty of harmonic resource is narrowly bound up with the evolution of 'pattern-music'. Few things so compellingly demonstrate the progressive shallowness which accompanied the increased mintings of Harmonic Progress.

Minor composers who dare not trust intuition naturally welcome Laws of Harmony and Form, because these assess the artist's civic virtues for all to see. Here is good reason for musicians to believe in a genuine science presiding over legislation. Where that exists, anybody can, with industry, acquire an acknowledged craft chartered by law-makers in the light of recent discoveries.

Every product gains respectability when it can deny the use of recipes, and refer inquisitors to an Eternal Synthesis. Unfortunately for the repose of the artistic middle classes, legislature is suspect when none but people who make a living out of it find a defence for it.

A flexible harmonic and rhythmical frame should function like the human skeleton. This is not a continuous, coherent structure. It is kept in its proper shape by muscles and tendons. In the same way the harmonic frame, while giving rigidity and support to the whole body, is held together by the muscles and tendons of melody.

Physiologists have successfully kept fragments of muscular tissue alive and functioning 'in vitro'. But no one has ever made the bones alone do anything similar. Such tissues were kept in salt solution and no longer dependent on the blood which is formed in the bone-marrow.

Melody can exist by itself, but neither harmony nor rhythm

can. One can imagine a shape without substance, but not a substance without shape; a partner without love, but not love without a partner; a cloud without rain, not rain without a cloud. We can even believe that the first human body was without a navel, but we cannot very well conceive a navel without a body. We have to go to Lewis Carroll again to find a grin without a cat.

This anatomical versatility has been too subtle for most musicians. They felt better supported by a cast-iron corset, and while they sacrificed elasticity they hoped that a variety of coverings might hide its presence. Popular academic technique taught one how to operate with grooved casts such as electricians use to build continuous, insulating containers for a network of wires. The casts are few in number; but all crossings, curves, and elbow-joints can as easily be put together as the lines of nursery railway models. This allows for a fair number of patterns; only, with whatever ingenuity the single blocks are arranged, the varied designs of the possible groupings cannot be expected to give genuine freedom. But flexibility is a primary requirement when we are dealing with such living, moving substances as the strands of the musical tissue. The number of standard moulds we call chords, and the narrow selection of stock cadences combination of them permits, allow no liberty of movement to the melodic lines which have to run through the few channels that can be formed.

In the course of the last few centuries, composers trained in this technique have, with increasing subjection, treated melody as a mere function of harmony. Admittedly, from time to time a chord has been added to the stock. Its fate and effect are identical with those of a newly marketed switch that brings joy to hearts of engineers in the nursery. When the first thrilling experiments are over, when new patterns have been tried, the latest addition proves to have given no more than a fugitive sensation. The engine must still run over fixed curves with a sameness that through growing disillusionment remains at every moment verifiable. The new chord, hailed with enthusiasm, brings no intrinsic enrichment—the ephemeral power of novelty passes, and the chariot of melody can no more than before be driven unimpeded along the path of imagination.

The most noticeable effect of the eager application of 'modern harmony' is to make its users' productions all the sooner seem like photographs of uncles and aunts in the daring fashions of their youth. Just that appealing aspect which to exploiters of novelty seem most promisingly impressive, later appears the most pathetic and ludicrous. Just that fur collar and those pointed shoes that made Jack look so dashing, make Uncle James look so dowdy in his nephew's eyes, and the hat of which Jenny was so proud makes Aunt Jane look a pitiful frump to her niece. And what about Uncle Franck's best chromatic sequence, and Auntie Claude's best whole-tone scales? Ahimè!

The one chance is to grip the hearer's attention with that sheer force of vitality which, despite passing fads, a Puccini's work exudes through all pores. But even such men, rare as they necessarily must be, pay their part of the penalty when what were meant to be crushing accents rapidly become the cloying commonplaces of routine harmony exploited by the morning-after composers who felt nothing of the first intoxication, nothing of the subsequent dejection; who are themselves the dun cats and the blue rats once seen by over-excited artists, and who mechanically set about their depressing business daily from ten to four, without knowing any qualms.

Mr. Bernard Shaw—to make a *salto mortale*—observed that chords which for Wagner personified the curses of his villains, chords calculated perpetually to shatter the nerves of listeners, now sound pleasing to our ears. It looks as if there were no issue from this Black Hole where we threaten to die for want of fresh harmony in the close crowd of Privates Chord and Generals Bass. But this has been the core of my argument:

there does exist one. If only composers overcome their fatal infatuation for the 'mews' that keeps them in a stifling embrace once they come too close—if they order their harmonies according to the controlled designs of polyphony, they may feel relief, they may breathe again.

I am too acutely aware of possible false interpretations to shirk restatement of the thesis I have spread over this diffuse exposition. I call to my aid Balzac's answer to an exasperated critic. The critic wails: 'I say, this is like the three hundred goats of Sancho!' Balzac replies: 'That is the whole of literature, my friend! "Clarissa" is a masterpiece, and it is in fourteen volumes, yet the densest scenario-writer will tell you the whole story in a single act. If only I entertain you, what do you complain about?' I do not for a moment hope that I am entertaining. I would never pretend to the speed of Richardson at his slowest. I can only pray that I may not be *very* much more boring.

I am anxious to reiterate that I never meant that any and every harmonic clash or rhythmical contradiction is justified as long as separate parts are polyphonically delineated with reasonable precision.

A skilful polyphonist will rarely experience the need for ruthlessness. He systematizes his harmony in the course of innumerable, patient experiments, and then honestly adheres to it. This is no more than artistic decency. He would not, when he is faced with a difficulty, conveniently recall his privileges, and settle the matter by stating that 'tel est mon plaisir'. He need never stoop to meanness to extricate himself. Anyhow, the strictest procedure does not lead to harmonic starvation. On the contrary, polyphony often provides prospectors and claim-jumpers with shimmering samples of 'modern' chord progressions. Most of them, however, are so preoccupied with their distrust of hypothesized laws of nature that they erect their fears as the conventional barricades of revolution. This soon becomes a convention itself, and their barricades hem in their movements as much as those of their opponents. Their consolation is that of the circus lion in his cage who nightly pities the poor audience for being kept behind bars. In transition periods a brief stay of execution is usually possible. As the creditor-hunted buck had to stay indoors before sunset, so the doubtful cases only appear in darkness, or otherwise they masquerade as their own butlers and bodyguard bruisers. Here lies the explanation of the perverse use of opposed conventions, the mixing of two vocabularies, which we know as the modern harmonizing of old tunes. The tune is right, and the harmony is right, but wait till the bailiff finds out that the one leaves the house in the clothes of the other. Then the game is up. The retarded dissolution is all the more final the longer it has been warded off. Melodic outline may be cunningly disguised by the plaiting round it of many-coloured, startlingly unexpected harmonies, but the ear is not long deceived by this unforeseen coupling, *mésalliance* as well as bigamy.

Once the ear is no longer startled into confusion, it will again single out the essential melodic line, and judge it on its intrinsic merits. However favourably one is disposed, and however great one's early affection for music which thrilled one as the first green of spring seen in the first consciousness of youth, there comes a time when one detects under this entrancing approximation only a nostalgic restatement of faded hopes.

The oldest old masters have been as young as the youngest of young fools can ever be. Fashion's latest darling cannot make himself younger than Homer at sixteen, and probably nods oftener than the blind bard did at any time of life. But it is a long way from the bold searching of genius to the rash impudence of experimenters who resent the loss of any useful note garnered in the twilight on the field of thought.

As long as composers can compose; as long as the fountains of music do not run dry in the shrivelled breasts; no one feels enticed by lust for speculation into making of his works a vehicle to carry his speculative ideas. He may conduct experiments in private. He may write treatises on theory, and even give them such artistic merit that they give rise to a new manner which he himself did not attain, although it might have suited his thought best. But he cannot wait for that any more than a child can, with patience, become its own father; or should it be brother, or step-brother? . . . Wagner only knows. The experiment has been allegorized on the stage, but not conducted in the laboratory, or the alcove where nature hides her deepest secrets.

VIII

When the theoretical conclusions of a musician are presented in the form of compositions, they thrill few but his colleagues and disciples. The disciples know all about it beforehand, and delight in a fresh smack prepared for the collective cheek of Philistinism; if they ever feel regret it is that the master has not gone farther. But the ordinary public suspect that their attention is being claimed on false pretences.

The next question is whether it is more pernicious to repeat the interesting experiments of a recent methodist, or to imitate the idiomatic mannerisms of established masters. For all we know, they have been as much irritated by its perfection as we could possibly be ourselves.

Where I recommended the example of polyphonists who wrote for the Catholic Ritual, I did not mean that one should copy them. The practical reasons that determined them do not always hold good for us. There is no wisdom in uncritical acceptance of another man's stylistic principles. But we may with profit remember them.

Judging by results, by the finished works, one understands how fruitful even the experiments of polyphonic writers of five and six centuries ago have been. If we learn to understand the works, we may be inspired to similar experiments. That should prove more useful than the memorizing of handy cribs which permit every musician to 'press the button', after which the rest comes automatically.

FORMALISTS, FORMULAS, FORMALITIES

Emotional intimacy, not analysis, supplies final understanding. But what do most musicians know of Okeghem, Obrecht, Dufay, Lassus, Byrd, Tallis, Vittoria? To the average student these are so many names. He usually knows of them only through fossilized assumptions embedded in the dreary wastes of musical history. He cannot know that they may give him the illumination which he seeks in vain in the toy-shop philosophy of Strauss, the Noah's Ark of the 'Ring', the Theosophical lucubrations of a Scriabin, the Chinoiseries of Ravel, the late-new dandyism of Stravinsky, or the catchpenny je-m'en-fichism and Max-and-Moritz wickedness of Hindemythology.

A form that raises no hindrance to thought, that has no limits of adaptability, allows complete manifestation of what originality a composer possesses.

Originality is an endowment one cannot help having or missing. It is as fatal a gift as the beauty of Little Sister White, or Conjunctivitis Neonatorum.

It is not an achievement, but a quality which one may even lose. Since it can stand so much in the way of a career, many composers must have been relieved to see it disappear as time went on. But they have not always kept to honest opus numbers that allow us to share the secret. Here we touch another question. Is it better to make money by making a name, or make a name by making money? Champions of these two methods affect contempt for each other, and no cynic has ever extracted enough information to tell us whether the *homme arrivé* considers that either name or money has made or broken him.

Originality need never be sacrificed in the employment of forms already applied with perfected workmanship. We must not confound these with forms brought to perfection; their usefulness has come to an end, a stage has been reached where association with them results in anti-climax. It is not simply a matter of relative talent or the degeneration of a school. For the communication of fresh ideas the old forms have to be given suitable reformation. Some fundamental principles may be preserved, but while a fugue remains a fugue as long as it does not become something else, sonata form retains its title only by courtesy. We call a work a sonata because the composer has thus designated it. This does not imply that he has thus designed it; without his appellation we might never have guessed as much. When, however, the essential character of the most representative works of the name is preserved while the shape is adapted to new needs and a wider grasp, an extended version of the form is created. This is what Berlioz did with his 'Symphonie Fantastique'. But, for exactly such reasons he incurred the wrath of the guardians of traditions who in their half-baked but overdone zeal sit tight on the strongbox before it is full of treasure, and in their anxiety for the half-empty vessel would keep any one without authorization from depositing his tribute. The academic oblates who try to keep a pure flame burning from the rancid fat of half-decomposed conventions through the sluggish wick of caste-interest, stormed and raged with property lightning-and-thunder from their dusty priest-holes!

Starting from the premiss that a form has been employed for perfect music, the simplest argument by *reductio ad absurdum* shows that this in itself does not entail its subsequent uselessness. We need but consider the alternative; it is definitely ascertainable that no pioneer ever established a permanent claim to originality by his primary exploitation of a virgin idiom. Usually, all he achieved was to break the thread of a guiding tradition which invests a form with definite aesthetic standing. This is what, almost without exception, happens when the form is all his own invention, as of the White Knight, that prototype of the Modern Composer.

When he fails in this particular object, your modern composer has an excuse the classics had not thought of—he tells you that he was being facetious. And modern composers are whales for facetiousness. They stand so far above their subjects that they cannot even feel humiliation if they fail. They are like jugglers who, every time they don't catch the ball, wink an eye at the public, meaning that it was all clowning, anyhow, that a guess is as good as guile, that of course one could if one tried, but one wasn't really this time. Your composer becomes so detached that he knows no longer where he is. When he is insipid he makes it clear that he is sarcastically so. All his clumsiness is as intentional as that of the clown who gets rolled up in the carpet. The composer gets rolled up in his own music, but he just peeps out at the side to make you understand that it is part of the show. One step higher on the intellectual ladder he passes off his helplessness as supercilious renunciation. He parodies the ridiculous classics. Still, when we look at contemporary music, we cannot help noticing that a capable craftsman like Elgar, in spite of the Spirit of our Time, does not revert to Biting Irony. Neither does a man of such intensive convictions and searching ideas as Delius fight shy of emotion and ask us to interpret every unusualness as sarcasm. The clever protégés of Diaghilev were the fellows who set the pace for the bright sprints and spurts of offhand you-know-what-I-meanness. A dashing new generation loudly advertised its intellectual aversion to intellect and its sentimental distaste of sentiment. A comic side-aspect was that they despised Beethoven for it, Beethoven who said that music should not be touching or moving—'That is good for females only'—but that 'Music should Knock Sparks off the Heart of a Man!' One would think that he, of all people, should have been their chosen example, but they could no more understand him than they could see where their own smartness was leading. Could there be anything so grotesquely futile as our dapper, slashing young bloods shouting that the old masters are a sickly crowd of yellow-bellied slabber-chops and puff-paste boobies? All this tremendously up-to-date slickness pales like last year's recollected moonshine in noon's broiling sun, before a couple of bars of real music written by a whole man with all his fists and pluck and guts and wits about him. What have these unblackballed ragged timers to say for themselves when they are confronted with something really vital? Something like 'O vos omnes', or 'Deh! vieni'? It is unjust, however, to presume that aridity of soul and imagination are more characteristic attributes of our day than glib cleverness. They have always existed, but they never supplied the stuff from which great works are made. The hundred per cent. commercial travellers and high-powered salesmen of music have been at their pitiable job in every century, but they did not always have the brazen cheek to claim the attention of the few who regard art as the essence of our most exalted hopes and ambitions. The notorious Spirits of the Times may welcome Spirited Time-servers, but the artist's occupation is with his own spirit first. If that happens to be a good spirit it will be for later generations the extract of all that mattered. The poor that are always with us are not only people who fail to make an income, they are also people out of whom nothing goes: sterile sceptics, and the rational, radical utilitarian. Ironical ghoulies dissecting sympathy, sarcastic ghaesties sniggering at generosity, and high-browety beasties, have reared their vile heads all through the nights of ages. But no creepy and crawly purity of verminous race bestows creative power, not to speak of spiritual cleanliness.

There are composers who exist by the extras which academic analysis advises us to remove from florid music before we judge its intrinsic worth. The theory-whetted pruning knife is supposed to have the power of removing enough from the ornamental classical trees for us to recognize the bare trunk of some simple hymn-like tune.

This method of musical detection is as unsound as the corresponding one of criminal investigation, the procedure that is recommended in the 'Malleus Maleficarum' for catching witches.

Some frilled melodies may be unmasked by every one who knows the Wardour Street stock-in-trade, but there never was a beautiful puss of a tune that could, with the aid of the inquisitor's hammer, be shown to hide a terrifying old hag of a dirge. The richly bedecked work of some of the old Netherlanders, for all its canonic splendour, always obeyed an exacting discipline shaped by demands of execution; strict logic in every detail was an ever-present necessity.

The purely emotional tone-poet obeys other needs. By climaxes and collapses he conveys the intoxication in which he lives himself, through an infinite capacity for provoking a state of epileptic frenzy. Tchaikovsky was the first considerable composer to give those bowel-griping sensations of the starting elevator which in modern opera are all-taking and yet giving so little.

The narcissist composer asking public attention for the cosmic vastness of his neuropathic wallowings and retchings is really no more than a sentimental confidence-trickster. By devious means he exacts tribute for the maintenance of his private miseries. Society-gossip journalists and professional practical jokers have something more valuable to offer. The world buys a very sorry pig in a very nasty poke every time it walks away with the piteous musical shivers of these nerve-sufferers who flee from truth and from battle through one symphony after another. They are like deserters who wheedle the fare back to their unit from every man who ought to run them in. The hard-luck tale they tell grows more and more heart-breaking as they improve their beggarly practice.

Many an unwary music-lover has had his receptive faculties blunted by frequent subjection to the gibbering of eroto-maniacs whose hysterical outbursts appear on almost every orchestral programme. The hectic oscillation between paroxysms of sobbing despair and frantic laughter is bound to wear out the nerves of any one who has to bear it. When asked to suffer with such composers, one suspects even their sincerity —that last refuge of impotence. If they actually felt the devastating inner strife they publicly lament, would they not soon find the peace of the padded room and the cooling-helmet? If we listen to their shrieks it must blunt our perceptions; if we become inured to them, all finer shades are wasted on our ears. Mozart, Purcell, Vittoria, or Bellini contain a depth of emotion that surely suffices for the utter degree of what humans can bear. But the outworn apparatus of the sensation-seeker-and-finder fails to register it. With his deadened sensibilities, he calls 'that kind of music' insipid. Such tame stuff bores him; he needs at least a Tannhäuser Bacchanal to make him sit up and take notice.

When 'Pierrot Lunaire' was only a year old, a few young enthusiasts arranged a performance of it in Busoni's house. When it was over, and when the 'schweigende Dandy von Bergamo' and the 'Alte Duft aus Märchenzeit' had left floating the subtle fragrance of their exotic beauty, Busoni, the Florentine, with a moist eye thanked Schönberg. Ah! if he saw Bergamo's vales he would recognize the truth of his own music; had he known them he might have conceived something even more lovely than this ending, if that were possible. Schönberg at once plunged into a flamboyant disquisition on how no personal experience could add to the intensity of his conceptions. Not only could imagination outstride reality, but he saw to it that it should, every time. Once given a text, he would never stop squeezing the poetic lemon until the pips musically squeaked. A blue sky?—the bluest clarinet! A green tree?—the greenest horn! Every time complete concentration of all conceivable associations that ever seared their traces on the soul. This is largesse indeed, even if not artistic economy. Can one do more than empty the whole chest of drawers when asked for the loan of a shirt? It is the recipe of Elia's young Chinaman for roast sucking-pig. Such prodigality is bound to exhaust one's resources prematurely. Mr. Ernest Newman aptly stigmatized this tendency when he described Liszt's setting of 'Die tote Nachtigall' as 'musical elephantiasis'.

Once a listener's ears have been over-stimulated, there is only one method of resuscitating his paralysed receptivity, that is by a direct attack on his nerves. What Fleet Street once called the 'meteoric career of Verismo', opened a way which led from Wagner, via Richard 'Elektra' Strauss, to Hollywood.

The international hotch-potch style, that took from every school and every master whatever is easiest to swallow and most exciting in its effect, has been with great material profit exploited by composers like D'Albert and Wolf-Ferrari.[1] These were the real perverters of taste, not Meyerbeer, as superannuated criticism maintains. They were the people that first gathered a slaveringly eager following of musical masochists to whom they could preach lyrical exhibitionism from the stage, with elucidating action.

Where must the young composer go for models, if he wants to be 'live' but not indecent? Not to the neurotic Grand-Guignol knowingness of those ups-and-downs see-saw merchants with their 'Jean qui rit et Jean qui pleure' hysterics. Nor to those who specialize in banging blown-up bags behind the ears of listeners whose nerves have been set all on edge by queer noises behind the wainscot and wailings down the operatic chimney.

If he acquires those tricks, and it is much easier than to learn to write a fairish thriller, he has a good chance of being smiled on by pushing publishers and by enterprising *entrepreneurs*. We must keep in mind that every spirited young musician runs the risk of being frightened into up-to-dateness by his elder's eternal praises of the austerity, and the sedate beauty, and the serenity of old composers. He has a bleak, chilly impression of castrated dignity. Or, at best, of Fra-Angelesque sweetness turned into music, sung, in Mr. Bernard Shaw's words, by angelic doctors around the Papal Throne. But if the same young man got to know the works that are with cruel injustice thus belauded, he would discover that the most unctuous fawning and sawdery flummerdulation may be smeared on art

---

[1] Probably the greatest inspiration of D'Albert occurs in 'Tiefland', where the 'reine Thor', more foolish than ever, if not quite so pure, lays him down to sleep after having sung a long bed-time story with the refrain 'Der Wolf kommt heute nicht!' (He prophetically referred to what has lately acquired new notoriety as the Big Bad One.)

which for its size and power deserves better. He will be astonished to find there all the muscularity and all the bite he had come to expect in the disappointing modern products, which he has heard mentioned as models of concision, incisiveness, efficiency, clarity, and no-nonsense-about-it-ness. Even where he finds them not completely empty, he finds them on the whole completely useless in his quest for reliable examples of clear thinking and precise execution.

The classics of the Service must appear particularly instructive to youthful idealism by their logical function within a vital organism. A parallel does not obviously present itself anywhere to-day. Perhaps the marches of the military band provide one, and possibly such dance music as can be utilized for dancing. In these domains, where music still fulfils a definable social function, an almost exclusive right of exploitation has, unfortunately, been acquired by the manufacturers of Tin-Pan-Alley. For the whole of the past century there were only a few occasions, such as the 'Aïda' première in Cairo, where music played a dignified and notable role in important happenings. Nearest probably came the performance of the 'Symphonie Funèbre et Triomphale' of Berlioz, 'at the entombment of the fallen in the July Revolution'. The impressiveness of such a work, played on such an occasion, may be approximately gauged by the irritation it caused in quarters where similar ambitions had been frustrated. Wagner peevishly remarked that it was just the kind of stuff that every blue-bloused labourer would sing after one hearing, and his spitefulness was almost as significant as the surly admission of Habeneck that 'ce bougre a du talent'.

In spite of all suspect protestations of aesthetic disinterestedness by aspiring tone-poets who dare call the grapes of popularity too sour for their spoilt palate, one finds it difficult to believe in a composer who would not feel elated if he saw so honourable a position assigned to his work. With society constituted as it is to-day, the Church seems to provide practically the sole desirable opportunity. There a composer, while he works for his own artistic ends, contributes to an ideal purpose of wider appeal. It was some such combination many artists of Baudelaire's day sought. They were not, as is vulgarly assumed, popularity-hunters who hid their disappointments under a high-sounding phrase, 'L'art pour l'art'. The loftily detached state of mind in which that watchword was coined did not proceed from thwarted ambition. It meant that the artist dedicates his individual work to the greater glory of the whole of Art which symbolizes humanity's ideals. He should therefore find full satisfaction in the perfection of his own work which furthers this, but he need not despise the public's applause or official recognition when it comes uninvited. Only he must not seek it by studying fashionable taste, or by intrigue. An honest creative artist has no wish to be approachable only for the elect. He would not close his soul to friendly visitors, or haughtily warn them off as trespassers; no more than a genuine grand seigneur would grudge people a walk in his grounds. If they overlook beauties it is their loss.

Whether a composer's work is completely esoteric, or frankly autobiographical, whether he is anecdotal or flees the subjective as original sin, concerns exclusively himself. The gayest dog may be melancholy in his closet, and the sourest cynic and immoralist may sob over a dead mouse when his public is not watching.

Only this much is certain, that as no mother bears children to see them blown to rags or choked in poison gas, so no composer plans his works for the monstrous fate of falling into the conventional concert programme, to hang there like a soldier's body on the barbed wire.

The one satisfactory type of concert, in spite of superior critics, is still that designed by a genuine virtuoso to display a surpassing technical brilliance and originality to an audience of hero-worshippers. I do not speak of an adored tenor blubbering a number of achingly familiar arias. I am thinking of an event that now has become rare, the triumphal tour of the capitals by a Paganini, or a Liszt, or a Busoni—who was perhaps the last of them. Busoni certainly suffered under the genteel shrinking of tired reporters, who consider it due to dignity and culture to be supercilious about exciting performances that perpetuate the Liszt-Paganini legend. His standing as a composer was unacceptable to them for this reason alone. Paganini is still neglected to-day by people who keep their heads so high in the clouds that they distrust brilliance only one degree more than success. It is significant that the vast majority of them only know him by a ridiculous version with Siegfried-Idyll orchestra of one movement of his first Concerto, for which Wilhelmj is responsible. Yet they will, without hesitation, call his music contemptible. That it is unique for its mordant wit, its passionate fervour, and a spirited originality which raise it far above the prodigiously ambitious symphonies of some of his famous contemporaries, is unknown even to violinists, who dare not risk incurring the critics' displeasure by presenting his works. There are, undoubtedly, some features of his concertos and his concert variations that, in comparison with the mighty seriousness of Beethoven's string quartets, could be called frivolous. But who has really ordained, with the whole musical world meekly accepting, that music shall always be solemn, and that it shall not have the right of other arts to be frivolous on occasions? When the wizard of legend, 'un possédé du génie', as Berlioz described Paganini, appeared on the platform before an excited public rightly expecting to hear something the like of which had never been heard before, a lengthy tumultuous orchestral *tutti* was a perfectly fitting introduction to his first solo. The very pressure of anticipation thus legitimately achieved was an aesthetically justified procedure. It gave a well-balanced approach to the dazzling manifestation of a mobile but incisive, burning but strictly controlled spirit. There could be no more appropriate atmosphere in which to listen to his highly individual music, with its magic of intricate ornament, and an unequalled dexterity that maintains thematic unity through the course of the boldest episodic designs,

UN-LOCAL COLOUR

whose tissue never loses lucidity in spite of all its ingenious embroidery. Here, for once, we meet that harmonious equilibrium of many contributing factors which makes a public performance an artistic event.

This cannot be achieved by the playing of a shamefaced transcription of a fragment of one of his works between Mozart's 'Ave Verum Corpus' and the '1812 Overture'. It appears there only because the last advertised pupil of some famous trainer must be given a chance of showing off his deadly faultless technique. I have heard famous fiddlers confess that they only played Paganini because it made a good exhibition, but that they thought the music dreadful. Under such conditions every one concerned is bound to suffer; the work itself most. Its ignominious position, however, is responsible for this; not its defects. Our modern concert is simply a ridiculous institution where most works are as much out of place as a painting by Fra Lippo Lippi would be in the mess-room of a colonial regiment, or a motet of Tallis played on the barrel-organ of a roundabout at Hampstead Heath on Bank Holiday.

Yet musicians usually believe that as long as a work is good, it comes off always and everywhere. If it does not, they think there must be something wrong with the work. When similar superstitions are possible, one cannot wonder that improvement in our methods of concert-giving does not easily come about.

Meanwhile, if we hope to see music socially reinstated to anything like its past glories, we ought to teach young composers respect for their art, and interest in forms which grew, through musical logic, from a social need.

They are, in truth, few, and they demand more application than composers are, on the whole, prepared to give. Strictly ordered polyphony is the one with the most impressive lineage. It is also the one that has remained unassailable where others lost any prestige they ever possessed.

The Catholic Church is practically the sole institution that regularly presents music cast in this form, and under exactly those conditions whose absence makes most modern performances the depressing affairs they are.

We might substitute the study of works written for it, and rendered in it, for the conventional occupation with outworn methods sleepily approved by the academies, and the 'new rationality' of their lately opened Pep Departments where students are instructed in the bright art of jazzing-in Quick 'Recapitulations'.

Here are two unpleasant things to forget, and one artistically profitable fact to remember. They might point the way to a revival of aesthetic decency by the cultivation of truly organic forms, and restore music to much of its lost dignity.

Let us go on hoping against hope, however much in our own time we see a foul determination to pull down tender Euterpe to the level of a lady cashier whose chief earnings are made on the sly in her rag-time. The ghastly popularity of music in the last few years, and the deep, nostalgic dissatisfaction of all thinking musicians, constitute a warning too stern for any one to disregard.

When we yearn for a faith and a discipline, we must remember that there are inspiring examples in existence, before, in despair, we seek salvation in determined speculation, or come to turn the search for restored balance and formal vitality into a game of blind-man's-buff.

www.ingramcontent.com/pod-product-compliance
Lightning Source LLC
Chambersburg PA
CBHW021056080526
44587CB00010B/262